Priesthood in the Evangelical and Orthodox Traditions

A Comparative Study

Iacob Coman (Ed.)

VTR

Bibliographic information published by the Deutsche Nationalbibliothek
The Deutsche Nationalbibliothek lists this publication in the Deutsche
Nationalbibliografie; detailed bibliographic data are available in the Internet
at http://dnb.d-nb.de.

ISBN 978-3-941750-56-2

© 2011
VTR Publications
Gogolstr. 33, 90475 Nürnberg, Germany
http://www.vtr-online.eu

Layout: VTR Publications

Printed by Lightning Source

Contents

Foreword
(Iacob Coman) 5

A Biblical Perspective on Priesthood
(John Tipei) 9

An Orthodox Dogmatic Perspective on the Priesthood
(Iacob Coman) 45

Priestertum aller Gläubigen: Eine evangelikale Perspektive
(Christian Krumbacher) 115

A Comparative Study of the Orthodox and the Evangelical Perspective
in Light of Historical and Biblical Teaching on Priesthood
(Eugen Jugaru) 143

Contributors 188

Foreword

Two thousand years after our Lord Jesus Christ's Ascension to heaven, approximately one thousand years after the Great Schism, and more than five hundred years after the Reformation movement, every church still smolders over the idea of how the ministering to God and to his people should or should not be understood as an office.

The priestly office in traditional churches, the pastoral ministry in the evangelical ones, or the renouncement to any qualification for ministering in other Christian churches, all these are still issuing debates and strong replies when it comes to the issue of authority of the church. The same debate includes the authority which Christ invested in those who are serving Him as church clerks, be they priests, pastors etc.

Questions regarding the apostolic authority and the way it could have been passed on, or regarding the similarities and differences between today's priesthood or pastoral ministry, on the one hand, and the priesthood of the Old Testament, on the other hand, are still valid now as they were in the past. A background consisting of contemporary Christian-theological behavior and ecumenical atmosphere generated the necessity of such a study entitled: "Priesthood in the Evangelical and Orthodox Traditions: A Comparative Study".

The book we offer was first intended to clarify this issue, first for ourselves and then for others. Therefore, we are not coming with an apologetic discourse against the priesthood of the traditional churches, but rather we are presenting again and in a comparative manner the problematic of such a subject. Starting with this common debate, we will try to conduct this discussion on priesthood not only in a comparative manner – Evangelical and Eastern – but also by appealing to an interdisciplinary approach. We are presenting a biblical perspective, *A Biblical Perspective on Priesthood – John Fleter Tipei*, a dogmatic and an Orthodox dogmatic perspective, *An Orthodox Dogmatic Perspective – Iacob Coman*, an Evangelical perspective, *An Evangelical Perspective on Priesthood – Christian Krumbacher* and, finally, a comparative synthesis through the Pentecostal dogmatic perspective, *A Comparative Study of the Orthodox and the Evangelical Perspective in Light of Historical and Biblical Teaching on Priesthood – Eugen Jugaru*.

The present book, as already mentioned, bears the mark of a research from different fields and theological areas. The unity of such a work will not reside in the agreement of the authors, but in their complementarity. The way we intended this book was not to necessarily bring its authors to an agreement, although here and there some sort of agreement is obvious; the unity of this book comes from the academic honesty regarding the Holy Scriptures text, from the academic honesty regarding the way the Eastern Church formulated its creed with respect to priesthood, and from the academic honesty regarding the evolution of the concept of priesthood in the Patristic Thought and the Reformers' Thought.

From a biblical perspective, John Tipei takes us on a terminology journey, first in the Old Testament, over the meanings of the terms that define the priestly office. Having as a textbook the basic versions of the Old Testament (the Hebrew canon, the Septuagint and the Latin version of St. Jerome), the author presents the authenticity of Levitical and Aaronical priesthood, and its exclusivity up to the time of Temple's destruction by the Romans when – the author argues – the priestly office and the sacrificial ceremonies were completely ended. Over such a biblical meaning and consensus, John Tipei brings to discussion the issue of priesthood in the New Testament. There is a tension in terminology and a complementarity in terminology – priest and priesthood compared to presbyter, bishop – that are managed with honesty and followed by their respective conclusions. Due to this study we can present in the book a biblical and exegetical foundation which will help us understand the rationale involved in the dogmatic and Orthodox dogmatic perspective, the Protestant perspective and the comparative perspective.

The dogmatic and Orthodox dogmatic perspective does not intend to underscore some theological dimensions of the priesthood. The highlights are generally made for those aspects that can face the trial of a Bible text, then follow the debated ones and in the end the ones in the conflict zone regarding the way Jesus Christ viewed the ordained ministry following His Ascension. Accordingly, the dogmatic perspective does not belong to the debate area but to the research area, an area still waiting for answers to all the questions raised.

From the Evangelical perspective, Krumbacher sets out with the development of the terminology. He limits the High Priest Office to Christ only and then extrapolates the priesthood, based on exegesis of 1Peter 2,5-9, to all the believers describing and implicitly proving the way Evangelicals approach this issue and makes it an article of faith. Such an approach paves the way for Eugen Jugaru's comparative perspective and allows us to draw certain conclusions. At the same time, Krumbacher's analysis offers the chance for dialogue over the ministry as an office. The ministerial office, be it priesthood or pastoral ministry, is an office that abides. In Jugaru's opinion, this office is a privilege that every believer should be aware of and responsible for. The one who ministers to believers (priest, pastor etc.) does not have anymore the authority to mediate; instead, he has the authority to call people to Christ (the High Priest), and to proclaim the Gospel of Christ (the High Priest).

Surely, the results of this research effort will show the academic interest of the authors. At the same time, we hope to be able to underscore the importance of ministry for those who are consecrated by ordination and for those who are not ordained. With no claim of treating the subject exhaustively, we still hope that our present work will encourage the writing of new papers on this issue, works that will improve our research and correct it, where it would be the case.

Finally, we hope that you will enjoy the reading and that, eventually, we would have successfully met your expectations raised by the title and the foreword of this book.

Project coordinator Iacob Coman

John Tipei
A Biblical Perspective on Priesthood

Introduction

The theme of priests and priesthood is prominent within the Scriptures. It appears in the first book of the Bible and lingers until the book of Revelation. The office of priest is mentioned about 700 times in the Old Testament and approximately 80 times in the New Testament. Evidently, such a vast theme offers a large scope for one interested in the subject. The aim of this study is, however, limited to the investigation of all the relevant passages in the Old Testament and the New Testament, referring to the office of a "priest" or to the general term "priesthood", in order to establish whether such an office was assimilated in the Christian Church of the New Testament period.

Therefore, we will proceed by presenting in short the priestly office of the Israelite religion, insisting mainly on the functions of the Levitical priest. The analysis of the relevant passages in the New Testament will be preceded by a discussion on the terminology used in the New Testament to refer to the office in Judaism, Christianity or pagan religions. As a general definition for "priest", most dictionaries refer to a person whose function is to make sacrificial offerings and perform other religious rites as an intermediary between deity and worshipers. The closest description of priesthood as a definition found in Scripture is probably Hebrew 5:1: *"For every high priest, being taken from among men, is appointed for men in things pertaining to God, that he may offer both gifts and sacrifices for sins."*

In any religion, a priest is viewed as intermediary between deity and worshipers. The need for an intermediary is based on the idea that the regular worshiper is inadequate to present himself or herself before the deity. Access to the deity is permitted only to consecrated people who prepare themselves for such an encounter through established rites of purification.

1. Priesthood in the Old Testament

In the Israelite religion of the Old Testament period, the priesthood is present at three levels, namely, the high priests, the ministerial priests and the universal priesthood. At the time of the Exodus, the high priest was Aaron (Ex 31:30), the ministerial priests were his four sons (Ex 28:21; Aaron's sons – Nadab, Abihu, Eleazar, and Ithamar), and the universal priests were the people of Israel as a whole (Ex 19:6). Whether such a model was carried over into the New Testament Church is a matter which we will be investigating in this present study. However, it is useful to mention at this point that only the first two levels are present in the Judaism of the first Christian century; there is not a reference to the universal priesthood of the Israelites in the context of the Jewish religion.

The Hebrew word used to designate the priestly function, *kohen*, refers to the custodian of a shrine in the earlier books of the Old Testament, to the "Levite priests" in the book of Deuteronomy, and to the "priests the sons of Aaron" in the Priestly Code.[1] The term is rendered in the Septuagint by ἱερεύς and in the Vulgate by *sacerdos*.

The main role of the Levitical priest was that of mediator between the people and God. He accomplished his mediating duty in a distinctive manner, namely, by offering sacrifices to God on behalf of the people – *sin-offerings, burnt-offerings, peace-offerings* and the special sacrifices as *inaugurating a covenant* (Ex 24:8) or the *sacrifice of Passover*. In the case of animal sacrifices, the priest's responsibilities were related to the most significant part of the ritual – the pouring or sprinkling of blood upon the altar. Such a duty might not be performed by a lay person. Other ritualistic responsibilities included: the daily offering of incense (Ex 30:7), the weekly renewal of the loaves of proposition (Lev 24:9), and the filling of the oil-lamps (Lev 24:1), the maintenance of the sacred fire on the altar for burnt offerings (Lev 6:9), declaring the lepers clean or unclean (Lev 13-14; Deut 24:8; cf. Mt 8:4), blowing of the trumpets to announce the holy days (Num 10:1), offering of sacrifices for those who broke the law of Nazarites (Num 6:1-21), etc.

The duties of the Israelite priest went beyond the cultic responsibilities. They also included teaching the Law (Lev 10:11; Num 35:1ff; Deut 33:10; Hag 2:11; Zech 7:8; Hos 4:6; Mal 2:7), in which the priests were assisted by the Levites, and settling the difficult lawsuits among the people on issues not explicitly covered in the Sinai revelation (Deut 17:8, 9; 19:17; 21:5).

---

[1] A.E.J. Rawlinson, "Priesthood and Sacrifice in Judaism and Christianity", in *Expository Times* 60, 1949, p. 116.

The priests were assisted in their cultic duties by the Levites who were servants and assistants of the priests, given to the latter as "a gift from the Lord" (Num 18:6). The Levites had to prepare different oblations and keep the sacred vessels in proper condition. Their main responsibility was to be the guardians of and care for the tent of meeting and the ark of the covenant (Num 18:20ff), although, they were not permitted to come close to the furnishings of the sanctuary or the altar, nor to perform the sacrificial act, especially the sprinkling of the blood (Num 18:2-6, 19). It was only after the building of the Temple in Jerusalem when the Levites were given the authorization to instruct the people in the Law (2Chr 17:8; Neh 8:7) and some judicial powers (2Chr 19:11).

Among the priests, the high priest had a unique role, being "the highest embodiment of theocracy, the monarch of the whole priesthood, the special mediator between God and the People of the Covenant".[2] His special garments and priestly accessories (Ex 28; Lev 8:7-8) and his specific functions distinguished him from the other priests. As Wenham correctly states, "Israel could see in the glorious figure of the high priest the personal embodiment of all that the nation ought to be, both individually and corporately."[3] Apart from supervising the other priests in their daily duties related to sacrifices, he was uniquely entrusted with the responsibility to bring the "most holy" sacrifice on behalf of the people, each year, on the Day of Atonement (Lev 16:1ff). This sacrifice, which was to atone for all the sins of the Israelites, was preceded by a special sacrifice for Aaron's own sins and for those of his household (Lev 16:6) and by the cleansing of the sanctuary and the altars (Lev 16:16, 19-20). The high priest had also the prerogative to seek counsel of Jahweh on various occasions in the history of Israel, through Urim and Thummim (e.g. Num 27:21; Deut 33:8; 1Sam 14:41 (LXX); Ezra 2:63; Neh 7:65).

One last aspect which pertains to our discussion is the selection and the appointment of the Old Testament priesthood. Although there seems to have been priests among the Israelites even before the giving of the Law at Sinai (Ex 5:3; 19:22, 24), the formal priesthood of the Old Testament was strictly selected from the tribe of Levi, namely from Aaron's lineage (Ex 3:5-13; 32:26-29; Num 3:10; Lev 21:17-23). Therefore, is also known as the "Levitical" or "Aaronic priesthood". The consecration of priests was performed in elaborate ceremonies which lasted for seven days, involving washings with pure water, the wearing of special garments, anointing with oil, the sacrifice of bullocks

---

[2] J. Pohle, J. (1911), "Priesthood", *The Catholic Encyclopedia*, New York, Robert Appleton Company. Retrieved October 29, 2010 from New Advent: http://www.newadvent.org/cathen/12409a.htm

[3] G.J. Wenham, *The Book of Leviticus*, NICOT 3; Grand Rapids: Eerdmans, 1979, p. 141.

and rams, participation in the laying of hands on the sacrifices, and the sprinkling of the blood on each priest-elect (Ex 29-30; Lev 8-9; cf. Num 8:5-21).

In the first century AD, the high priest was the head of the Sanhedrin, thus occupying the highest position in Jewish society. With the destruction of the Temple in 70 AD by the Romans, the Jewish high priesthood and sacrificial system disappeared completely.

2. Priesthood in the New Testament

There are five types of priesthoods mentioned in the New Testament: pagan priests, the Jewish priesthood, the priesthood of Melkizedek ("a priest of the Most High", Heb 7:1), the High-priesthood of Christ and the priesthood of all believers. There is only one instance in the New Testament when pagan priests are mentioned. During their first missionary trip and following the healing of the lame in Listra, Paul and Barnabas are welcomed as deities by the priest of Zeus (ὅ ἱερεὺς τοῦ Διὸς). Together with the crowd, this pagan priest brings bulls and garlands with the intention to worship the two missionaries and offer sacrifices to them (Acts 14:13). The obscure priestly status of Melkizedek is mentioned in the Epistle to the Hebrews in connection with the priesthood of Christ. It is not the purpose of this study to discuss this personage and his priestly role. Therefore, after presenting the terminology used in the New Testament for various ranks of priests, we will be discussing the three remaining categories of priesthood, in terms of status and attributions.

2.1 Terminology Used in the New Testament

In the New Testament, the Greek term for "priest," ἱερεύς, is used exclusively for the priests of the Gentiles and Jews. There is not one instance in the New Testament (or in the writings of the Apostolic Fathers) when the term is used in the Christian church to distinguish a minister from a layman. This avoidance is remarkable and, at the same time, striking, especially in the light of the fact that all the writers of the New Testament books were Jews, with the exception of Luke, and, as Griffith Thomas noted, "were steeped in sacerdotal ideas, language, and associations from their earliest childhood."[4] According to Fr. Benedict Ashley, the avoidance of the term "priest" is Christian circles was intentional:

> Thus it is clear that in preparing and leaving leaders in his Church, Jesus intended that they should share in his headship of the Church not only as shepherds and teachers but also as ministers of his sacraments, that is, as priests. That the term "priest", is not used of them is explained by the need of the infant

---

[4] Thomas, W.H. Griffith, "Is the New Testament Minister a Priest", *Bibliotheca Sacra* 136, no. 541 (1979), p. 67.

Church to avoid any suggestion that its leaders claimed to be Jewish priests. As Hebrews argues, the Christian priesthood is the reality of which the Aaronic priesthood is only a metaphor.[5]

But, taking into consideration this "eloquent silence of the apostolic writings",[6] Thomas sees in it the guiding role of the Holy Spirit in the composition of the Holy Scriptures. In his words:

Humanly speaking, the chances against avoiding the use of ἱερεύς in this connection are like ten thousand to one. Indeed, it may be said that to refuse to explain it by the guiding of the Holy Spirit is to require for its explanation what is virtually a miracle of human thought, foresight, and mutual prearrangement among several writers.[7]

The reasons for the avoidance of the term priest for Christian ministry will be presented later in detail. At this stage it is sufficient to note that, in light of the one and only, inviolable and permanent priesthood of Christ, the only mediator between God and humankind, a special human priesthood would be irreconcilable with the apostolic Christianity. As Lightfoot argues, in this respect "Christianity stands apart from all the other religions"[8] and the lack of a special Christian priesthood is the "characteristic distinction of Christianity".[9]

Those who argue for the existence of a Christian office called "priesthood" in the New Testament church establish their position on the etymological derivation of the English word *priest*. According to the Merriam-Webster Dictionary, the English word *priest* is derived from the Middle English *preist*, which, in turn, developed from the Old English *prēost*. Ultimately, the latter is derived from Late Latin *presbyter*, a Latinized form of the Greek πρεσβύτερος.

While such etymological derivation might be correct, our focus is not on the English translation, but on the words used in the first century Christian church.

---

[5] Benedict Ashley, "Who is a priest?", online article, 2007, http://www.ignatiusinsight.com/features2007/bashley_whoisapriest2_oct07.asp . A similar view is held by Theodore Stylianopoulos, who suggests that the Jewish priests who converted to the Christian Faith (Acts 6:7) may have continued to serve in the Temple for some time. In order to avoid the identification of the Christian ministers with the former Jewish priests, the Church refrained from using the term "priest" for its ministers – Theodore Stylianopoulos, "Holy Eucharist and the Priesthood in the New Testament", in *The Greek Orthodox Theological Review* 23, 1978, p. 114.

[6] J.B. Lightfoot, *Saint Paul's Epistle to the Philippians,* London: Macmillan and Co., 1879, p. 264.

[7] Thomas, W.H. Griffith, op. cit., p. 67.

[8] J.B. Lightfoot, *Saint Paul's Epistle to the Philippians*, p. 182.

[9] Ibid.

The terms we are dealing with in the New Testament are: ἱερεύς – *priest* and ἱεράτευμα – *priesthood*. From the usage of the terms, it is clear that ἱερεύς was never used interchangeably with πρεσβύτερος in the New Testament. While ἱερεύς was used exclusively to designate the priestly office in Judaism or pagan religions, πρεσβύτερος is a word that covers a variety of meanings: elder of age, forefathers, member of the Sanhedrin, judges in smaller cities, an office of the Christian church, a member of the heavenly court seated around the throne of God.[10]

The word ἱερεύς is used in a literal sense exclusively for the priests of the Jews and once for the priest of Zeus (Acts 14:13). When used to designate the officers of the Jewish cult, it takes two forms: the simple noun ἱερεύς, priest (Mt 8:4; 12:4, 5; Mk 1:44; 2:26; Lk 1:5, 8; 6:4; 10:31; 17:14; Jn 1:19; Acts 4:1; 6:7; Heb 8:4; 9:6; 10:11; Rev 1:6;), the compound noun ἀρχιερεύς. When used in the singular, ἀρχιερεύς the reference is invariably to the person holding the office of *high priest* at that particular time or to the high priesthood of Christ (Mt 26:3, 57, 62, 63, 65; Mk 14:53, 60, 61, 63; Lk 3:2; Jn 11:49, 51; 18:13, 15, 16, 19, 22, 24; 19:15; Acts 4:6, 23; 5:17, 21, 27; 7:1; 9:2; 19:14; 22:5; 23:2, 4, 5; 24:1; Heb 4:15; 8:3; 9:7, 25; 13:11). In most situations, the noun appears in the plural and is usually translated by *chief priests* (Mt 2:4; 16:21; 20:18; 21:15, 23, 45; 26:3, 14, 47, 59; 27:1, 3, 5, 12, 20, 41, 62; 28:11; Mk 8:31; 10:33; 11:18, 27; 14:1, 10, 43, 53, 55; 15:1, 3, 10, 11, 31; Lk 9:22; 19:47; 20:1, 19; 22:2, 4, 52, 66; 23:4, 10, 13; 24:20; Jn 7:32, 45; 11:47, 57; 18:3, 35; 19:6, 21; Acts 5:24; 9:14, 21; 25:2, 15; 26:10, 12).

There are several instances when the two Greek words are used about Christ: ἱερεύς, *priest* (Heb 5:6; 6:20) and ἀρχιερεύς, *high priest* (Heb 2:17; 3:1; 4:14; 5:5, 10; 8:1; 9:11). In connection with the priesthood of Christ, the author of Hebrews refers to Melchizedek – "priest of the most high God", for whom he uses the simple ἱερεύς (Heb 7:1; cf. v. 3).

The term ἱερεύς is used also metaphorically of Christians, as they sacrifice their life to God and to Christ (Rev 1:6; 5:10; 20:6). The word ἱεράτευμα, *priesthood*, is either a common noun referring to the status of being a priest or a collective noun referring to a body of ordained religious practitioners. In the New Testament, it is reserved for the Christian community as formed of priests (1Pet 2:5, 9) and is never used to refer to the priesthood of the Old Testament or the Jewish priesthood. A related noun, ἱερωσύνη is used both for the Levitical priestly office (Heb 7:11, 12, 14) and the priestly office of Christ (Heb 7:24). A verbal form, ἱρατεύειν, can be found in Lk 1:8 with reference to the execution of priestly duties by Zechariah.

---

[10] Cf. *Theological Dictionary of the New Testament* 6: 651, 931.

2.2 The Jewish Priesthood

The Levitical priesthood continued in the land of the Jews from the time of Moses until the destruction of the Second Temple in 70 AD. The numerous references to Jewish priesthood in the New Testament, especially in the narrative books, are, therefore, normal. At the same time, in full accord with the writings of ancient historians and the Jewish literature, they reflect the religious life of the Jewish nation in the first century of our era. Basically, from the information we gather from the New Testament references on Jewish priesthood, results that the attributions of the priests remained the same as it was established by the Law of Moses. We will take a brief look at the relevant references in the New Testament to the Jewish priesthood in order to assess the Jewish religious life and community in terms of structure and cultic responsibilities of each level of priestly service.

Our primary concern in studying the issue of priesthood in the New Testament is to see whether the three levels of priesthood seen in the Old Testament, namely, the high priests, the ministerial priests and the universal priesthood have been carried over in the structure of the Christian church. A second very important aspect is to see whether the ministries in the Christian church of the New Testament preserved the sacerdotal function of the Old Testament priesthood.

The main role of the Old Testament priest was to present the people before God, through sacrifices. Basically, the attributions of the Mosaic priesthood remained the same from the time of Moses until the fall of Jerusalem in 70 AD. The Jewish priesthood at the time of Jesus was structured on three levels of ministry: the office of: a) the high priest (ἀρχιερεύς), b) the chief priests (ἀρχιερεῖς) and, c) the regular priest (ἱερεύς).

a) During the first century AD, the office of the high priest conferred the holder the status of the head of the nation, both ritually and politically, as the high priest was *ex officio* presiding over the Sanhedrin. The high priest before the Exile was appointed for life (cf. Num 35:25, 28), but during the first century AD, it seems, he was appointed at will, possibly annually (cf. Jn 11:51), by the secular powers (Jos., "Ant"., XV, iii, 1; XX, x). Evidence from the New Testament indicates that members of the family of Annas and Caiaphas were often reappointed in the first century (Mt 26:3, 57; Lk 3:2; Jn 11:49; 18:12-28; Acts 4:6). Although in normal situations the high priest would be appointed by the Great Sanhedrin, sometimes content to only confirm the appointment of this office. It is known that Herod the Great appointed six high priests. The Roman legate Quirinius and his successors also exercised the right to appoint high priests. This explains the fact that the number of high priests from Aaron to the Exile was not greater than that of the last sixty years before the destruction of the Second Temple.[11] Biblical evidence shows that some of the high priests were held in high esteem even after being replaced by another person. Annas, for example, retained not only the title belonging to his former dignity but also some of the prerogatives of his former high priestly office, perhaps as consultant (cf. Jn 18:12-28).

The high priest exercised supreme authority in all things, political, legal and sacerdotal. The main duties of the high priest in the first century AD were to preside over the Great Sanhedrin, to perform the ceremony on the Day of Atonement by entering in the Holy of Holies to make atonement for his house and for the people, to officiate "on the seventh days and new moons" and annual festivals (Jos., *Bell.Jud.*, V, v, 7), to offer sacrifices for his sins and those of the priests and to consecrate priests.[12]

b) The vast majority of the New Testament passages on priesthood refer to the second level of ministry in the Jewish cult, namely the office of chief priest.[13] The Greek word is the same as for the high priest, ἀρχιερεύς, but appears in the plural. It seems that the power of priesthood has been absorbed by an elitist group of priests, a sort of priestly aristocracy. According to one view, this group was formed of deposed Jewish high priests and those who sat in the Sanhedrin as heads of priestly families. It is known, however, that the chief priests had a great influence on the high priest and in the Sanhedrin.[14] The gospels present the chief priests as being the group which constantly opposed Jesus, sought to arrest and kill him, and eventually condemned him to death, in cooperation with the Roman governor.

c) According to G.F. Moore, the main function of the Jewish priest in New Testament times was cultic, the teaching of the Law being taken over by the *soferim*, i.e. scribes.[15] Until the fall of Jerusalem, the duties of the Jewish

---

[11] Emil G. Hirsch, "High priest", in *Jewish Encyclopedia*, p. 390.

[12] For a more detailed description of the high priest's responsibilities, see Emil G. Hirsch, "High priest", pp. 391-393; W.H. Horbury, "The Aaronic Priesthood in the Epistle to the Hebrews", in *Journal for the Study of the New Testament* 19 (1983): 43-71.

[13] Mt 2:4; 16:21; 20:18; 21:15, 23, 45; 26:3, 14, 47, 59; 27:1, 3, 6, 12, 20, 41, 62; 28:11; Mk 8:31; 10:33; 11:18, 27; 14:1, 10, 43. 53, 55; 15:1, 3, 10, 11, 31; Lk 9:22; 19:47; 20:1, 19; 22:2, 4, 52, 66; 23:4, 10, 13; 24:20; Jn 7:32, 45; 11:47, 57; 12:10; 18:3, 35; 19:6, 21; Acts 5:24; 9:14, 21; 22:30, 23:14; 25:2, 15; 26:10, 15.

[14] E. Schürer, *The History of the Jewish People in the Age of Jesus Christ*. rev. by G. Vermès, F. Millar and M. Black; Edinburgh: T.&T. Clark, 1979-1987, vol. 2, pp. 204-207. See also David Foster Estes, "Priesthood in the New Testament", in *International Standard Bible Encyclopedia*, online version, http://net.bible.org/dictionary.php?word=Priesthood%20In%20The%20New%20Testament.

[15] G.F. Moore, *Judaism in the First Centuries of the Christian Era: The Age of Tannaim*, vol. 1, Peabody MA, Hendrickson Publishers, 1997 (originally published in 1927), p. 308f.

priests were carried in accordance with the prescriptions of the Mosaic Law. They offered the sacrifices prescribed in the Law and took care of other cultic/ritual concerns in the temple (Mk 1:44; Mt 12:4-5; Lk 1:5-23; etc.). Other duties include pronouncing benedictions (Num 6:22-27; Deut 21:5), teaching the Law (Lev 10:11; Deut 24:8; 27:14), acting as scribes (Ezra 7:11; Neh 8:9), supervise tithing (Neh 10:38), examining lepers (Lev 13:19ff; 14:1-11; 14:34 ff; cf. Lk 17:14), purify the unclean (Lev 15:31), etc. Luke gives some important information about the work of the priests. Zachariah, a priest of the course of Abijah, the 8th of the 24 courses in which priests were divided (1Chr 24:7-18), was chosen by lot to burn incense in the temple (Lk 1:5-9). Thus, the priests ministered in turns by courses and, in these courses, they divided their duties by casting lots (v. 9).[16] The common priests of the Jews are mentioned together with the high priest in connection with the arrest and trial of Peter and John (Acts 4:1). Luke presents in a positive light the fact that "a great multitude of priests became obedient to the faith" (Acts 6:7).

2.3 The Priesthood and High-Priesthood of Christ

The Gospels and Apostle Paul never speak of Jesus as being a priest. In fact, his origin from the tribe of Judah disqualified him to be an Aaronic priest (8:4, 5). According to one view, some of Jesus' words and actions fall clearly in the category of priestly duties. For instance, it is claimed that what Jesus said and did at the Last Supper clearly indicates that the early Christians understood the Last Supper as a priestly act on Jesus' part, to be continued as a central practice in the church.[17] It is doubtful, however, that Jesus' words and actions at the Last Supper were understood this way. Surely, in the disciples' mind, a priest would present the people before God, not his own body to the people. In our opinion, there are no parallels between Jesus' act at the Last Supper and the duties of a priest.

In contrast to the Gospels and Pauline epistles, the Epistle to Hebrews set Jesus forth not only as a true priest, but as the only true priest, the genuine High Priest (2:17; 3:1) who presents himself as a sacrifice to God in behalf of the people and enters into the Most Holy Place with his own blood to make atonement for the people's sins.

---

[16] For more details, see Chapter 11 in Shemuel Safrai and M. Stern, eds., *The Jewish people in the first century: Historical Geography, Political History, Social, Cultural and Religious Life and Institutions*, in Compendia Rerum Iudaicarum ad Novum Testamentum Series, vol. II, Philadelphia: Fortress Press, 1976. (pp. 561-630).

[17] Pohle, J. s.v. Priesthood, in *The Catholic Encyclopedia*, New York: Robert Appleton Co., 1911, Fr. Benedict Ashley, "Who is a Priest?", http://www.ignatiusinsight.com/features 2007/bashley_whoisapriest_oct07.asp.

In Hebrews, the priesthood of Jesus is declared to be after the order of Melchizedek (5:10; 7:11, 14), i.e. radically different (ἱερεὺς ἕτερος, 7:15) from that of the Levitical priests and superior to it. The emphasis here is clearly on the personality of the priest, not on his work. The intention of the writer, here and throughout the book, is clearly to indicate the superiority of Christianity over Judaism. Jesus did not become a priest on the basis of his descent or inheritance, but "by the power of an endless life" (7:16). The superiority of his priesthood is also evident in the fact that, in contrast to that of the Levitical priests, it is based on a better covenant (7:22; 8:6), and is eternal (7:20-28) and untransmissible (7:23, 24).

Further, after showing some resemblance between the high priesthood of Jesus and that of Jewish high priest (5:4, 5), the author of Hebrews contrasts the two, emphasizing the superiority of Jesus' high priesthood. The Levitical priesthood was merely pictorial and thus preparatory (9:9; 10:1; cf. 8:5) of the priesthood of Christ. While the work of the high priest was conducted in the "second tabernacle", i.e. the Holy of Holies, Christ conducts his priestly activity in a "more perfect tabernacle" (8:1-5), i.e. "into heaven itself" (9:11, 24). The next contrast is made between the types of the sacrifices offered. While the ancient high priests offered the blood of goats and calves, Christ offered "his own blood" (9:12). Lastly, the contrast has to do with the effectiveness of the sacrifices offered. The ancient high priest had to enter into the Holy of Holies every year, but Christ's sacrifice is better and much more effective in that "he entered once for all in the most holy place" to "bear the sins of many" (9:12, 28).

The priesthood of Christ is the central doctrine of Hebrews. The entire book is dedicated to proving that, by presenting himself as a sacrifice before God, Jesus Christ annulled the old system of priesthood. Priests are no longer necessary to offer expiatory sacrifices or to perform rituals because these things were only a shadow of the reality which is the Priesthood of Christ. As Ryrie puts it, "What the old had to do repeatedly and could never do finally Jesus had done once and for all."[18]

Men no longer need other men to mediate between them and God, because Jesus, by his own blood, torn the veil from top to bottom and gave them direct access into the Holy of Holies, i.e. in the presence of God (Heb 10:19, 20; cf. Mt 27:51; Mk 15:38; Lk 23:45). Here in the Most High Place, believers are invited to enter and offer spiritual sacrifices: the fruit of the lips, good deeds and sharing with others (Heb 13:15, 16), as priests in Christ. But there is no resemblance between these sacrifices and the blood sacrifices of the Old Tes-

---

[18] Charles C. Ryrie, *Biblical Theology of the New Testament*, Chicago, Moody Press, 1959, p. 248.

tament; they are of a spiritual nature and are presented by each believer for himself, not on behalf of others. The bringing of sacrifices to God, in word and deed, is both a privilege and a duty of all Christians.

2.4 The Priesthood of Believers

There are a few texts in the New Testament which attribute the priestly status to all believers,[19] rather than to a special class of people. The idea is not really new, for such collective language is used in the Old Testament: The Israelites are promised to be made "a kingdom of priests" (Heb. *memleket kohanim*) among the nations of the world (Ex 19:6). Israel's role was "to be the vehicle of the knowledge and salvation of God to the nations of the earth."[20]

2.4.1   Texts in the NT on the priesthood of all believers

There are three places in the New Testament where the notion of the general priesthood of believers is set forth: the First Epistle of St Peter (2:9) and the Book of Revelation (1:6) and (5:10).

1Pet 2:9 Ὑμεῖς δὲ γένος ἐκλεκτόν βασίλειον ἱεράτευμα ἔθνος ἅγιον λαὸς εἰς περιποίησιν ὅπως τὰς ἀρετὰς ἐξαγγείλητε τοῦ ἐκ σκότους ὑμᾶς καλέσαντος εἰς τὸ θαυμαστὸν αὐτοῦ φῶς

Rev 1:6 καὶ ἐποίησεν ἡμᾶς βασιλείαν, ἱερεῖς τῷ θεῷ καὶ πατρὶ αὐτοῦ - αὐτῷ ἡ δόξα καὶ τὸ κράτος εἰς τοὺς αἰῶνας τῶν αἰώνων ἀμήν.

Rev 5:10 καὶ ἐποίησας αὐτοὺς τῷ θεῷ ἡμῶν βασιλείαν καὶ ἱερεῖς[21] και βασιλεύσουσιν ἐπὶ τῆς γῆς

It should be noted that the term "priesthood", ἱεράτευμα, is found in the New Testament only here in v. 9 and in v. 5 of the same chapter. In v. 5, Christians "are built up as a spiritual house to be a holy priesthood (ἱεράτευμα ἅγιον)." The expression "a royal priesthood" (βασίλειον ἱεράτευμα) in 1Pet 2:9 and the juxtaposition of "kingdom" and "priests" in Rev 1:6 and 5:10, used with reference to the believers, are taken from the Book of Exodus (19:6). Here, God is

---

[19] In his article "Womb of the World", Peter J. Leithart examines how baptism is an effective sign of the socio-religious reorganization of the world in the New Covenant. The article maintains that the phrase 'our bodies washed with pure water' in Heb 10:22 refers to baptism, and therefore implies in context that baptism initiates into the Christian priesthood. Peter J. Leithart, "Womb of the World: Baptism and the Priesthood of the New Covenant in Heb 10:19-22", in *Journal for the Study of the New Testament* 78 (2000), pp. 49-65.

[20] Thomas D. Lea, "The Priesthood of all Christians", in Southwestern Journal of Theology 30/2 (1988), p. 16.

[21] The reference to "kingdom and priests" (βασιλείαν καὶ ἱερεῖς) here may be a hendiadys: "priestly kingdom".

offering a covenant to the people of Israel, that they may be God's inheritance and may become "a kingdom of priests" in the midst of the nations. The New Testament people of God, like the Israelites of the Old Covenant, form the universal priesthood.

The word βασίλειον could be understood as an adjective (the neuter form of βασίλειος, *royal*) or as a noun, *palace* or *king's house*. Arguing for a parallel between verses 5 and 9, Elliot suggests that the word is intended as noun, with the meaning of "king's house" or "royal palace".[22] On this interpretation, the words βασίλειον and ἱεράτευμα are two distinct designation for the Christians Peter is addressing. They are both "king's house" (in the sense of "palace", not family) and "priesthood". Such a separation of the two terms is found in Revelation 1:6 ("he made us a kingdom, priests") and it seems to reflect John's understanding of God's promise to Israel in Exodus 19:6. Israel will be "God's house" and "a priesthood".

There are, however, some indications in 1Pet 2:9 that βασίλειον ἱεράτευμα should be seen as a noun and a modifier. The phrase is part of a list of designations for the Christian community formed in the same way: "a chosen race, *a royal priesthood*, a holy nation, a people destined for vindication." Elliott objects that out of the four pairs in this verse, the other three have the noun followed by the modifier, but here the modifier precedes the noun. If the author intended the word as an adjective, he would have been consistent in terms of the position of the modifier in reference to the noun.[23] Therefore, in Elliot's opinion, the position of βασίλειον before the noun is a sign that it is not a modifier, but should be understood as a noun. Elliot, however, overlooks the fact that the reversal of the two words is not Peter's work. The wording of this and the next designation is identical with that of the LXX translation of Exodus 19:6: βασίλειον ἱεράτευμα καὶ ἔθνος ἅγιον, except for the conjunction καὶ which connects the two designations in the LXX. It becomes clear that Peter imports two designations from the LXX translation of Exodus 19:6 and adds two more to describe the Christians as the New Israel. The phrase βασίλειον ἱεράτευμα should be translated, then, by "royal priesthood". Its meaning is quite different from that of the MT – מַמְלֶכֶת כֹּהֲנִים "a kingdom of priests".[24]

---

[22] J.H. Elliott, *The Elect and the Holy: An Exegetical Examination of 1 Peter 2:4-10 and the Phrase* βασίλειον ἱεράτευμα (NovTSup 12, Leiden: EJ Brill, 1966), pp. 149-154. It seems that Elliott is forcing the meaning of the word here.

[23] Ibid., p. 151.

[24] Following Hort, Ernest Best argues that βασίλειον should be understood as "a body of kings" and, thus, supports the translation of βασίλειον ἱεράτευμα "kings and priests" or "a body of kings and priests". Ernest Best, "1 Peter 2:4-10: A Reconsideration", in *Novum*

God's promise to Moses, "You shall be unto Me a kingdom of priests and a holy nation", was fulfilled in the Christian Church. We may infer that the new "priesthood of all believers", like the old one, is bound to perform some sort of priestly functions in the new Temple of God (1Cor 3:16). In the next section we will investigate the nature of the priestly functions of each believer.

2.4.2 Priestly duties of each believer

In his commentary on Hebrews, F.F. Bruce gives us an excellent statement about the sacrificial nature of Christianity: "Christianity is sacrificial through and through; it is founded on the one self-offering of Christ, and the offering of His people's praise and property, of their service and their lives, is caught up into the perfection of His acceptable sacrifice, and is accepted in Him."[25] Evidently, the reference is not to the ordained ministries of the church, but to the general priesthood of all believers. On the same note, Bishop Demetrios Trakatellis' article entitled "'Ακολούθει μοι / Follow me' (Mk 2:14) Discipleship and Priesthood" makes a connection between discipleship and priesthood in order to underline the "dimension and richness of discipleship inherent in any genuine and integral priesthood."[26] While we can agree with Bishop Trakatellis that "one of the most important contributions of the New Testament to a proper understanding of the nature and function of the priesthood is the idea of discipleship"[27], we must say that such an idea, in itself, is not useful to distinguish between the general priesthood of believers and the ordained ministry.

Returning to F.F. Bruce's statement on the sacrificial nature of Christianity, we may say that, like the priesthood of the Old Testament, Christians, as priests of the New Covenant, approach God without having to make offerings for their sins (Heb 10:22). They offer, nonetheless sacrifices but these do not consist of slaughtered animals but of their own bodies, offered as *a living sacrifice*, holy, and acceptable to God, which is our "reasonable service" (λογικὴ λατρεία) or worship (Ro 12:1). The reason why the body is to be sacrificed is because it is "the vehicle that implements the desires and choices of the redeemed spirit".[28] It represents the whole personality which is called to offer *the*

Testamentum 11, no. 4, pp. 288-291. The ending -ιον allows for this rendering, although the evidence for this usage is extremely limited.

[25] F.F. Bruce, *The Epistle to the Hebrews*, The New International Commentary on the New Testament (Grand Rapids: Eerdmans, 1964), p. 407.

[26] Demetrios Trakatellis, "'Ακολούθει μοι / Follow me' (Mk 2:14) Discipleship and Priesthood", in *Greek Orthodox Theological Review* 30/3 (1985), pp. 271-285.

[27] Ibid., p. 271.

[28] Everett F. Harrison, "Romans", *Romans-Galatians,* in The Expositor's Bible Commentary, vol. 10, ed. Frank E. Gaebelein *et al.*, Grand Rapids: Zondervan Publishing House, 1976, p. 127.

sacrifice of obedience. They offer *the sacrifice of praise* continually to God, that is, "the fruit of lips" which make confession to His name (Heb 13:15). Also, they "do not neglect to do good and to share what [they] have with others, for with *such sacrifices* God is well pleased" (Heb 13:16). Obviously, the sacrifices that are pleasing to God consist of both the sacrifices of praise of v. 15 and the almsgiving and the deeds of mercy of v. 16. Lastly, like the Temple priests *they offer incense*, and the smoke of their prayers goes right up into the presence of God (Rev 5:8; 8:4).

According to J.M. Ross, there are four aspects which characterize the activity of the Christian priesthood: **1) personal access to God, 2) public worship, 3) service of the church and 4) the service of the world.**[29] His points are detailed below:

> 1. The direct access to the very presence of God is a privilege which we are too ready to evade. The reasons are various: the minister is already praying for us; we are not skilled to pray adequately; it is much more comfortable to stay in the outer courts burning incense than to enter into God's presence where our sin is exposed; the ritual, although more costly than a regular and consistent life of prayer is preferred by many Christians, because it does not involve too much effort.
>
> 2. The public worship is another privilege of each Christian which is many times evaded, either because it is much easier to let the "professional" worshippers do it or because we let it slip into a form of entertainment.
>
> 3. The service of the church is that part of the priestly duty of each believer by which he or she builds up the church according to his/her particular gifts and abilities. To substitute one's gifts and talents with money is a wrong idea.
>
> 4. All members of the "royal priesthood of believers" are to function, like the Levitical priests, as intermediaries between God and the people. It is our responsibility to draw the unbelieving near God, to interpret God's will for them, to intercede for them before God. The Apostle Paul, in serving the Gentiles, saw himself as a "temple-servant" (λειτουργός) of Christ. In this capacity, said the apostle, "*I serve* the Gospel of God *like a priest*" (ἱερουργοῦντα τὸ εὐαγγέλιον τοῦ θεοῦ), so that the *offering consisting of the Gentiles* (ἡ προσφορὰ τῶν ἐθνῶν)[30] may be

---

[29] J.M. Ross, "The Priesthood of All Believers", *Expository Times* 62 (1951), p. 47 (whole article, pp. 45-48). In his extensive article on the general priesthood of believers, Ernest Best limits the priestly functions of a Christian to three: access to God, the offering of sacrifices and the blessings of the people. The third one, however, cannot be found in the New Testament. Ernest Best, "Spiritual Sacrifice: General Priesthood in the New Testament", in *Interpretation* 14 (1960), p. 294.

[30] The Gk. "the offering of the Gentiles" could be understood as "an offering belonging to the Gentiles" (possessive genitive), "an offering made by the Gentiles" (subjective geni-

acceptable [to God], sanctified by the Holy Spirit" (Rom 15.16, emphasis mine). It is the apostle who presents the Gentiles before God as an acceptable offering, most likely as a thanksgiving offering. Such responsibility belongs, however, not only to the ordained ministry of the church, but to all members. It derives from their status as members of the "royal priesthood".

As one can see, these priestly duties include privileges and responsibilities. But which of these duties of all Christians is the most important? They are all important, but it seems that responsibility is better emphasized than privilege. By virtue of his priestly function, the believer does have the right of access to God, but he/she must assume the sacrifices his status entails and commit to serve the church and the world. As Jerry Chance put it:

> An examination of scriptural references and allusions to the priestly traits and activities of the believer ... strongly suggests that the idea of universal priesthood denotes primarily the Christian's ministry of love, service, and witness to the neighbor rather than the Christian's privilege of access to God.[31]

According to Revelation 20:6, the general priesthood of believers will continue to the time of Jesus' return and beyond. The essential responsibility of this priesthood is to offer praise and adoration to God and the Lamb.

In both Romans and Hebrews, the collective aspect of the priestly ministry of believers is emphasized. Although each believer is singularly responsible for fulfilling or not fulfilling his/her priestly duties, he/she does not act in isolation. The texts are in plural, indicating that God is pleased when an entire group of Christians acts collectively rather than individually. It is more efficient in terms of reaching the target and more impressive to the world when Christians unite their efforts in order to save the lost and ameliorate the sufferings of the unprivileged.

The "priestly" status granted to each believer denotes that no other human priesthood is needed as an ecclesiastical structure. All Christians have equal access to all priestly functions and, therefore, they need no representation from any other person in the bringing of their sacrifices. This is not to say that the idea of representation is eliminated altogether. The author of the Epistle to the Hebrews, immediately after presenting the priestly duty of each believer to bring sacrifices of praise and of good works, goes on and exhorts his readers to

---

tive), or "an offering consisting of the Gentiles" (appositive genitive). In view of Paul's role as a λειτουργός of Christ, the latter translation makes more sense than the other two. So J.D.G. Dunn, *Romans* (WBC 38), 2:860; C.E.B. Cranfield, Romans, Grand Rapids, Eerdmans, 1985, p. 365.

[31] Jerry M. Chance, "The Social Thrust of the Idea of the Priesthood of Believers", in *The Theological Educator 3*, June 1974, p. 7.

obey their leaders and submit to them (Heb 13:17). A presentation in parallel of the general priesthood and the ordained ministry is also found in 1 Peter: those who form "a holy priesthood" (2:5) are to "be subject to the elders" (5:8) whose duties he just described (5:1-5). Similarly, Apostle Paul states that not all members of the church can be apostles, or prophets, or teachers and pastors. The specialized ministry of the church as presented in the New Testament, in both its narrative and epistolary books, is the focus of the next section.

2.5 The Ordained Ministry of the Church

According to the New Testament, there are only two levels of leadership in the church – elders and deacons. Elders, also designated as *pastors* or *overseers*, are the principal leaders of the local church (Acts 20) and deacons are elder helpers, mainly in administrative matters (Acts 6:1-7; 1Tim 3:8-13). The qualifications for the two levels of ministry are stated in 1Timothy 3 and Titus 1.

The terms used in the New Testament with reference to the office of an elder are: πρεσβύτερος – elder, ἐπίσκοπος – overseer or bishop, and ποιμήν – shepherd or pastor. The three terms are used interchangeably (e.g. Acts 20:17, 28), each one of them depicting a specific function for the office of elder. In Zens' opinion, "the term «elder» refers to maturity, «bishop» («overseer») refers to oversight and administration, and «pastor» refers to the elements of shepherding such as feeding and guarding."[32]

There is only one type of church government in the New Testament and that is provided by plural eldership.[33] The evidence shows that there is no example of a church in the New Testament ruled by one elder, not even the church at Jerusalem or the churches established by the Apostle Paul. The rule is always plu-

---

[32] Jon Zens. "The Major Concepts of Eldership in the New Testament", *Baptist Reformation Review*, Summer 1978, p. 29.

[33] The Catholic position on this is well represented by R. Benedict Ashley. In his view, the High Priesthood of Christ requires a "certain ecclesiology". Since we have a High Priest, says Ashley, the Church is "an hierarchical organization". In his words: "In fact it is derived from the Greek *hieros*, sacred, and *arche*, a principle of order, and hence simply means "sacred order". The Church is no mere mob or loose "Jesus Movement", but an organic, well-structured, dynamically acting community whose organization is determined by its spiritual mission." On the basis of biblical metaphors like "living stones" or "body" Fr. Benedict concludes that "the Church is hierarchical, that is, has a sacred order in which Christ as High Priest is the hierarch, the principle of that organic order." Then he goes on to say that "Since the Church is Christ's body by which he remains visibly present and active in mission in the world, its leaders must also sacramentally signify that priestly presence within the Church." http://www.ignatiusinsight.com/features2007/bashley_whoisapriest_oct07.asp. Unfortunately, there is no biblical evidence produced in order to support such theological statement.

ral leadership (Acts 14:23; Acts 20:17, 28; Phil 1:1; Tit 1:5 and James 5:14). But the reality of elder equality in the early church does *not* imply automatically similarity in the functions the elders performed. All elders were equal because they occupy the same office but, at the same time, they performed different duties, according to the gifts possessed by each one. But the possession of different spiritual gifts did not lead in the New Testament church to a "specialized eldership" classified in categories like "ruling elders", "teaching elders", "miracle-working elders", etc. According to some scholars, a division of this sort is found 1Timothy 5:17 where two types of elders are mentioned – the "ruling" and the "teaching" elders. It is our opinion that this text simply points out the diversity of gifts among the elders since *all* elders must rule and teach in the church (1Tim 3:2, 5). Those elders who rule well and labor in the Word are counted worthy of "double honor". Most likely, this "double honor" includes respect and financial support for the elders since "the laborer is worthy of his wages" (1Tim 5:18; cf. also 5:3 where "poor widows" are entitled to the same "honor"). However, whether some elders receive "honor" or "double honor", they still remain equal in authority with the other elders.

According to traditionalist scholars, the New Testament structure of the Church is seen in terms of the traditional historical threefold ministry of bishops, priests and deacons. In other words, from the very beginning there was no plurality of eldership, but three levels of authority.[34] This model, however, finds no support in the New Testament itself. It is a later reading of the New Testament, through the lenses of the patristic writers.[35]

In the following section, we will investigate the duties of the ordained ministry in the New Testament in order to assess whether such duties are compatible with the functions and roles of the priests and to prove or disprove the existence of a special Christian priesthood.

2.5.1 Duties of the ordained ministry

The duties performed by the elders of the local church include *governing* of the local church (1Tim 3:5; 5:17; 1Pet 5:2-3), *equipping* for the work of ministry (Eph 4:11-12), "*shepherding* the flock" (Acts 20:28; 1Pet 5:1-4), *preaching*

---

[34] E.g. Benedict Seraphim, "On the Priesthood in the New Testament", posted on 26 February 2005 at: *http://benedictseraphim.wordpress.com/2005/02/26/on-the-priesthood-and-the-new-testament/*

[35] The first among the Apostolic Fathers to mention the "three-order" structure of Church leadership was Ignatius of Antioch. In this order, presbyters and deacons are working under the authority of the monarchical episcopos. Such structure was a practical necessity, in Ignatius' view, for the unity and orthodoxy of the Church (Ignatius, To the Smyrnaeans, 8). In the post-Ignatian period, the bishop has been "adorned" with royal paraphernalia.

and *teaching* (Eph 4:12; 1Tim 5:17; 2Tim 2:2; Tit 1:9), *providing protection against false teaching* (Acts 20.27, 29; Titus 1.9), *providing exhortation* (1Tim 4:13; 6:2; Tit 1:9; 2:15), *appointment of leadership* (1Tim 4:14; 2Tim 1:6), *prayer for the sick* (James 5:13-16). What we know of the responsibilities of a deacon is even less: He cares for and leads his household well (1Tim 3:12), and perhaps provides food for needy widows (see Acts 6:1-7). But are these functions sacerdotal?

Those who affirm the existence of sacerdotal ministries in the New Testament church derive their arguments from a comparison of Christian ministry today with the role of the Levitical priesthood of the Old Testament. Such approach is at fault in that it does not filter the nature and the duties of the priesthood in contemporary churches through the ecclesiology of the New Testament period. For a correct assessment of the ordained ministry in contemporary churches, it is essential to know the nature and structure of the leadership in the church of the first century AD.

First of all, it should be made clear that the idea of sacerdotalism underlines the powers of priests as essential mediators between God and humankind.[36] Sacerdotal is, therefore, only that function which one cannot fulfill for himself, but needs a higher authority to act in behalf of him. In this section, we will analyze the functions of the ordained ministry (clergy) which have been understood by some as being sacerdotal in light of the New Testament ecclesiology. According to this view, the functions of the Christian "priests" are: to offer sacrifice (i.e. to celebrate the Eucharist), to forgive sins, to bless, to preach and to sanctify.

2.5.1.1 Bringing sacrifices in behalf of the people (The Eucharist)

Theologians of the historical churches see Eucharist as a New Covenant sacrificial meal corresponding to the Old Testament Passover, and, therefore, necessitating a priest to administer it. According to many Protestant and Evangelical theologians, the above interpretation is nothing more than theologizing the ministry of the New Testament church in light of the Old Testament. In this section we will be paying careful attention to the New Testament passages relevant to the Eucharist to see how the first century church understood the "sacrament" and how it was practiced. Our goal is, therefore, twofold: a) to find out if New Testament church understood *Eucharist as a sacrificial meal* and b) to see if there is any *connection in the New Testament between ordained ministry and the administration of Eucharist*.

Is Eucharist a sacrificial meal? According to the famous Protestant scholar Joachim Jeremias, in presenting the bread and wine as his "body", respectively

---

[36] http://www.merriam-webster.com/dictionary/sacerdotalism?show=0&t=1288792471.

his "blood", Jesus used cultic terms and, implicitly, compared himself to the Passover sacrifice:

> When Jesus speaks of 'his flesh' and 'his blood' ... he is applying to himself terms from the language of sacrifice ... Each of the two nouns presupposes a slaying that has separated flesh and blood. In other words: Jesus speaks of himself as a sacrifice.[37]

On the basis of an old Passover prayer which asks God to remember the Messiah, Jeremias translated the commandment "do this in remembrance of Me" by "do this so that God may remember Me". So, Jeremias understands Eucharist as an *anamnesis*, a memorial or commemorative sacrifice which is observed to "remind" God about the work that Jesus did on the cross for us.[38] Although we understand the "remembering" as being "manward" rather than "Godward", i.e. man is intended to remember Christ not God,[39] we can unhesitantly agree with Jeremias that Jesus conceived Eucharist as a "memorial" of the salvation he had accomplished through his death. In fact, this is plainly stated in 1Cor 11:26, where Paul adds to Jesus' words: "For every time you eat this bread and drink the cup, you proclaim the Lord's death until he comes." However, this is not to say, as Jeremias does, that a memorial is in itself a sacrifice. Even if verb ποιεῖν ("to do") and the noun ἀνάμνησις ("remembrance") can be used in the Old Testament with sacrificial overtones, as Akin suggests[40], it does not necessarily mean they were used in the same way here. As already shown above, the celebration is not understood by Paul as a memorial offering which one brings before God to prompt his remembrance of Jesus. It is a memorial in its plainest sense, by which the worshipper remembers the work of Christ on his behalf (1Cor 11:24, 26).

Other scholars see Eucharist *as a continuation of the Old Testament Passover?* The primary emphasis of the original Passover seems to have been the smearing of the door-posts of the houses with blood as a protection against the plague of death. In the later stages of development of the Israelite religion, it had come to be celebrated as a solemn annual rite of thanksgiving, a commemoration of God's deliverance of Israel from Egypt (Ex 12:26-27). Because of this latter significance, the Passover festival has been re-interpreted in the New Testament as a foreshadowing and symbol of redemption through Christ. Apostle Paul writes: "Christ our Passover has been sacrificed. So then, let us celebrate the Feast..." (1Cor 5:7-8).

---

[37] J. Jeremias, *The Eucharistic Words of Jesus*, Minneapolis MN, Fortress Press, 1977, p. 222.

[38] Ibid., p. 252.

[39] Gordon Fee, *1 Corinthians*, pp. 552-557.

[40] James Akin, "The Office of New Testament Priest", http://www.cin.org/users/james/files/ntpriest.htm.

Jesus' death on the cross, which otherwise was an execution by the Roman authority, is interpreted by Paul as a sacrifice, as a "Passover sacrifice". Such re-interpretation of the Israelite festival was enhanced by the historical fact that Jesus' crucifixion took place at the time of Passover. Now, having seen that the death of Jesus was understood by the church of the first century as a sacrifice, the next thing to investigate is the connection between Eucharist and the Passover meal.

The two were connected in the sense that, according to the Gospel writers, it was during the Passover meal that Jesus presented the bread and the fruit of the vine as his body and his blood and, in doing so, inaugurated the Eucharist. But, is there any other connection between Eucharist and the Jewish Passover to justify the idea that the former was understood by the first century church as a sacrificial meal?[41] It must be noted that, in depicting Christ as "our Passover", Apostle Paul does not mention at all the Eucharist. He, indeed, summons the Corinthians to "celebrate the festival" (5:8), but is he alluding to the Eucharist? Is he calling the believers to celebrate the Eucharist? The continuous present tense of the active subjunctive ἑορτάζωμεν must be understood as a call to an "ongoing feast of the celebration of God's forgiveness by holy living".[42] It was so understood by John Chrysostom in his homiletic commentary: "It is a festival, then, the whole time in which we live ... the whole of time is a festival to Christians, because of the excellence of the good things which have been given ... The Son of God ... freed you from death and called you to a kingdom."[43]

Even when one allows that an allusion is made here to the celebration of Eucharist, there is nothing in the text about the sacrificial nature of the Eucharist or the priestly functions of those who administer it.[44] On the contrary, the sacrifice of Christ is referred to in the past tense: "Christ, our Passover lamb,

---

[41] Such view was held by some scholars like Jean Héring, *The First Epistle of Saint Paul to the Corinthians*, London, 1962, p. 37; J.J. Lias, *The First Epistle to the Corinthians*, Cambridge, 1896, p. 61 and G.P. Wiles, *Paul's Intercessory Prayers*, SNTSMS 24, Cambridge, 1974, pp. 146f.

[42] Gordon Fee, *The First Epistle to the Corinthians*, NICNT, Grand Rapids, Eerdmans, 1987, p. 218; F. Godet, *First Epistle to the Corinthians*, vol. 1, p. 266. See also Anthony C. Thiselton, *The First Epistle to the Corinthians: a commentary on the Greek text*, in NICGT, Grand Rapids, Eerdmans, 2000, p. 406.

[43] *1Cor. Hom.*, 15:6.

[44] The idea of atoning for sins cannot be present in this passage, for the Passover lamb in the Old Testament was not sacrificed to atone for sins. It was rather a symbol of the deliverance of Israel from the Egyptian bondage. As Israel was set apart as a distinct people by being spared through the blood of the paschal lamb on the doorposts of their houses, so the believers in Corinth were set apart as a distinct people through the blood of Christ – Richard B. Hays, *First Corinthians*, Philadelphia, Westminster John Knox Press, 1997, p. 83.

has been sacrificed." In our opinion, this passage does not support the idea of continuation between the Israelite Passover and the Eucharist nor the view that the nature of Eucharist is sacrificial meal.

While I can agree with A.E.J. Rawlinson's assertion that "[it] is the Last Supper which makes Calvary sacrificial", in the sense that it was the Last Supper which afforded the clue for the sacrificial interpretation of Jesus' death, I must disagree with his contention that, it was during the New Testament period when Eucharist was regarded as being a sacrificial meal.[45] The earliest "proof" brought by Rawlinson is from Apostle Paul's contrast of the "table of the Lord" with the table of demons (1Cor 10:21). In his opinion, the placing of the two settings side by side demonstrates that Apostle Paul "regard the Christian observance as falling within the same general category as the sacrificial feasts of the non-Christian religious world".[46] But the analogy that Paul is making in the previous verses is not between pagan meals and the Eucharist, but between the pagan meals and the sacrifices of the Old Testament. What the apostle is saying is that those who participate in the pagan meals are sharers in what has been sacrificed to demons in the same way the old Israelites shared in the sacrifices offered to God. As Gordon Fee contends, Paul's recourse to an additional illustration from Israel is a clear indication that he did not see the Lord's Table as a sacrificial meal.[47] Another aspect which goes against the view which sees the Eucharist as a sacrificial meal is the fact that it violates the mosaic prohibition against the consumption of blood (Lev 17:10-11). In the Israelite sacrifices only the meat was consumed ("the body"), while in the Eucharist both the body and the blood are to be consumed.

According to our investigation, there is no indication in the New Testament that the apostolic churches understood the Eucharist as a sacrificial meal. It is true that the vocabulary used in some of the early Christian writings seems to indicate that this understanding of the Eucharist was part of an early development in the history of Christian thought. The author of Didache exhorts the believers "to break bread and hold Eucharist, after confessing your transgressions that your offering may be pure."[48] Apparently, the same understanding is found in Ignatius' letter to the Ephesians where the Lord's Table is described as an "altar".[49] The Eucharist came to be known as the "unbloody sacrifice"

---

[45] A.E.J. Rawlinson, "Priesthood and Sacrifice in Judaism and Christianity", in *Expository Times* 60, 1949, p. 118.

[46] Ibid.

[47] Gordon Fee, *1 Corinthians*, p. 472.

[48] *Didache*, 14:1-3

[49] Ignatius, *ad Eph* 5, "Let no man deceive himself: if anyone be not within the altar, he is deprived of the bread of God."

(ἀναίμακτος θυσία) around the middle of the fourth century, when the phrase was used by Cyril of Jerusalem and possibly, before him, by Athanasius.

Is there any connection in the New Testament between ordained ministry and the administration of Eucharist? According to Benedict Seraphim, there are some indications even in the New Testament that the elders and deacons had some liturgical functions in relation to the Eucharist at this time. His argument starts with the Apostle Paul's perception on his ministry in Romans 15, as one who is a "temple-servant" (λειτουργός) serving the Gospel of God *like a priest* (ἱερουργοῦντα). Then, continuing with Paul's responsibility to appoint elders in all the churches he established and the continual observance of the Eucharist, Benedict Seraphim reaches the conclusion that "one can, on the New Testament alone, build a strongly suggestive case that the *episkopoi*, *presbyteroi* and *diakonoi* served the Body and Blood of Christ in the elements of the bread and wine of the Eucharist."[50] In our opinion, Seraphim's argumentation is at fault here, nothing being strongly suggestive or, simply, suggestive of the connection between ordained ministry and the Eucharist.

First, he is narrowing the meaning of λειτουργός to read "temple-servant" and, in doing this, to get as close as possible to the notion of a "priest". It is well known that the meaning of λειτουργός and its cognates is more general, being translated simply by "minister", "ministry", "to minister" etc. The term is used with the same broad meaning of Epaphroditus (Phil 2:25), of angels (Heb 1:7) and Jesus (Heb 8:2). That any word from the word group λειτουργός, λειτουργία, and λειτουργεῖν could be used in a strict sense and a broad sense during the same time frame is proven by Luke. With reference to the service of Zacharia, the priest, he uses the noun λειτουργία in the strict sense of its OT usage, i.e. bringing sacrifices in temple (Lk 1:23). In a Christian context, he uses the same word (in its verbal form λειτουργεῖν) with reference to the common prayer and fasting of the church in Antioch (Acts 13:2).

Secondly, when the Apostle Paul refers to himself as one who is "serving the Gospel of God like a priest" (ἱερουργοῦντα), he is using the terms in a metaphorical sense, not in terms of Old Testament sacrificial duties of a priest. The term, a *hapax legomenon* in the New Testament, is used in connection with another metaphorical description of the Gentiles as an "offering" to God. The apostle was given the "priestly duty" [literally, "the priestly work"] of proclaiming the Gospel of God and, in doing this, to present the Gentiles as an *offering* acceptable to God. Neither the verb ἱερουργέω, *to serve as priest*, nor the noun προσφορά, *offering*, are to be taken literally. But, in fact, ἱερός means

---

[50] Benedict Seraphim, http://benedictseraphim.wordpress.com/2005/02/26/on-the-priesthood-and-the-new-testament.

sacred, holy – so, the primary meaning of the verb ἱερουργοῦντα is "performing the sacred duty of" or "performing the holy service of". Then, taking into consideration the primary meaning of the verb and the fact that the "sacred duty" is directly connected to the proclaiming of the Gospel and only secondarily to presenting the Gentiles as an "offering", it seems to me that the idea of a "priestly work" is not at the forefront of the text. Apostle Paul is describing himself as one who "received the grace to be a minister of Christ Jesus to the Gentiles, performing the sacred duty of the Gospel of God, so that the Gentiles may become an offering acceptable to God, sanctified by the Holy Spirit."

Turning to the main issue of this section, the connection between the special ministry and the Eucharist, we may say that there is not one passage in the New Testament to make this connection. The first association of this sort is apparently made by Ignatius of Antioch in his epistles (about 107 AD).[51] It is beyond our purpose to develop here a biblical theology of Eucharist. However, we reject the view that the Eucharist is a continued sacrifice and that, consequently, has to be administered by priests, i.e. Christian priests. In our view, it has no basis in the New Testament: 1) there is no passage in the New Testament to present the Eucharist in sacrificial terms, and 2) there is no connection made in the New Testament between the Eucharist and the ordained ministry. The New Testament never suggests that the person presiding over the "memorial ceremony" has to be a priest.

The "unperishable" priesthood of Christ is foundational for the New Testament priesthood of all believers and detrimental to the idea of special Christian priesthood. According to the writer of Hebrews, Jesus' priesthood is "unchangeable"[52] or better, "untransferable"[53] (ἀπαράβατος 7:24). This is a plain statement that there is no need for an intermediary between men and God other than Christ. In view of the general priesthood of believers presented above, each person has a direct access to God. The Roman Catholic view that Jesus Christ has appointed a special new priesthood whose work is to offer Him repeatedly as a sacrifice for sin is totally unbiblical, as the transubstantiation view is.[54]

---

[51] Ignatius, *ad Eph* 5; cf. also *ad Eph* 20.
[52] F.W. Danker, et al., *A Greek-English Lexicon of the New Testament*, Chicago, University of Chicago Press, 2000, p. 97.
[53] C. Spicq, *Theological Lexicon of the New Testament*, Peabody – MA, Hendrickson Publishers, 1994, 1.143-1.144.
[54] For an exposition of the Catholic view on the Eucharist, see e.g. James Gibbons, *The Faith of Our Fathers*, Baltimore, John Murphy, 1917, p. 387ff.

2.5.1.2 Receiving confession and forgiving sins

The authority to receive confession of sin and to forgive sins is seen as a sacerdotal function of the Christian priest. It is well known that, in the Old Testament, the forgiveness of sins was received through the mediation of the priests who offered sacrifices to God in behalf of the people. According to the Epistle to the Hebrews, that is no longer necessary because, through Jesus' sacrifice, we can approach God directly and boldly, without any human mediator (Heb 4:16). Jesus Christ is our great High Priest (Heb 4:14-15) and the only intermediary between God and humanity (1Tim 2:5). Moreover, one can find the plain statement in the Gospels that no man has to authority to forgive sins in the absolute sense of the verb; this is God's prerogative. The scribes criticize indirectly Jesus' pretension to have the authority to forgive sins: "Why does this man thus speak blasphemies? Who can forgive sins *but God only?*" (Mk 2:7, our emphasis). Jesus does not dispute the scribes' theology but, by linking the forgiveness of the sins and the healing, he gives them a sign of his messianic identity.

There are basically two texts in the New Testament that are used to support the practice of priests receiving confession from church members. The first one, Jn 20:23, does not mention the apostle's duty to receive confessions, but mentions their authority to forgive (ἀφίημι) sins. The second text, James 5:14-16, mentions both the confessing of sins and the forgiveness. In the following section, we will be making an analysis of each of the two verses (and the parallel passages) to determine if the contemporary practice of priests receiving confession of sins is endorsed here.

John 20.23. According to some interpreters, the Son of Man who had "the power to forgive sins" (Mt 9:6; Mk 2:7-10; Lk 5:21-24), communicated this authority to His apostles on Easter night: "Whose sins you shall forgive they are forgiven, whose sins you shall retain they are retained" (Jn 20:19-23). Jesus' statement finds its closest parallel in Mt 16:19, "I will give you the keys of the kingdom of heaven. Whatever you bind on earth will have been bound in heaven, and whatever you release on earth will have been released in heaven" and Mt 18:18, "I tell you the truth, whatever you bind on earth will have been bound in heaven, and whatever you release on earth will have been released in heaven." At least three points can be made at face about the three texts under discussion: (1) Confession of sin is not mentioned at all here. (2) The same authority of binding and releasing which was given to Peter at Caesarea Philippi, is given to the community in the context of the discussion on restoring broken relationships (Mt 18:15-22). 3) There is no promise in these texts, or even a hint, that the authority to forgive sins would be transferred to the successors of the apostles. Jesus' promise was specifically directed to the apostles.

The tenses of the verbs in John 20:23 impose the following translation: "Those whose sins you forgive have already been forgiven; those whose sins you do not forgive have not been forgiven." Having the first verb in each clause in the aorist and the second in the perfect, it results that the action of the second verb reflects an abiding state that began before the action of the first verb. Then, the message of the verse is: The forgiveness or the withholding of one's sins are not the results of the apostles' will or refuse to forgive, but the results of God's action. Apostles only proclaim that which has already taken place. The passive of the verb ("have been forgiven") is a divine passive[55], in agreement with John's perspective that only God can forgive sin through the blood of Jesus (Jn 1:29; 1Jn 1:7, 9). Christians can have a part in the forgiveness of others' sins at least by praying (1Jn 5:16-17) or by proclaiming the forgiveness of sins through Jesus (e.g. Acts 10:43; 13:38). The idea that only God has the prerogative to forgive sins is also present in Matthew 18:19, in the context of restoring relationships between disciples. Immediately after speaking about the disciples' authority to bind and release, Jesus assures them that anything they agree on and ask from the Father, it will be done for them. In this context of restoring relationships between his followers, Jesus' remark must be taken as referring primarily to "asking for forgiveness".[56]

In John 20:23, the "forgiving" and the "retaining" of sins by the apostles are mentioned in the context of believers' ministry to nonbelievers (vv. 21-23) and, therefore, are part of their proclamation of the Gospel. The sins of those who accept the Gospel are forgiven and, conversely, the sins of those who do not accept the Gospel are retained.[57] This interpretation is consistent with the main idea of the Farewell Discourse (cf. 15:27, 16:1-4, and 17:18), that the disciples are to continue the ministry of Jesus after he has departed from the world.

James 5:15. The action of confessing sins to "one another" is mentioned here in the context of the presbyters' prayer for the sick (v. 14). Although there is no injunction that confession has to be done before the presbyters who are called to pray for the sick, this type of confession cannot be excluded. Physical heal-

---

[55] Merrill C. Tenney, *John*, in Expositor's Bible Commentary vol. 9, ed. by Frank E. Gaebelein, Grand Rapids, Zondervan, 1981, pp. 193f. The same grammatical construction is present in Matthew 16:19 where, in each sentence, the verb of the second clause has the force of a future perfect. Its action precedes that of the first verb of each sentence.

[56] R.T. France, *The Gospel of Matthew*, in NICNT, Grand Rapids, Eerdmans, 2007, p. 697.

[57] Craig S. Keener, *The Gospel of John: A Commentary*, Peabody MA, Hendrickson Publishers, 2003, p. 1206f. In his comment to this verse, Calvin says: "While Christ enjoins the Apostles to *forgive sins,* he does not convey to them what is peculiar to himself. It belongs to him to *forgive sins.* This honor, so far as it belongs peculiarly to himself, he does not surrender to the Apostles, but enjoins them, in his name, to proclaim *the forgiveness of sins,* that through their agency he may reconcile men to God. In short, properly speaking, it is he alone who *forgives sins* through his apostles and ministers" – See commentary online: http://www.ccel.org/ccel/calvin/calcom35.x.iv.html.

ing and forgiveness are closely associated here[58], but healing is made dependent on the confession of sins as much as it is on the prayer of faith. Taking into account the fact that healing is expected to take place at the home of the sick believer, naturally confession is made in the very same context. Therefore, it is safe to say that the text alludes to the presbyters' role of receiving confession from the sick members of the church. But the confession of sins and the prayer are not prerogatives of the elders; they are also left to each individual member of the church. The members of the community are exhorted to confess the sins to one another (v. 16, ἀλλήλοις), possibly first of all to those wronged, and pray for one another. As Oda Wischmeyer noted, "the social context of prayer is not necessarily the assembly together with the πρεσβύτεροι, but the spiritual community of individual members of the group, and their mutual responsibility and sympathy."[59]

From the above analysis in James, we are in the position to draw the following conclusions: First, receiving confession of sins is not a prerogative of the ordained ministers of the church, but a right of each individual member. The only religious rite reserved here to the elders is the anointing of the sick with oil. Secondly, James 5:16 does not link forgiveness of sins with the confession of sins "to one another". Thirdly, neither the presbyters nor the individual members have the power to forgive sins. The forgiveness is received as a collateral blessing, together with healing. The prayer of the presbyters (v. 15) and that of the individual/community (v. 16) are intended primarily for healing. Fourthly, there is no suggestion in the text that the prayer of the presbyters would be more effective than the prayer of the simple member. It is "the fervent prayer of a righteous person [that] is very powerful in its working" (v. 16).

In conclusion, the concept of confession of sin to a priest is not taught in these texts which are the primary texts used to justify the sacrament of Penance. Believers are encouraged to confess their sins to one another and pray for each other in view of healing. Other passages refer to the confession of sins before God who is "is faithful and righteous, forgiving us our sins and cleansing us from all unrighteousness" (1John 1:9). As New Covenant believers, we do not need a human mediator between us and God in any respect, "for there is one God and one mediator between God and men, the man Christ Jesus" (1Tim 2:5).

---

[58] It is probably so because of the widespread idea that physical maladies are caused by sins committed or inherited. See Mt 9:2-5; Mk 2:1-12; Jn 5:14, 9:2; 1Cor 11:30.

[59] Oda Wischmeyer, "Reconstructing the Social and Religious Milieu of James: Methods, Sources, and Possible Results", in *Matthew, James and Didache*, edited by Huub van de Sandt and Jurgen K. Zangenberg, SBL Symposium Series 45, Society of Biblical Literature, Atlanta 2008, p. 39.

2.5.1.3 Praying in behalf of the people

Biblical leadership, as shown above, does not make the distinction laity/clergy as it is done in contemporary churches. On the contrary, it promotes a pattern of ministry in which all members "carry one another's burdens" and work together for the building up of the Body (Gal 6:2; 1Cor 12:12-27). There are several injunctions in the New Testament on the duty of Christians to pray for one another (e.g. Col 4:3, 4; 1Thes 5:25; 2Thes 3:1; Heb 13:8; Jas 5:16). Whether church members pray for the ordained ministers or vice versa, the act of praying for one another has nothing sacerdotal about it. According to Hebrews, each Christian has a direct access to the "Holy of Holies" and, therefore, does not need a human mediator before God (Heb 10:19-20).

Peter's and John's prayer for the Samaritans to receive the Holy Spirit was used sometimes as an argument that, at least in some situations, Christians need the mediation of their ordained ministers in order to secure blessings of some kind. The prayer of the two apostles, accompanied by the laying on of their hands, was seen as a priestly function. According to some scholars, the dispensing of the Holy Spirit is a prerogative of the apostles.[60] Philip had no authority to pray for the Samaritans to receive the Spirit, therefore the apostles Peter and John had to come from Jerusalem. This opinion is invalidated by other cases in the book of Acts when people other than the apostles lay hands for the reception of the Holy Spirit (9:17) or those situations when the Spirit comes without human mediation (2:4, 10:44).

According to some Christian traditions, the anointing of the sick with oil is another "priestly" duty of the professional priesthood. True, James 5:14-15 states clearly that those who should administer the anointing for healing[61] are the "presbyters"[62] of the church and that the gesture should be accompanied by

---

[60] A.J. Mason, *Relation of Confirmation to Baptism*, 1893, p. 23; F.H. Chase, *Confirmation in the Apostolic Age*, London, Macmillan, 1909, p. 26; Lowther Clarke, "The Laying on of Hands in the New Testament", in *Confirmation or the Laying on of Hands*, vol. 1 by various authors, London, SPCK, 1926, p. 8; M. Dibelius, *Studies in the Acts of the Apostles*, edited by H. Greeven, London, S.C.M., 1956, p. 17; N. Adler, *Taufe und Handauflegung*, p. 97; Kirsopp Lake, *Beginnings*, IV 92-93, V p. 53; B. Neunheuser, *Baptism and Confirmation*, translated by J.J. Hughes, New York, Herder and Herder, 1964, p. 44.

[61] In the Roman Catholic Church, the verse is a proof text for the doctrine of Extreme Unction. According to this doctrine, the priest anoints the eyes, ears, nostrils, hands and feet of a seriously ill person to give spiritual aid and comfort and spiritual health, including, if need be, the remission of sins. The footnote to James 5:14 in the official Roman Catholic English translation reads: "See here a plain warrant of scripture for the Sacrament of Extreme Unction, that any controversy against its institution would be against the express words of the sacred text in the plainest terms."

[62] The official Roman Catholic translation in English (Douay version) the term used for the elders is translated by "priests", in spite of the fact that the Latin Vulgate, used for translation, has *presbuteros* and not *sacerdotes*, the usual word for priests.

prayer. A legitimate question is whether the gesture is the prerogative of the ordained ministry and, if so, is it a sacrament? From the scarce information we have in the New Testament about the practice (Mk 6:13; Jas 5:14-15), it seems that, indeed, the anointing of the sick with oil is given to those who are sent with a special mission. But, is this a priestly function? The only thing the elders are to do and cannot be done by the members of the church is to anoint with oil. The anointing with oil, however, is not the main part of the ritual and the oil has no miraculous powers in itself. Therefore, the elders are not called because otherwise the healing would not be possible. According to verses 15 and 16, the healing is given to the prayer of faith and such prayer is by no means the prerogative of the elders. The whole community is called to confess sins to one another and pray for one another in order that those who are sick might be healed (5:16). The injunction that the presbyters are to be called can be explained by the fact that, most likely, they were primarily endowed with the gifts of healing in their respective congregations. At least in the earliest days of the movement, as recorded by Luke, leadership arose from the operation and recognition of spiritual gifts (Acts 6:3, 5, 8; 13:1, 2).[63] I acknowledge the possibility that James was familiar with the operation of the gifts of healing and that some of the elders possessed them (based on the analogy of Acts 6:3-5, 8; 8:6, 7 where, at least in Stephen's and Philip's case, the position of leadership is associated with spiritual gifts). It would, however, be precarious to assume that all elders were endowed with such a gift i.e. that healing the sick was a special function of this office.[64] The fact that "the elders of the church" *as a college* had to be called, shifts the emphasis from the gift to the office; they are to be called because of their official position in the church, rather than because of their possession of healing *charismata*. In other words, they are called not as healers but as intercessors. To connect the *charisma* of healing with the office of "elders", as Dibelius suggests,[65] would necessarily mean to assume a late development characterized by the institutionalization of the *charismata*.

In conclusion, the prayer "for one another", mentioned several times in the New Testament, is not reserved to the priestly class, but is the right of the whole community, as an act of Christian solidarity and compassion. And this is

---

[63] J.B. Mayor, *Epistle of James*, Minneapolis MN, Klock & Klock, 1892, p. 169; S. Laws, *The Epistle of James,* San Francisco, Harper & Row, 1980, pp. 230-231. R.V.G. Tasker, *James*, in TNTC, Leicester, Inter-Varsity Press, 1983, p. 131. Cf. also John F. Tipei, *The Laying on of Hands: Its significance, techniques and effects*, Lanham MD, University Press of America, 2009, p. 148.

[64] J. Wilkinson, "Healing in the Epistle of James", in *Scottish Journal of Theology* 24 (1971), p. 335.

[65] M. Dibelius, *A Commentary on the Epistle of James*, revised by H. Greeven. ET, Philadelphia: Fortress Press, 1976, p. 252f.

true in all situations the prayer is needed: for the reception of the Holy Spirit (Acts 8:15), for healing and forgiveness (Jas 5:14, 16) etc.

1.5.1.4 Preaching the Word

According to the teaching of the historical churches, the main duty of a Christian priest is that of imparting the Word of God to the faithful and to be the herald of the Gospel of Jesus Christ to those outside the church.[66] There are several references in the Old Testament pointing to the priestly duty of teaching the Law (Lev 10:11; Num 35:1ff; Deut 33:10; Hag 2:11; Zech 7:8; Hos 4:6; Mal 2:7). But when it comes to proclamation, as William Adams correctly notes, "the Levitical priest had no special Divine message to the people. He had no Gospel to preach, no glad tidings to proclaim. But, when, in times of national apostasy or national calamity, the people needed warning or guidance or consolation, it was not to the priest that they looked for help."[67]

In the New Testament, the duty of the elder to "feed the flock", by that meaning to impart the word of God, is clearly emphasized. It is difficult, however, to regard this duty as a priestly function. Earlier we defined that a priest is a mediator between man and God, performing in behalf of the former those actions which he cannot do for himself. According to the New Testament, preaching and interpreting the Word of God to the people are pastoral duties, rather than priestly functions. There is no indication in the New Testament that the Word of God has to be given to Christians and interpreted to them because this would be actions they cannot do for themselves. On the contrary, the Jews in Berea are presented on a positive note as people with an "open mind", precisely because they did not received blindly the words of the Apostle Paul, but they were "examining the scriptures carefully every day to see if these things were so" (Acts 17:11). The teaching that only the church is authorized to interpret the Scripture for her members is not found in the New Testament but reflects a later development in the theology of the Early Church.

As for the duty to communicate the Word of God to the faithful and unfaithful, the New Testament shows clearly that this is the prominent mission of an elder (1Tim 5:17; 2Tim 2:2). But, in preaching the Word, the Christian minister functions more like the Old Testament prophet who transmitted the oracles of God to His people. Likewise, in the New Testament, the Christian minister has the sacred duty to bring God's Word of reconciliation, the Good News, to the

---

[66] E.g. *Presbyterorum Ordinis,* teaches: "Priests ... have the primary duty of proclaiming the Gospel of God to all." In this way, "the spark of faith is lit in the hearts of unbelievers ..." (*PO*, 4)

[67] William J. Adams, "The Christian Ministry viewed in the Light of the Ancient Jewish Priesthood", in *Expository Times* 2 (1891), p. 277.

people. But, again, this is not a priestly duty. The minister is God's ambassador rather than one who acts before God on behalf of the people. According to Griffith Thomas, "this is the New Testament «ministry of the Word» and all of it is ministerial and instrumental, not mediatorial and vicarious."[68] Moreover, the mandate to witness the word is a prerogative of the ordained ministry. It belongs to all believers (Lk 9:60; Acts 8:5; Phil 1:14).

In concluding this section, we reiterate the fact that the prominent idea in the Old Testament priesthood was sacerdotal, i.e. that it emphasized the intermediary role of the priest between God and humankind. When one looks at the duties of the Christian ministers, listed above, it would be difficult to find anything sacerdotal about any of them. As Andrew Bonar said almost two centuries ago, "ministers of Christ *approach men* in behalf of God, who sends them as ambassadors, but these [Levitical] priests *approached God* in behalf of guilty men."[69]

There are situations in the public worship of a church when a minister would act in a representative capacity, performing actions which cannot be performed collectively, e.g. the breaking of the bread at the Eucharist or the anointing with oil of the sick. But when he does so, there is no special anointing upon him which is denied to other Christians.[70] Ordained ministry in the Church is not based on priestly prerogatives which other members of the church cannot perform. The special acts they do on behalf of the community are not part of the priestly functions shown above but merely representative and are performed by virtue of a special call or endowment by the Holy Spirit (Rom 12:6; 1Cor 12:7; Eph 4:7; 1Pet 4:10).

---

[68] Griffith Thomas, "Is the New Testament Minister a Priest?", p. 71.

[69] A. Bonar, *Leviticus* (Geneva Series of Commentaries; Carlisle PA, The Banner of Truth, 1846), p. 13.

[70] J.M. Ross, "The Priesthood", p. 47.

3. Conclusions

In the present study we analyzed the relevant New Testament passages to the issue of priesthood in order to see if the office of "priest" had been assimilated from the Israelite religion. Our investigation has shown that one of the central teachings of the New Testament is that the Old Testament priesthood was completely abolished through the sacrifice of Christ. No longer, are men to come to God through other men, but they have now direct access to God through the gateway opened by the atonement of Christ. (Heb 4:16) Through his death, Christ restored men and women to a personal relationship with God and established himself as a High Priest before God, with a permanent office. Now "there is one God and one intermediary between God and humanity, Christ Jesus, himself human" (1Tim 2:5) and there is no need for priests to do blood offerings. This explains why the New Testament nowhere uses the word "priest" to describe a leader in Christian service. As J.B. Lightfoot noted, "the kingdom of Christ has no sacerdotal system."[71]

Our study confirmed the thesis that there are only two kinds of priesthood recognized by the New Testament: 1) the High Priesthood of Christ and 2) the priesthood of all believers. If the first one must be taken literally, as the culmination of the whole sacrificial system of the Old Testament, the second one is metaphorical, in the sense that the sacrifices offered are no longer blood sacrifices but spiritual offerings. Another aspect which was underlined during our study is that the priesthood of all believers does not rule out the existence of a specialized, ordained, ministry: deacons, presbyters and bishops. We cannot emphasize enough Griffith Thomas' statement that, in the New Testament, "the essential idea of the ministry is *diakonia,* not *hieratum,* service not sacerdotalism, and it can never be too frequently asserted that the fundamental concept of the Christian ministry is that it represents God to the church rather than the church to God, that it is prophetic and not priestly."[72]

The doctrine of sacerdotalism made its way into the Christian dogma in the second and third centuries, especially through the writings of Cyprian, the Bishop of Carthage. By the end of the second century, the bishops of the church were called priests. The priestly office was vested primarily in the bishop, but a presbyter shared in his "priestly" function in the sense that, in the bishop's absence, he could act as his delegate. When, later on, the spread of Christianity dictated the establishment of parish churches, the presbyter became the principal celebrant of the Eucharist and, thus, was perceived as a parish priest. By virtue of his performing the Eucharist, hearing confession and

---

[71] J.B. Lightfoot, Saint Paul's Epistle to the Philippians, p. 182.
[72] Griffith Thomas, "Is the Christian Minister a Priest?", p. 70.

granting absolution of sins, the priest eventually became the church's main representative of God to the people and vice versa. But, as mentioned above, there is no idea in the New Testament of sacerdotal duties reserved for Christian ministers, no indication that salvation is deposited in the priesthood and dispensed through sacraments. Such teachings were developed later on in conjunction with other doctrines like the apostolic succession and will be the subject matter of another study which is part of the present research project.

Bibliography

Adams, William J., "The Christian Ministry viewed in the Light of the Ancient Jewish Priesthood", in *Expository Times* 2 (1891), pp. 276-277.

Adler, N., *Taufe und Handauflegung: Eine exegetisch-theologische Untersuchung von Apg 8,14-17*. Ed. M. Meinertz. NTAbh 19/3. Münster, Westfalia, 1951.

Ashley, Benedict, "Who is a priest?", online article, 2007, http://www.ignatiusinsight.com/features2007/bashley_whoisapriest2_oct07.asp

Akin, James, "The Office of New Testament Priest", online article, http://www.cin.org/users/james/files/ntpriest.htm

Best, Ernest, "Spiritual Sacrifice: General Priesthood in the New Testament", in *Interpretation* 14 (1960), pp. 273-299.

_____, 1969. "1 Peter 2:4-10 : A Reconsideration." *Novum testamentum* 11, no. 4: pp. 270-293. *ATLA Religion Database with ATLASerials*, EBSCO*host* (accessed January 3, 2011).

Bonar, A., *Leviticus* (Geneva Series of Commentaries), Carlisle PA, Banner of Truth, 1846.

Bornkamm, Günther, "*presbus*", in *TDNT* 6, pp. 651-683.

Bruce, F.F., *The Epistle to the Hebrews* (NICNT), Grand Rapids, Eerdmans, 1964.

Calvin, Jean, *Commentary to the Gospel of John*, online version: http://www.ccel.org/ccel/calvin/calcom35.x.iv.htmlChance, Jerry M. "The Social Thrust of the Idea of the Priesthood of Believers", in *Theological Educator* 3, June 1974, pp. 7-9.

Chase, F.H., *Confirmation in the Apostolic Age*. London: Macmillan, 1909.

Clarke, W.K. Lowther, "Laying on of Hands in the New Testament", in *Confirmation or the Laying on of Hands*, Vol. I, by various authors. London: SPCK, 1926.

Danker, F.W. et al., eds., *A Greek-English Lexicon of the New Testament*, Chicago, University of Chicago Press, 2000.

Dibelius, Martin, *Studies in the Acts of the Apostles*, edited by H. Greeven, London, S.C.M., 1956.

Dibelius, Martin, *A Commentary on the Epistle of James*, revised by H. Greeven. ET, Philadelphia: Fortress Press, 1976.

Dunn, James D.G., *Romans* (WBC 38, 2 vols.), Dallas, Word Books, 1988.

Elliott, John H., *The Elect and the Holy: An Exegetical Examination of I Peter 2:4-10 and the Phrase* βασίλειον ἱεράτευμα (NovTSup 12), Leiden: E.J. Brill, 1966.

Estes, David Foster. "Priesthood in the New Testament", in *ISBE*, online version, http://net.bible.org/dictionary.php?word=Priesthood%20In%20The%20New%20TestamentFee, Gordon. *The First Epistle to the Corinthians* (NICNT), Grand Rapids, Eerdmans, 1987.

France, R.T., *The Gospel of Matthew* (NICNT), Grand Rapids, Eerdmans, 2007.

Gibbons, James, *The Faith of Our Fathers*, Baltimore, John Murphy, 1917.

Gill, Theodore A., "Priesthood of Believers", in *Theology Today* 15/3 (Oct 1958), pp. 302-303.

Godet, F.L., *First Epistle to the Corinthians*, Edinburg, T. & T. Clark, 1889.

Harrison, Everett F., "Romans", in *Romans-Galatians*, in The Expositor's Bible Commentary, vol. 10, ed. Frank E. Gaebelein *et al.*, Grand Rapids: Zondervan Publishing House, 1976.

Hays, Richard B., *First Corinthians*, Philadelphia, Westminster John Knox Press, 1997.

Héring, Jean, The First Epistle of Saint Paul to the Corinthians, E.T., London, 1962.

Hirsch, Emil G., "High priest", in *Jewish Encyclopedia*, New York: Funk and Wagnalls, 1905, pp. 389-393, or http://www.jewishencyclopedia.com/view.jsp?artid=721&letter=H

Horbury, W.H., "The Aaronic Priesthood in the Epistle to the Hebrews", in *JSNT* 19 (1983), pp. 43-71.

Ignatius, *To the Smyrnaeans*, in *Early Christian Fathers*, ed. by Cyril C. Richardson, New York, Collier Books, 1970.

_____, *To the Ephesians,* in *Early Christian Fathers*, ed. by Cyril C. Richardson, New York, Collier Books, 1970.

Jeremias, Joachim, *The Eucharistic Words of Jesus*, Minneapolis MN, Fortress Press, 1977.

Keener, Craig S., *The Gospel of John: A Commentary*, Peabody MA, Hendrickson Publishers, 2003.

Laws, Sophie, *The Epistle of James*. San Francisco: Harper & Row, 1980.

Lea, Thomas D., "The Priesthood of all Christians according to the New Testament", in *Southwestern Journal of Theology* 30/2 (1988), pp. 15-21.

Leithart, Peter J., "Womb of the World: Baptism and the Priesthood of the New Covenant in Hebrews 10:19-22", in *Journal for the Study of the New Testament* 78 (2000), pp. 49-65.

Lias, J.J., *The First Epistle to the Corinthians*, Cambridge, University Press, 1896.

Lightfoot, J.B., *Saint Paul's Epistle to the Philippians*. London, Macmillan and Co., 1879.

Mason, A.J., *Relation of Confirmation to Baptism as Taught in the Holy Scriptures and the Fathers*, New York, 1891.

Mayor, J.B., The *Epistle of St. James*. Minneapolis MN, Klock & Klock, 1892.

Moore, G.F., *Judaism in the First Centuries of the Christian Era: The Age of Tannaim*, vol 1, Peabody MA, Hendrickson Publishers, 1997 (originally published in 1927).

Neunheuser, B., *Baptism and Confirmation*. trans. J.J. Hughes, New York, Herder and Herder, 1964.

Pohle, J., "Priesthood", in *The Catholic Encyclopedia*, New York, Robert Appleton Company, 1911.

Presbyterorum Ordinis, online document of the Catholic Church, http://www.vatican.va/archive/hist_councils/ii_vatican_council/documents/vat-ii_decree_19651207_presbyterorum-ordinis_en.html

Rawlinson, A.E.J., "Priesthood and Sacrifice in Judaism and Christianity", in *Expository Times* 60, 1949, pp. 116-121.

Ross, J.M., "The Priesthood of All Believers", in *Expository Times* 62 (1951), pp. 45-48.

Ryrie, Charles C., *Biblical Theology of the New Testament*, Chicago, Moody Press, 1959.

Safrai, Shemuel and M. Stern, eds., The Jewish people in the first century: Historical Geography, Political History, Social, Cultural and Religious Life and Institutions, in Compendia Rerum Iudaicarum ad Novum Testamentum Series, vol. II, Philadelphia: Fortress Press, 1976.

Schürer, E., *The History of the Jewish People in the Age of Jesus Christ*. rev. by G. Vermès, F. Millar and M. Black; Edinburgh: T. & T. Clark, 1979-1987.

Scott, William M. F., "Priesthood in the New Testament." *Scottish Journal of Theology* 10, no. 4 (December 1, 1957): pp. 399-415. *ATLA Religion Database with ATLASerials*, EBSCO*host* (accessed January 3, 2011).

Seraphim, Benedict, "On the Priesthood in the New Testament", posted on 26 February 2005 at: http://benedictseraphim.wordpress.com/2005/02/26/on-the-priesthood-and-the-new-testament/

Spicq, Ceslas, *Theological Lexicon of the New Testament*, Peabody – MA, Hendrickson Publishers, 1994.

Stylianopoulos, Theodore, "Holy Eucharist and the Priesthood in the New Testament", in *Greek Orthodox Theological Review* 23 (1978): pp. 113-130.

Tasker, R.V.G., *James*, in TNTC. Leicester, Inter-Varsity Press, 1983.

Tenney, Merrill C., *John*, in Expositor's Bible Commentary vol. 9, ed. by Frank E. Gaebelein, Grand Rapids, Zondervan, 1981.

Thiselton, Anthony C., *The First Epistle to the Corinthians: a commentary on the Greek text*, in NICGT, Grand Rapids, Eerdmans, 2000.

Thomas, W.H. Griffith, "Is the New Testament minister a priest", in *Bibliotheca Sacra* 136, no. 541 (January 1, 1979): pp. 65-73, *ATLA Religion Database with ATLASerials*, EBSCO*host* (accessed January 3, 2011).

Tierney, John, "The High Priest", in The Catholic Encyclopedia. vol. 12. New York, Robert Appleton Company, 1911. 29 Dec. 2009 http://www.newadvent.org/cathen/12407b.htm

Tipei, John F., *The Laying on of Hands: Its Significance, Techniques and Effects*, Lanham MD, University Press of America, 2009.

Trakatellis, Demetrios, "'Akolou, qei moi / Follow me' (Mk 2:14) Discipleship and Priesthood", in *Greek Orthodox Theological Review* 30/3 (1985), pp. 271-285.

Van de Sandt, Huub and Jurgen K. Zangenberg, eds., *Matthew, James and Didache*, SBL Symposium Series 45, Society of Biblical Literature, Atlanta 2008.

Wenham, G.J., *The Book of Leviticus* (NICOT 3), Grand Rapids, Eerdmans, 1979.

Wiles, G.P., *Paul's Intercessory Prayers* (SNTSMS 24), Cambridge, University Press, 1974.

Wilkinson, J., "Healing in the Epistle of James", in *Scottish Journal of Theology* 24 (1971): pp. 326-345.

Wischmeyer, Oda, "Reconstructing the Social and Religious Milieu of James: Methods, Sources, and Possible Results", in *Matthew, James and Didache*, edited by Huub van de Sandt and Jurgen K. Zangenberg, SBL Symposium Series 45, Society of Biblical Literature, Atlanta 2008.

Zens, Jon, "The Major Concepts of Eldership in the New Testament", in *Baptist Reformation Review* 7/2, Summer 1978, pp. 26-33.

Abstract

The official ministry in contemporary churches, as well as in churches of the last five or six centuries, is different from one tradition to the other in terms of terminology used, form and contents. The historical churches introduced the priestly office, similar to the Old Testament one, the principal role of which is to assure the mediation between men and divinity. The Reformed and Evangelical churches reject the need for any human mediation between man and God on the grounds that Christ, through his sacrificial death, had done away with the old sacrificial system and inaugurated a new system in which he is the High Priest and the only Mediator between humanity and God. Through the same act, Christ provided free access before God to each believer, making each of his disciples a "priest" before God. This study is meant to investigate the biblical texts relevant to the subject of priesthood in order to build a biblical foundation for the next chapters of the present project, i.e. the dogmatic approach of the concept of priesthood. After analyzing the New Testament terminology on the official ministries of the church, the author investigates the unique role of Christ as High Priest and Mediator between man and God and conducts an exegetical study of the passages relevant for the "priesthood of all believers" concept, emphasizing the metaphorical sense of this priesthood. Another aspect which is underlined during our study is that the "priesthood of all believers" does not rule out the existence of a specialized, ordained, ministry: deacons, presbyters and bishops. Lastly, the author makes a detailed investigation on the place and role the official ministry had in the New Testament church. It is argued that, from the standpoint of the New Testament writings, none of the duties of the ordained ministry is sacerdotal. The official minister acts always in a representative capacity, performing those actions which cannot be performed collectively. The conclusion of this study is that the roots of the priestly office, existant in historical churches today, are not to be found in the New Testament. This office appeared as a post-apostolic development of the Christian thought, in conjunction with other doctrines like the apostolic succession.

Iacob Coman
An Orthodox Dogmatic Perspective on the Priesthood

Introduction

The following research is integrated in the general theme of the comparative study regarding the priesthood – ***Priesthood in the Evangelical and Orthodox Traditions: A Comparative Study*** – and considers capitalising on the way the Eastern Church recuperates parts of the biblical text and of the tradition regarding the tasks of those who had the laying of hands and who have thus become partners with God in a spiritual activity, with the purpose of saving their neighbour, "... There is only one sacerdotal priesthood, the one that comes from Christ the Saviour, through the Holy Apostles, fulfilled through election and ordination, by the bishops, priests and deacons. The dignity of each level of the church hierarchy requests the same preparation and moral conduct. The priesthood is ordained by God."[1] This type of justification and declaration of the priesthood is filled with eastern theology and is justified through the text of the Holy Scripture and through the attitude of the Lord Jesus Christ himself, whom through his personal ministry and that of the Holy Spirit established a spiritual authority in the church. "He who descended is the very One who ascended higher than all the heavens, in order to fill the whole universe. It was he who gave some to be apostles, some to be prophets, some to be evangelists, and some to be pastors and teachers, to prepare God's people for works of service, so that the body of Christ may be built up until we all reach unity in the faith and in the knowledge of the Son of God and become mature, attaining to the whole measure of the fullness of Christ..." (Eph 4,10-13) A cut above the polemics regarding the transfer of semantic content of the word priest over the term of pastor and a cut above the translation divergences on which the Eastern Church bases its argumentation regarding the priestly office in the New Testament, we shall have to observe that God intended for *someone* to exist in cooperation with him in order to effect the salvation of his people.

As we have already observed, it is not our intention to follow a polemical or argumentative approach to the detriment of eastern thought. Our approach is one honestly appreciative, but, at the same time, we shall not overlook, when needed, the departing tendencies of the Eastern Church from the biblical index.

---

[1] Ștefan Alexe, Sfinții Trei Ierarhi și actualitatea gândirii lor despre preoție, [f.d] [f.l].

In eastern thought, the priestly status is, still, significant not only from a theological or religious perspective. The priestly status is significant because, in rural areas, and even in larger cities, the political, communal and private lives gravitate around the priest and is determined by him. The priests prestige add light and honour to those who belong to the Church and people's lives are determined positively because of the priest's presence. In eastern thought, not only in scholarly thought, the priest gives meaning to existence: "The priesthood is hanged by the highest firmament; it enters with no impediment into the highest heavens and walks splendidly and easily amidst the angels and the bodiless powers."[2] Man believes this and behaves deep within oneself determined by this reality.

In most cases, the priest's authority is higher than the mayor's is and of other official institutions in eastern rural society. This authority does not come from laws or civil norms, but from the moral authority of the priest and from the way in which each easterner considers oneself as belonging to the church from the perspective of longing after one's own eternity. "The dogma of salvation in the church and through the sacraments only prolongs the idea of cosmic solidarity and of the necessity of godly help in escaping evil, in the acclivity towards perfection. Only the conscience of one's need of the Church and of the sacraments for personal salvation, meaning the need for something that meets you from the outside, can pull you out of the individualist arrogance."[3] The indissoluble unity between the spiritual and lay life, between perennial and eternal destiny, between one's people and religion, between social and religious precedence, makes society's attachment to the priest and his self-accountability to be a serious and contemporary problem.

The priestly office from within the Church can never be confounded with High Priestly ministry of the Lord Jesus Christ. Even if at times certain prerogatives that are appropriated by the Church for the priests seem to be more than the biblical text allows, still the priestly office in the Church is clearly delimited and inconfoundable with what Christ the Lord enacts for our salvation. It is true that at times, some of the terms become interchangeable and some things become slightly confusing, but, as we shall see later on, the intention is to declare Jesus Christ as Lord and to offer possibilities for people to become members of Christ's body, namely the Church. Terminologically speaking, the above-mentioned are deducible also from the fact that in eastern theology, when there is a reference to the priestly office within the church, certain expressions are used such as churchly priesthood, serving priesthood, sacramental

---

[2] Sfântul Ioan Gură de Aur – Sfântul Grigore de Nazians – Sfântul Efrem Sirul, *Despre Preoție*, p. 310.

[3] Dumitru Stăniloae, *Ortodoxie și românism*, p. 37.

priesthood, saintly priesthood, etc., formulations that are not attributed to Christ. In the present research, in order to be honest to the presentation of eastern thought regarding the priesthood, we shall be faithful to this terminology in order to express as correctly and honestly as possible that which this theology declares about the priestly office and not that which we suppose it declares.

In conclusion, in this research we propose to answer the exigency that eastern theology has itself concerning the priesthood. The coordinates and perspectives of protestant theology shall be used less and not in contradiction, but complementarily and toning. We are interested to find what the East declares about the priesthood, not what we suppose it declares. In addition, we do not find important the evidence of biblical sliding in our research; instead, we focus on the way eastern theology regards the priestly office to be biblical, one that takes over the priestly office of the Lord Jesus Christ and continues it until the end of time.

I. The Priesthood in the Eastern Chruch: Origin and Relevance

In eastern theology the priestly office, and consequently, the priest are seen as a reality which is higher than the evaluations of the usual socio-religious thinking. Priesthood is considered as a divine dignity, the priest being the dignitary of God. This is the reason for which the realities that qualify someone as priest and which impose nobility are foreign to the conventional realities that have to do with academic preparations, professional competence or age. "Priesthood, the gift one partakes through the laying of bishop's hands, is not bound to old age, as it may be said, equally that it is not bound to youthfulness as well, in a word, it has is not bound to age, but to the virtue of the one to whom it is given."[4] In other words, neither the qualities of a priest, nor the evaluation criteria of this quality are of human descent, but the priesthood and its qualities, which are required for this, must be of divine origin.

The theological discourse that lead to these conclusions are well anchored in the teachings of the orthodox Tradition and, likewise, in the orthodoxy's specific understanding and application of the biblical text, the Old Testament as well as the New Testament. In the Eastern Church, the text of the Holy Scriptures is not secondary, as the protestant or evangelical churches often state it. In Eastern Church theology, the text of the Holy Scriptures or the revelation is an integral part of the life and spirit of the Church. "The connection between the Holy Scriptures and the Holy Tradition is so indissoluble, that one cannot be conceived without the other, and, even more so, one cannot be understood

---

[4] Nicolae Corneanu, *Credință și viață*, p. 314.

or deepened without the other, because those who have truly lived the true word of God – some of them as apostolic fathers, the immediate disciples of the apostles – are a precious help in the understand of the scriptural text, contributing to the continuation of the Church Tradition."[5] The positive and necessary evaluation of the priestly office in the New Testament stage is based, therefore, in the Eastern Church, on the "correct" understanding of the Holy Scriptures, understanding provided by the church fathers' tradition, on the teachings they left to Christ's Church. This approach of reality, unknown to the West, but not to the Bible and the Tradition from the approach of the East, have made possible the development of a wide tradition related to the priesthood, regarding its need, its origin and it's relevance.

When we discuss the problem of priesthood from an eastern perspective, we talk of the Lord Jesus Christ himself. The origin of the priestly office in the Orthodox Church is tightly tied to the person of the Lord Jesus Christ and to his ministry and High Priest, as sacrificed Lamb for the atonement of sin and as mediator between God and people. In this context, the priestly office in the Eastern Church is intrinsically tied to sacrifice, to forgiveness and salvation. A religious life outside these elements cannot be spiritual and cannot rise above the perishable. The argument through which man can rise above death as destiny, towards eternity, is sacrifice. "But this sacrifice cannot be brought 'for all', but each would bring it for oneself. It must be brought by One for all, that is by Christ, who, as One, brings himself for all. This is the priest, the servant of the church with responsibility for a community. Through this, he is shows himself at the same time to the believer's consciousness that he needs Christ as Mediator. The priest symbolizes Christ as mediator, the fact that man cannot enter through himself into the loving and never-ending relationship with God."[6] We can notice that at this level the priesthood signifies that which Jesus Christ has done in humans favour. The whole activity of the Lord Jesus Christ, as redeemer, forgiver of sins and saviour, can be found in the priestly office, as symbol.

However, the liturgical and priestly reality shows that the priestly office in the Eastern Church goes beyond the idea of symbol and imposes a sort of substitution of Jesus Christ. From the perspective of the theological discourse, the above mentioned by Stăniloaie presented correctly and biblically, but, from the perspective of practice and orthodox communities faith, things are with shades of difference or flagrantly different. The believer does not understand the priest as symbol, but as an authority that stands between him (the believer) and Him (Christ, the Son of God). This forces us to understand that there exists a wrong

---

[5] Dumitru Radu, *Îndrumări misionare*, p. 37.
[6] Dumitru Stăniloae, *Teologia dogmatică ortodoxă*, vol. 2, pp. 156-157.

understanding of orthodox theology within the Orthodox Church or that orthodox theology is as the church understands it, not as it is expressed.

We shall present two examples: confession and priestly intercession.

Confession, one of the most important events in the believers' lives, is also known as the sacrament of confession, or the sacrament of repentance. Defined in a complete and complex way, confession comes to aid the believers' relation with God. "Repentance or Confession is the Sacrament in which God forgives through the father confessor the sins of Christians who repent sincerely and confess them before him."[7] Apparently, it is an open door to the seekers of forgiveness, but at the same time a substitution of the Jesus Christ's prerogatives or even a blocking of the believers to reach him. It is possible that at the level of argumentation, through which the need and obligation to confess is justified, the situation is as correct and honest as possible; but at the level of the development of the act itself and at the level of the attitude of the one who seeks Christ, confession is another added element through which man is distanced from Christ under the care of a spiritual comfort that pretends to help the approach to the Savior or souls. Under these conditions the perplexity and doubt are not necessarily oriented towards the Sacrament of Confession. The sacrament of confession can have intrinsically both purpose and biblical argument. That which comports suspicion is the priestly office's attitude, which demands that man, even if one has added grace, to belong to the equation of forgiveness, where the authority and the prime and ultimate right belongs to Jesus Christ alone. "Priests", writes Nectar of Eghina, "are also given the other arrangements by the bishop: baptizing and unction with the Great Mire of the baptized, to commit the Sacrament of the Wedding, to confess and **forgive the sins of the repenters...**"[8] (added bold). Such a statement, however lenient we might be with the meaning of certain biblical texts, seems to be an overstatement. The Bible, when referring to such issues is quite radical: *"Salvation is found in no-one else, for there is no other name under heaven given to men by which we must be saved."* (Acts 4:12). *"In him we have redemption through his blood, the forgiveness of sins, in accordance with the riches of God's grace that he lavished on us with all wisdom and understanding. And he made known to us the sacrament of his will according to his good pleasure, which he purposed in Christ, to be put into effect when the times will have reached their fulfillment to bring all things in heaven and on earth together under one head, even Christ."* (Eph 1:7-10). First and last, the love and the right of forgiveness belong exclusively to Christ the Lord.

---

[7] Dumitru Radu, *Îndrumări misionare*, p. 547.
[8] Sfântul Nectarie de Eghina, *Despre preoție*, p. 27.

The second example, priestly intercession, is very sensitive. It is completely true that in the Holy Scriptures we are encouraged to mediate for one another and to pray for one another. Because of this reality, honestly, we can affirm that the priest's pastoral prayer and his pastoral intercession are most important because all the believers desire it. Things change a little when man begins to understand that the priest's intervention is not an optional one or one that can be solicited as help, instead, it is one without which we cannot have access to God. "The entire ministry of the priest in the parish he was given to pastor is fulfilled by delegation, through the almighty power of the Saviour. 'In my name', he told the Apostles, 'demons shall they exorcise, in new tongues shall they speak'. Therefore, the priest is a delegate, **a locum of the Saviour** (added bold), continuing the ministry in his name and, as a legal representative, he has the Apostles' plenitude ... His calling and the power regarding the souls comes to him from Christ."[9] Such affirmations and all the creeds that gravitate around certain nuclei give priesthood an authority and an origin superior to the honest ministry that is generally evoked. In spite of this, those of us who wish to know the Eastern Church's dogmatic confession of faith regarding the priesthood have the obligation to start from the hypothesis of honesty that characterises this Church and from the premise that there is nothing hidden; rather that it's intention is the worship of God and the pastoring of the believer towards repentance and salvation. God places a great responsibility on those whom we call pastors and others call the priests, a responsibility from which they cannot escape through any exegetical or homiletical trick. It is about the pastoral care that God himself asks for. "If it is useful for him who maddens only one man, even the least one, to have a mill stone tied to his neck and be thrown into the sea (Mt 18:6) and if all those who wound the souls of the brethren sin against Christ (1Cor 8:12), what would happen to the priests, what punishment would they receive when they lose not one or two or three, but such a great number of believers?"[10]

Even if the also situation implies the interpretation we gave, the problem does not derive from the fact that there is a sacrament of confession or of repentance and neither from the fact that there is a in the priest a disposition to pray for the people and to intercess for this. The biblical meaning of confession and its necessity is kept, the meaning of the need for prayer and intercession is also kept, and, not least, the biblical meaning of the pastor is also kept. There is a need for discussion and questions with regard to the add-ons that pass over the

---

[9] Petre Vintilescu, *Preotul în fața chemării sale de păstor al sufletelor*, p. 41.

[10] Sfântul Ioan Gură de Aur – Sfântul Grigore de Nazians – Sfântul Efrem Sirul, *Despre Preoție*, p. 171.

Scriptures' Word or the add-ons that are given birth by the isolation of certain textual meanings, leaving on a secondary level the ensemble of the Revelation.

The Contemporary Priestly Office –
Origins from an Orthodox Dogmatic Perspective

Orthodox theology, as we have anticipated, develops a very wide discourse regarding priesthood and its role in humanity's salvation. The Church Fathers as well as later theologians up to this day are not reticent in taking any element from the Old Testament and contextualizing it through the teachings of the New Testament in the development of a theology regarding the serving priesthood, a priesthood that represents the royal one; that is the one of the Lord Jesus Christ. Starting from certain rites (incensing, sanctifying water, etc.) up to the garments, most of these elements of form and content declare that the creed's formulation about priesthood is not only a dogmatic one, but also a biblical one. Due to this reason, the Eastern Church considers itself a protector of the traditional early church teachings of Christianity and of Christ's teachings left of the Holy Apostles.

Referring strictly to the priesthood, the Eastern Church connects the sense and significance of the priestly office to the most important declarations within the Holy Scripture regarding Jesus Christ and his ministry as High Priest. In this context, the origin and purpose of the Church's priestly office must be regarded in the same way as the priestly office that Jesus Christ assumed. "The priesthood after Melchisedec's order is 'without father or mother, without genealogy'" (Heb 7:3) , besides any immanent transmission or purely human delegation. The sacerdotal power is inspired by Christ to the twelve apostles, and it's origin is strictly divine: 'You did not choose me, but I chose you and appointed you' (Jn 15:16). 'Axios' and 'Amin' pronounced by the people at the elections are still indispensable, but only as elements of theandrism: the human condition of the charism, with its purely divine source."[11] In this sense, the origin of the priesthood in the Eastern Church is divine one, strictly divine. Priesthood is seen as a tradition, as a dowry that God had taken care of through Jesus Christ and the Holy Apostles, so that we might have it. Its sense is not that it belongs to us, but one through which we belong to it. In this context we deal with o spiritual reality that comes from Christ towards us with an intention to unite us with one another and then to appropriate us in God's Self and in godly power, thus making possible the unity of Christ's body and declaring the theandric nature of the Holy Church. This is made possible also through the Sacrament of Priesthood; that is in the way that Jesus Christ through the Apostles has given divine grace until the present day to those who pastor the Holy Church:

---

[11] Paul Evdokimov, *Ortodoxia*, p. 179.

"The apostolic worthiness is not limited only to the person of the apostles, but is succession based because the Holy Apostles' *apostolicity* is eternal because of the eternal character of the saving worship of the Church that humanity's Saviour established ... And, just as the ministry of the Church extends into eternity, so the apostles worthy succession will carry on and it will last forever. Thus, as long as people's communion on earth and the prosperity of the humankind will endure, the apostolic succession will endure just as long through the laying of the archiepiscopate."[12] We can observe that the sense of the priesthood's origin in the Eastern Church is continually one of continuity, a sense that does not justify itself, but one that results from something divine cu functionality and divine purpose. The Eastern Church does not argue priesthood but declares its continuity; it declares Christ in it and declares it in Christ.

This is even more evident as assuming the priestly office is an irrevocable act. Just as Christ does not adhere to the reality of ceasing to be Christ, so the priest cannot adhere tot he reality of ceasing to be a priest. "... this character of priesthood as a sacrament that makes any servant of the divine word and caretaker of the divine sacraments, without reference to his moral quality, shows that the grace that is given to the ordained one inerasable and a new ordination, or the passing from a priestly order to a laic one is not allowed."[13] We observe therefore, that in eastern theology regarding the priesthood, we deal not only with the fact that priesthood is of divine origin, but also from its own being, it obligates itself to behave divinely. The law regarding priesthood, the cannons that depict the way this office works within the Church underlines the right that this office reserves for itself, namely not to behave at any time in any other way but as derived from the divine, continuing the divine and serving it for the sanctification of those who believe and who belong to the church.

The origin of the priesthood in Christ and its spiritual behaviour, superior to the normal and a bearer of the divine, must be understood in Eastern theology as wonders of grace and an additions to this. To be a priest presupposes a surplus of grace, not just in receiving it, but also in offering it. The priest is the beneficiary of a surplus of grace in what he is and what he offers. Without the priestly office, it is theoretically impossible for man to be the beneficiary of the grace-filled works of God for man's salvation. Due to this reason, when we speak of the origin of the priesthood in the Eastern Church, we also speak of it's origin in the Grace God offered in and through Jesus Christ. To be ordained, that is to be a priest, is also a matter of grace and offering of grace. "The sacrament of ordination or of priesthood is the Sacrament in which, through the laying of the bishops hands and through prayer, it is imparted to

---

[12] Sfântul Nectarie de Eghina, *Despre preoție*, p. 29.

[13] Hr. Andruțos, *Simbolica*, p. 316.

the specially trained person, in the Church and for the Church, ***the divine grace*** at one of the priesthood's levels ... That is why it is also called the Sacrament of sacramental priesthood or ***gracious*** in the Church."[14] That is why the way in which the laymen relates to the priest is first of all a problem of spiritual nature, and then or not at all, one of social-administrative nature. The priest is perceived as one to whom God has given a surplus of precedence regarding all of life's aspects which must compete to sanctify man, and, respectively, to save him. "The priesthood as activity in God's sensitive plan of the unseen priesthood of Christ, or of his intercession before God, is a gift from God. The believers constantly need the visible priest, different from them, because they always need Christ, as Mediator ... Just as Christ, as Mediator, was sent by the Father, so are the priests and bishops sent by Christ as the ones through whom He fulfils in an unseen way his ministry of intercession or salvation. This is why they receive from Christ his Spirit, so that Christ would fulfil through them his salvation ministry."[15] Due to this reason, we cannot speak about a shortened entry to God, an act through which the priest would remain an appendix with an optional utility. This type of attitude, considered as belonging to the Protestant and Evangelical Churches is one that annuls grace's purpose, or, simply put, it refuses grace.

In Eastern theology, the priestly office must be regarded as an intrinsic element of the divine grace. The sense and purpose of salvation is, actually, the sense and purpose of grace, which in itself, presupposes the sense and purpose of the priesthood. Due tot he fact that the orthodox option regarding grace is not similar to that of the West, that is grace is an uncreated energy[16], is an eternal given of God's way of being, when we speak about priesthood as having it's origin in Christ's grace, we speak of a superior origin to times and dates, a priesthood identical to that of Melchisedec, without a starting point and without ceasing. The origin of the priestly office in grace and considered as a carrier of grace is a characteristic of the Orthodox Church, with who's help is the necessity of the priesthood is explained and imposed, through which all the members of the body can be coagulated around the Head, which is Christ.

---

[14] Dumitru Radu, *Îndrumări misionare*, p. 567.

[15] Dumitru Stăniloae, *Teologia dogmatică ortodoxă*, vol. 2, p. 156.

[16] "The teaching on the divine uncreated energies constitutes a an essential characteristic of Orthodoxy and it the basis for the faith in the personal character of God, for the deification of man and the transfiguration of matter and creation. Orthodox theology understands grace as divine energy and work, personal and uncreated, through which man become 'participate in the divine nature' (2Pt 1:4)" Ion Bria, *Dicționar de teologie ortodoxă*, pp. 141-142.

Finally yet importantly, when we speak of the priesthood's origin in Eastern thought, we must take account of the Holy Spirit's person and the work he has done at Pentecost. The Holy Spirit makes the priestly office that has its origin in Christ and his Grace, to be a bearer of Christ and Grace. In other words, being a priest presupposes being at the same time *christoforical, charisoforical* and *pneumatoforical*. The overflowing of the Holy Spirit at Pentecost does not only confirm that the Apostles are departing from within Christ and the divine Grace, but it also declares the departing from and through the Holy Spirit. "... It follows clearly that the church hierarchy is built upon the Spirit's descent and that each received his place in the hierarchy, according to the measure of Christ's gift. The twelve apostles are on the highest level in the church's hierarchy, meaning the bishops' level."[17] This reality, as we shall later observe, explains why the priestly office is connected tightly and consistently to the sacraments' problem, elements in which the Holy Spirit's activity is defining. Only through the Holy Spirit, everything happens at the holy Eucharist, at the baptizing, at the confession, etc. can be lifted over the simple human manifestations, and becoming Sacraments with whose help Grace transcends history and time and makes the participants contemporaries with eternity.

The priestly heritage in Christ, in the divine Grace and in the Holy Spirit is not to be regarded as a historical date, but as a responsibility that regulates the relationship between man and God regarding the reconciliation. "The priest represents and serves that category of interests within human society that has to do and which derive from the relation between man and God; his whole authority of his functioning comes from above, it is a grace that is not within the grasp of people to give."[18] Thus, the priest is the seen segment through which Christ works in an unseen manner and at the same time the priest is the seen one, who offers a segment of unseen power through the Sacraments that he administers.

Considering the origin of the priesthood in Jesus Christ, and the Grace of God shown in Christ, from the Eastern Church's perspective, comports a risk and confusion from the Protestant and Evangelical perspective. Because of the build up of rational elements in the protestant life and creed, sometimes complementary to faith, other times to its detriment, one can observe that the priestly office in the East becomes almost identical with the ministry of Christ and sometime it substitutes it. These types of conclusions make us more reticent concerning the priesthood and its sense in the Christian faith. Usually, looking back to the ceasing of the priestly office at the Temple because Jesus Christ is involved in this, protestant, and especially evangelical theology declared this subject a taboo. Yet, if we observe honestly and strictly what hap-

---

[17] Sfântul Nectarie de Eghina, *Despre preoție*, p. 23.
[18] Petre Vintilescu, *Preotul în fața chemării sale de păstor al sufletelor*, p. 39.

pens within these churches, we shall notice that although some terms have changed (priest became pastor, sacraments became sacraments or commemorative acts, etc.) these churches continue from a ritualistic perspective, exactly that which, in some sense, they dispute. We point this out not to increase the polemical tension, but to make possible the transcending of the biblical text through both perspectives with the purpose of becoming honest to the biblical text and towards our own confession of faith.

It is very true that in some liturgical manifestations, from our perspective, the priest appears as Christ himself or at least as *a someone* similar in the sense of Christ's substitution, but at the level of theological declarations, the Eastern Church either shades the affirmation or even denies it. "Only Christ is priest, everyone else is priest through participation, some ore bishops or elders. We must remember that in New Testament Greek, the term ἱερεύς – priest – is reserved the royal priesthood, and the priest, through ordination, is named elder or bishop. Christ is the only priest through unction (the early Church ordains her servants through the laying of hands), actually, the only sacerdotal ordination through unction is of the unction of the royal priesthood."[19] We deduce from this affirmation, as well as from others of this kind, that the priestly office in the Eastern Church is not estimated in the way in which it was estimated in the Old Testament. From an Eastern perspective, the New Testament priesthood is the fulfilment of a mandate that Jesus Christ the Lord trusted with the Holy Apostles and through them to those that have chosen to serve him. Due to this reason, the reality that needs to be researched is not the priestly office in itself, but the way in which this office, through those who represent it, fulfils its mandate. The reformation and the neo-reformation did not have as purpose the questioning of the priestly office; there was a sideslip on this subject. The reformation and the neo-reformation questioned the way in which those who were in the priestly office, that is the priests from a certain location and from a certain historical period, fulfilled correctly and biblically, or incorrectly and non-biblically the mandate Christ had left them. In Luther's open letter to Pope Leo X, he describes this reality explicitly. Luther did not question neither the priestly office nor the holy sea, but they behaviour in connection with the mission and destiny they had to fulfil. Next we shall present a few snippets of the letter: "This is why, Holy Father Leo, receive this apology of mine and consider me one of those who does not want to bring any harm to your person, and who only desires the best for you, as you are entitled to; also, consider me as one who does not desire envy or quarrel due to one's unlawful life, but only out of the love for the truth of the divine Word. In any other matter, I would gladly stay out of anyone's path, but I cannot and I do not want to abandon or

---

[19] Paul Evdokimov, *Ortodoxia*, p. 180.

deny God's Word. If anyone has another opinion or understands something else from my letters, he is mistaken and did not understand me correctly."[20] This perspective of Luther was not rigidly personal, but every believer at his turn had his own disappointment and his own spiritual difficulties. The sideslip regarding the accusation of the office itself as well as the biblical argumentation does not answer the desire to cast off the people that are put aside for God, but the desire to eliminate the behaviour of these people, even if they are priests.

When talking about this aspect in eastern theology things do not change significantly. The argumentative discourse in favour of the priesthood must start from the biblical text and to the detriment of any conciliatory attitude between holiness and sin. The thing that burdens this aspect is the mentioning that the grace of priesthood remains over the priest regardless of his way of life. "As the shining gold is not harmed when mingled with earth, and as glittering pearl does not change its light when placed next to unclean matter, neither does priesthood become filthy with anything, even if he who is priest is unworthy."[21] Even if the priestly virtues are very beautifully presented, departing from them is not that problematic as one might wish, and sometimes the priestly virtues must correspond to the priestly cast not Revelation. This reality determined the Scripture lovers from the age of the Reformation to deny even the office itself[22] and to proceed towards a terminological parallelism, which brought out as unique, certain biblical values that have been neglected. Continuing the debate over the relation between the sacramental acts and the spiritually human quality of the priest, we shall observe that in orthodox theology the Sacraments cannot be affected by the priests life. "… The Holy Sacraments maintain their power whatever the life of the priest is like. Holy Chrysostom says 'If grace were to search for everywhere for worthiness, there would be no baptising, no Body of Christ, nor would there be intercession through them. But because God works through the unworthy ones, the grace of Baptising is not harmed in any way by the priest's life.'"[23] If we were to assess this statement comparatively, that is considering all the Christian churches, we might notice that it transcends through its content and its reality all servant categories (priests, pastors, preachers, elders, bishops, etc.) The differences are at most on

---

[20] Martin Luther, *Scrieri*, vol. 1, p. 143.

[21] Sfântul Ioan Gură de Aur – Sfântul Grigore de Nazians – Sfântul Efrem Sirul, *Despre Preoție*, p. 315

[22] It is most likely that from the perspective of the complexity of the biblical truth, that this fact might not have been necessary. Perhaps some of the priesthood's attributes come into contradiction with that which serving means as sacerdotium in the church, but this might have been remedied without the radical measures that were taken.

[23] *Credința ortodoxă*, p. 144.

a declarative level or at the level of confessions of faith, but the concrete reality regarding the spiritual human life of the ordained is the same. This thing does not leave room to believe that the private life of the ones set aside for God does not matter, but it declares that the ministry of God for and towards the salvation of man rises above human imperfection. "Anyone who is, among people, a priest, is small and unimportant, compared to the priest about whom God said: 'You are a priest for ever according to the order of Melchisedec.' For High Priest is the one who walks in the heavens, who can surpass all creation and rise to the One who lives in the inaccessible light, to God and the Father of the Universe."[24]

In conclusion, the orthodox dogmatic perspective regarding the priesthood resumes the fact that Christ institutes this office, and it derives from Him as a gesture of divine love with the purpose of saving humanity. Priesthood was not taken by anybody for oneself, but it is succesoral and, at the same time, it is offered today as in the apostolic period. The succesorship accentuates the fact that from the Apostles, through the laying of hands, the transmission of the office was kept to this day, and when it is *offered today*, it presupposes the direct implication of the Lord Jesus Christ through the Holy Spirit at the ordination, an implication that does not confirm the authenticity of the apostolic tradition, but that is offers in grace to the ordained the Holy Spirit of the true God and the grace of priesthood that derives from the priesthood of Christ. Also, this investment, as well as its sobriety, bring Christ in the Church not to make him common but to proclaim his singularity and holiness, which is above all the things that can represent his ministry

II. Church Priesthood – The Extension of the Priestly Office Assumed by Christ

As we have already anticipated, in the Eastern Church, the priestly office is tightly connected to the Sacraments' enacting. Through them, God distributes grace and, consequently, salvation cannot exist outside the Sacraments. One of the reasons for which the reconciliation between Protestants and Orthodox is almost impossible is exactly the fact that the Protestant Churches do not recognize the Sacraments or at best recognize only two: baptising and the holy supper. The discourse begins from the fact that Jesus Christ Himself is the One that instituted the Sacraments and He is the one that enacted them first. Under these conditions, the priestly ministry is regarded as Christ's specific intention with the purpose of keeping within the communion with him those who belong to him. "Jesus Christ wants to extend the unity that he realised within Himself

---

[24] Origen, *Omilii și adnotări la Levitic*, p. 433.

to all those who believe in Him. This is not in an individualistic manner but a communal one, because the more he unites all with himself, the more he unites them among them, forming the His Church. That is why this unifying ministry of Christ is at the same time a ministry of the Church."[25] Here we speak of the communion that Christ has in Himself with the Father. This type of communion He wishes to impart to the members of his pneumatised body, that is the Church. In this spiritual process, the priest has a significant role, without his implication the presence of the Holy Spirit is almost impossible and the actualization of the Lord Jesus Christ's presence cannot take place. The extension of this unity corresponds to the most significant purpose of repentance, namely, deification. Christ became incarnate thus becoming man in order that man might proceed to becoming god. "The holy Fathers mention the dynamic relation of the Holy Spirit with Christ's human nature. His spiritual deification continues in those who commune with his 'Holy Body'. They are not only configured after the likeness of Christ, but are made Christ-like, filled with the Word of God, actually, associated with this fullness (Col 2:9), 'co-body like' and 'co-sanguinical' with Christ."[26] The priestly office, through the administration of the Holy Sacraments brings the graceful presence of Christ in the Church and, at the same time, creates the context for communion between the High priest, the Head of the Church, and the Church through the serving or churchly priesthood.

From the perspective of the priestly authority, that of administrating the sacraments and the saving grace, things are not different between the Apostles of the Lord Jesus Christ and those that bear priestly commission today. In order for the Apostles to be strengthened for administering the sacraments of God's kingdom, it was necessary for them to receive exactly that which the priests receive today when are ordained through the laying of hands. This aspect is justified by evoking the day of Pentecost, a day in which the Apostles, as persons that had been together with them, needed, in the same manner, the descending of the Holy Spirit. "In the Church of Christ, the priesthood has its beginning from the descending of the Holy Spirit over the holy apprentices and the apostles of Christ the Saviour. Before the descending, the apostles, did not have the worthiness of the priesthood, because the Holy Spirit, the One that completes all things and Who completes the priests, had not yet come to them."[27] Therefore, we observe that the definitive role for prolonging the priesthood the Lord Jesus Christ in the the priestly office the Church belongs to the Holy Spirit. This aspect requests an understanding that at the level of the

---

[25] Ștefan Buchiu, *Întrupare și unitate*, pp. 174-175.
[26] Paul Evdokimov, *Prezența Duhului Sfânt în Tradiția Ortodoxă*, p. 125.
[27] Sfântul Nectarie de Eghina, *Despre preoție*, p. 20.

confession of faith, the Eastern Church declares the priestly authority and it's serving only on the basis of the filling of these persons with the Holy Spirit.

The prolonging of the priestly office assumed by Christ in the serving priesthood, presupposes not so much the declaring of the salvation ministry's continuity as it's validation. Through the priest, God validates the implication of the heavens in the life of those that come near forgiveness and salvation and he fulfils this through the priest as well. "... The priest is at the same time a tool of the Holy Spirit, with who's assistance he continues the work of the Saviour in the world, as he himself had instructed and encouraged his holy Apostles, in the night of his capture ..."[28] Because of this, the individual closeness cannot declare or constitute the communion that Jesus requests from the Father in Jn 17, namely, that "all might be one" in the way in which Jesus Christ is one with the Father. The communion that is accomplished through the participation in the Sacraments, a participation that is mediated and realised by the priest is the only one that can attest the theandric character of the Church and, at the same time, confirm he belonging to the body of Christ. This communion is realised, generally speaking, at the enacting of the Sacrament of the Holy Eucharist. "We worship the Holy Gifts in the Sacrament of communion, because Christ is present in them, who gives himself to those who commune ..."[29] It results that worshiping the gifts and, implicitly, God is the moment in which communion is accomplished, the highest degree of closeness and living with Christ. In this type of communion, Christ offers himself to those who participate. Here, through the descent of the Holy Spirit over the bread and the wine, which become the body and blood of the Lord Jesus Christ, all the members, that is all the believers enact the communion becoming partakers to the Holy Body of the Lord, a spiritualised Body, anticipated on mount Tabor. "This transfiguration of the universe remains a hidden, mysterious irradiation, in which, therefore, we return mystically, through the Holy Sacraments."[30] The meaning of this communion is even more complete and profound because the Sacrament of the Eucharist, through the serving priest, the believers receive not only the transfigured body on Mount Tabor, but the communion is realised with the Body of the Lord hallowed in the fullness of the Spirit, which was after the resurrection and ascension to the Father.

Within the liturgy, the church singing, church prayer and the exaltation of the believers are tied to Heaven through he priest who mediates this manifestation, him being the visible connecting element. "In the Christian church, the connec-

---

[28] Petre Vintilescu, *Preotul în fața chemării sale de păstor al sufletelor*, p. 42.

[29] Serghei Bulgakov, *Dogma euharistică*, p. 71.

[30] Oliver Clement, *Trupul morții și al slavei*, p. 21.

tion of the priest to the divine masterwork is much more accentuated and full, because the purpose is to continue in the world the masterwork of the Saviour. He is the agent through whom the heavenly inheritance of Christ continues to spread in this world."[31] In this case, the entire worship atmosphere receives a doxologically liturgical dimension and through the faith of the entire transfigured community evokes in an anticipatory way the Kingdom that is to come. This reality makes the priestly office unable to be mistaken for a human hierarchy, but the priestly office brings out, on the one hand, our equality before God, making us partakers to the communion with himself, and, on the other hand, makes us known the cosmic order of God which includes in itself that which we call church hierarchy.

The extension of the priestly office assumed by Christ in the office of the serving priesthood does not presuppose any dilution of its quality. All has the value and sacredness that the presence of Jesus Christ always had, whether before the crucifixion or after the resurrection, or the ascendance to Heaven. "The priest does not commemorate or imitate the sacrifice of Christ, but through the power of the Holy Spirit, he actualises the effects of Christ's priesthood. Therefore, only because of this permanent actuality of his sacrifice, Christ is priest in eternity, and the serving priesthood , a participation in the unique sacerdotium of Christ, to the extent that the priests consecrate and offer God the body and blood of Christ; they are the visible extension of Christ over the eons."[32] The serving priesthood in the Eastern Church is declared to be of the same essence and strength as that of the Apostles at the overflowing of the Holy Spirit. According to those written by Mihălțan, the church priest enacts a sermon by sacrificing not a lamb or a kid, as in the Old Testament, but by bringing Jesus Christ as sacrifice.

The ecclesial authority in the east does not reside, as it sometimes results even from certain affirmations made by different hierarchs, in its old age; instead, the ecclesial authority resides from the belief that each priest has this ordination just as contemporary and alive as the Apostles had in the time the Lord Jesus Christ and after the descending of the Holy Spirit. "Each bishop is the follower of all the Apostles, because each Apostle is in communion with all the other Apostles. And then, each bishop is ordained by more bishops in the name of the entire bishopric, receiving the same grace and the same teaching that all the other Apostles and bishops received and, at the same time, becoming able to impart to the priests and through them to the all the believers from his bishopric, the same grace and the same unchanged teachings, that is in the entire Church, or placing them in the same communion with the Same Christ, who,

---

[31] Petre Vintilescu, *Preotul în fața chemării sale de păstor al sufletelor*, p. 40.

[32] Ioan Mihălțan, *Preoția Mântuitorului Hristos și preoția bisericească*, p. 85.

by bringing himself continually as sacrifice to the Father, maintains his humanity in the bond of the eternal unending love with the Father."[33] In this context, in eastern theology the priest is different from a delegate. The priest is of the same quality with that of the Apostles, he represents qualitatively and with authority, the mission handed by Christ, a mission declared even now, but also inherited from the apostles.

Two coordinates operate in this extension: the succession coordinate and the sacrament coordinate. If any of the two is missing, the office of the serving priesthood in the church represents neither God nor his intention in the church. The succession coordinate or *the belt of laying hands* reveals the beauty of continuity of Christ's followers from the moment of his ascendance to this day. Through this belt of the laying hands, the group of apostles and later the group of bishops received authority and right from God to put aside certain vessels that can be declared vessels of honour. Without these Vessels, the church would actually cease to exist. "… The bishop is a successor of the Apostles through the laying of hands and through and the invocation of the Spirit, having received through succession the power given by God to forgive and untie. He is a living icon of God on earth and thanks tot he divine work and power of the Holy Spirit, he is the plentiful river of all the sacraments of the Church through which salvation is received. We believe the bishop to be as important to the church as breathing is to man and the sun for the worlds."[34] God has chosen to bind himself to fill with priestly grace those that are put aside for the group of apostles and later to that of the bishops. Public authority and validation operate on this coordinate regarding those put aside.

The second coordinate is the sacrament. Here, the group of Apostles and the group of bishops have no contribution whatsoever; instead it is the direct and unmitigated intervention of God. "The prayer of the laying of hands over bishop mentions: 'not through the laying of my hands, but through the imparting of your gifts has grace been offered.' If hands are needed, it is only so that the gifts that emanate from the divine might be given. It is not about the prerogatives of any of the apostles or of the bishops collegiate, instead it is about the presence of the only Sacrificer: Christ. His unique word becomes in time the four Gospels, the unique cup, the multitude of eucharistical liturgies, his power extends over the his entire body in different ministries, functions, charisms, and gifts."[35] Within the sacrament of the extension of the assumed office by Christ, takes place the miracle of the filling with the priestly grace, grace that the bishops are not able to offer to anybody. Therefore, the bishop's

---

[33] Dumitru Stăniloae, *Teologia dogmatică ortodoxă*, vol. 2, p. 157.
[34] George Florovski, *Biserica, Scriptura, Tradiția – Trupul viu al lui Hristos*, p. 243.
[35] Paul Evdokimov, *Ortodoxia*, p. 179.

authority consists in putting aside a vessel, and in this vessel is filled at the bishop's prayer with priestly grace by Christ in an unmediated and unrepeatable way. "Therefore, the Sacrament of priesthood qualifies the visible person itself that enacts the Sacraments, through which Christ imparts to us the through the Holy Spirit, his saving grace, as well as his body and blood."[36] Under these circumstances, the priest receives graceful powers superior to all other believers and becomes not only precedence but also responsible with the salvation of the souls he pastors and the salvation of the souls that have not yet become members of Christ's body, that is of the church. All this complex manifestation, eastern theology affirms, is part of the Church Tradition that it expresses. That is why the Tradition cannot be considered as representing that which we deduce from the forms of religious manifestations of the Christian masses, instead it has a superior origin in connection to this conclusion and a superior content in connection to that of human origin. "The tradition is not a Church archaeology, but spiritual life. It is Church memory. It is, firstly, an uninterrupted current of spiritual life that originates in the Abode from above."[37] Due to this reason, the priestly office in the east is considered as *homofany*, that a representation of man flowed through by the Holy Spirit and in whom Jesus Christ, the Head of the Church, meets his Body, the Church. Under these conditions, the Eastern Church hierarchy justifies it's pretences regarding the people with its eternal responsibilities towards it and with a form of theocracy it expresses in relation to the state.

In the church priesthood or the serving priesthood are found in a viable way the most important elements from the Lord Jesus Christ's priesthood. If in the Old Testament priesthood important elements from the priesthood that Jesus Christ was to assume were found as symbol, which were fulfilled in what Christ worked among us, in the serving of eastern priesthood or churchly priesthood we do not find symbols but fundamental elements of this priesthood are on earth that which they are in heaven. For example, the confession of sins to the priest[38] is found within the Sacrament of Confession that which it is also in Heaven. If the Old Testament priesthood symbolised the priesthood of the Lord Jesus Christ, the New Testament priesthood works in a visibly the invisible priesthood of our Saviour. Therefore, the mystery of the priesthood from an

---

[36] Dumitru Radu, *Îndrumări misionare*, p. 566.

[37] George Florovski, *Biserica, Scriptura, Tradiția – Trupul viu al lui Hristos*, p. 246.

[38] Even if there are at least two biblical passages that speak of this subject, from a protestant and evangelical perspective, the exegesis that allows the Sacrament of Confession is at least forced. According to these passages those who wrong one another must also confess the sins to one another in order to forgive one another and to grow in holiness. The respective texts do not allow us to understand that we can wrong one another, confess, and ask for forgiveness from others, might they be even pastors or priests.

eastern perspective presupposes the existence of a few spiritual dilemmas that give an even clearer importance to the priest. The mystery of the priesthood is the visible Unseen, the temporary Eternal, the blemish Righteousness, it is a second incarnation, that is, the incarnate Christ who sanctified human nature and rose with it to the heavens, takes again, in the priesthoods sacrament, a human body, enacting in continuity and towards finality the last grace operation for the salvation of his Church.

Another significant characteristic in which we clearly see that the eastern priestly office considers itself an extension of the priestly office assumed by Christ is tied tot he quality of continuity regarding the competence and the authority to teach. Before the Lord Jesus Christ parted with the Apostles, he gave them a mandate known as the "great sending". "Then Jesus came to them and said, 'All authority in heaven and on earth has been given to me. Therefore go and make disciples of all nations, baptizing them in the name of the Father and of the Son and of the Holy Spirit, and *teaching* them to obey everything I have commanded you. And surely I am with you always, to the very end of the age'" (Mt 28:18-20). In this passage, Jesus Christ entrusts the duty and authority to teach to the Holy Apostles. Taking this passage rigidly we shall notice that the capacity to teach people about the eternal things, in the complex and responsible way of the text, is given only to those who received this mandate, namely the Apostles and their invested followers. This particular way of understanding the text created in the Eastern Church, a reality that maintains this Eastern Churchly Body well knit together. It is actually the faith and conscience of the believers regarding the fact that only the priest is the one who should know the teachings from God and he is the only one who can offer it correctly and in a saving way. This reality is a declaration of the believing masses, a declaration that strengthens the eastern perspective, namely, that the priestly office comes through Christ from God, without any alteration and without any kind of interruption: "Christ is therefore from God, and the Apostles are from Christ. Christ transmitted to the Apostles all that he had heard from the Father. From then on, those who came after the apostles who were ordained bishops in different regions, are after Jesus Christ's decision. They follow according to Saint Ignatius, the Apostles as Jesus Christ follows God, continuing their work."[39] This mysterious structure expresses the natural through which Jesus Christ extended his priesthood in the serving priesthood and transformed it into one of the most significant sacraments.

That which surprises us in this research is that the authority of teaching is not conveyed the quality of a sacrament. That is, even though the clergy relates very radically regarding who has the authority to teach, radically as in the ad-

---

[39] Dumitru Stăniloae, Teologia dogmatică ortodoxă, vol. 2, p. 157.

ministration of the sacraments, still, from a dogmatic point of view, the authority to teach does not belong to the priest in the shape of a monopoly that he has over the administration of the Sacraments. Here we deal with a behaviour of reciprocal faithfulness that solidifies the unity between the clergy and its lay members. We did not manage to deduce whether this happened due to the desire to keep the number seven or due to other reasons. That which is certain from the perspective of implementing the dogmatic orientation regarding this matter, is the fact that the authority to teach is reserved exclusively to the clergy.

Even though there does not exist such a formulation, due to the importance with which it is treated, we can speak of the authority to teach as a sacrament, *the sacrament of teaching,* or the *sacrament of preach.* Even if this example is not used, the subject itself is one that attests and imposes the fact that the priestly office is an extension of the priesthood of the Lord Jesus Christ and of his authority. Only Christ is the Word, only he is the Word incarnate, only he is the Teacher. Due to this reality, we shall speak of an extension from the perspective of being, and not one related to inheritance, that is what we are left with. Christ did not ascend to the heavens so the he might not be anymore and that the authority of teaching was left to the bishops, instead Christ exists. Therefore, the authority received by the bishops is not one that was left to them, but one that is related to being. The priest teaches as Christ taught and later that which Christ taught. The accent fall on **how,** on **in the same way** and then on **what,** on **content.** Of course that there is no reserve whatsoever, in the eastern theology, regarding the fact that the teaching of the priest is overlapping identically with the teachings of the Lord Jesus Christ.

The priestly grace given through the laying of hands qualifies singularly the bishop in order for him to have the authority to give the teachings. He makes contemporary the risen and glorified Christ in such a way that the believer's presence at Church is a presence next to and together with Christ. This opinion continues to maintain, in spite of secularisation, in most Christians of eastern rite, a spirituality that is very hard to justify, but sometimes desired by western protestant and evangelical Christendom. The authority to teach and to offer the Word to the believers, an authority given to the bishops who make Christ contemporary with today's people, is possible to be found in the same way in lay member. "*The right to teach and to confess in the Church is given only to the hierarchy* [...] The fact of confession in the name of the Church is given only to the bishop. It can also be formulated as follows: the right to an opinion and advice is given to all, but '*the power to teach*' is given only to the hierarchy – of course within the untouched fraternity of *ecumenicity.*"[40] Even though out-

---

[40] George Florovski, *Biserica, Scriptura, Tradiția – Trupul viu al lui Hristos*, pp. 250-251.

side the sacraments, the service of teaching is still one of the main coordinates that attest that in eastern theology the priestly church office is still one that prolongs the priestly office assumed by Jesus Christ. This aspect declares once again that the resemblances between the priestly office in the Eastern Church and the pastoral office in the evangelical churches are not sufficient to declare that we speak of the same thing. The serving priesthood is a different cast than that of the laymen in another manner than the difference between evangelical pastors and laymen. This reality asks and allows eastern dogmatic to speak of the canonical and non-canonical ordination. Based on this differentiation the conversion of a canonically ordained priest to orthodoxy does not necessitate him to be ordained again, even more so, such a practice is forbidden. However, when a non-canonically ordained priest converts to orthodoxy, he must be ordained.

In conclusion, from the perspective of the ministry that Christ Jesus executes as High Priest for the atonement of our sins, eastern theology mentions that the visible way that is just as important, of this heavenly activity is that accomplished by the priestly office from within the Church. Here, in the Church, the priest is he once who brings and prolongs Christ's activity, and through the Liturgy, through the teachings, and mostly, through the administration of the Sacraments, the holy hierarchs are co-workers with Christ and offer meaning to this service with the purpose of sanctifying and saving the members of the body. This dedication was offered y Jesus Christ to the Apostles. "The twelve Apostles must be considered as continuators and keepers of the Saviour's ministry and of the Holy Sacraments, the twelve pillars that were build on the stone that is our Saviour Jesus Christ, who built his Church, in order that it might be forever."[41] In addition, through them this hierarchical authority was offered on through the laying of hands and the presence of the Holy Spirit to all those whom had received the grace of priesthood. In the liturgical activity in the Church, and only in it, the bishop and the priest bring the heavenly Liturgy and makes visible the One who is invisible and makes the One who is inaccessible accessible. This miracle is accomplished through the pneumatisation of the Church, that is by the mysterious work of the Holy Spirit, who fills and flows through the Church, and the realities that are apparently common and human are expressed on a superior doxological level, declaring them heavenly and eternal realities.

The contemporanization of the heavenly sermon of forgiveness and intercession that the priest enacts as servant in the church, that is the prolonging of the Christological priestly office, is the most important ministry on earth. It is accomplished as a model of the heavenly one, it represents the one in the heavens and it has heavenly authority. The climax of this ministry is reached in the

---

[41] Sfântul Nectarie de Eghina, *Despre preoție*, p. 25.

moment of epiclesis. Once the priest administers the Sacrament of Holy Eucharist and through the invocation of the Holy Spirit, the bread and wine become the Body and Blood of Christ, on earth it is not accomplished that which is in heaven, instead the *Heaven does*, the heavenly powers are engaged in an action. The entire atmosphere is recuperated from time and space, and the body of Christ participates at the doxology of redemption that will find its meaning and fulfilment in eternity to come. When speaking about the evoking of the eternity to come or even about the matter of the eternity to come, we cannot doe it outside the space and doxological manifestation, because the eternity to come is unmediatedly doxological. The entire heavenly world, together with the redeemed human nature will amplify through their existence and manifestation the glory of God. The theology of the Sacraments and especially the Sacrament of the priesthood cannot be dissociated from this reality, because in the Sacraments the perishable is communicated, that is time, and likewise, eternity is reflected. God gives us the joy of his fullness, namely, to live in the present that which is to come with exaltation and glory in the future.

The serving priesthood in exercise is in fact the enacting in the present of the heavenly non-time, that is that which is eternal become liveable and experienced by the worshippers. This is done by and through the priest when he is in the churchly liturgical exercise.

III. The Sacrament of the Priesthood, Method of Administration of the Divine Grace

As mentioned above, the main body of the Eastern Church's life is constituted by the Sacraments. Their validity and necessity results from the fact that in them the miracle of meeting Jesus Christ takes place in them, the Comforter Holy Spirit fulfils his ministry of sanctifying the members of Christ's body and outside them the possibility of salvation is compromised. The seven Mysteries point to life's significant events that have both human and divine aspects at the same time. The Sacrament of Baptising – the new birth, the Sacrament of Unction – the unction with the Great and Holy Mire in order to receive the Holy Spirit, a ministry which was executed at the time of the Apostles by the laying of hands, the Sacrament of Holy Eucharist – the communion with the body and blood of the Saviour, the Sacrament of repentance or confession – the complete forgiveness of sins done after baptising, the Sacrament of Priesthood, the Sacrament of Wedding – two become one as an adding of grace and the Sacrament of the Holy Extreme Unction – the anointing with oil of the ill one in order to be healed[42], all these declare the happening of a super-physical phenomenon.

---

[42] The order is according to the one by Ioan Mircea in: Ioanichie Bălan, *Convorbiri Duhovnicești, vol. 2*, pp. 321-324.

This super-physical event is called in eastern theology Sacrament and Jesus Christ is considered as being the founder of each one of them.

In this chapter of our study, we shall evaluate the priestly office from the perspective of its quality as Sacrament. This is important because even if it is a Sacrament as all the other, the Sacrament of priesthood administers all obtaining a special status and special authority. "Sacramental or sanctifying priesthood is one of the seven Sacraments of the Church and the most important one, because it enacts all the other, and without which no other Sacrament is valid. As mentioned before, this priesthood is instituted by our heavenly Saviour, in the day of his resurrection, through the Breath of the Holy Spirit over the Apostles, when he also gave them the power to forgive the sins of men."[43] Approaching the subject from this perspective as well completes the image regarding the orthodox dogmatic orientation on the priesthood and it's quality.

The Sacrament: Introductive Aspects

If the term itself points to something mysterious, towards something abstract, to something inaccessible and beyond reason and proof, in reality, eastern theology offers this word another shade of semantic content. The Sacrament or the Holy Sacraments receive a richer meaning in eastern thought, a meaning superior to the natural reactions of the limited being, which reacts to any miracle: "… The sacraments are not abstract or magical things at all. It is about concrete manifestations in the unity of the sensitive and intelligible. Therefore, any sacrament in general and any particular sacrament of the concrete body of the church's unity, cannot be in any way separated by the natural and historical reality."[44] Everything that happens when the priest administers the sacraments are normal and natural manifestations. They are normal and natural not in the secular sense of the word and not in the normality of the human nature. Here we are talking about another order of normality. We are used tot talking about natural and supernatural phenomenon. The natural ones are those which we can control and which are specific to the perishable, while the supernatural are the ones which we cannot control and which declare through themselves superior to what is perishable. Thus, we name sickness and death as normal things, while we name the idea of eternity as supernatural. In reality, it is the other way round. The things that we name as being normal on earth are actually abnormal because normality is that in which God lives. The sacraments, as eastern theology underlines, are the manifestation of a normal situation because they and within them, man can be in the presence of God, that is, in state of normality.

---

[43] Ioan Mircea in: Ioanichie Bălan, *Convorbiri Duhovnicești*, vol. 2, p. 354.
[44] Nikolaos Matsoukas, *Teologia dogmatică și simbolică*, vol. 2, p. 346.

The sacrament is a means for God's grace, a means through which God comes near to man and man is near to God, without God becoming stained, but this nearness sanctifies man. The immanence of God are at work in the Sacraments in a most complex way, his uncreated energies, God's superior way of being, that is not found in anybody but in the Persons of the Trinity. When speaking about the Sacrament of Priesthood we must consider all this rhetorical complexity through which it is clear that the priestly office takes upon it, manages and transmits God's characteristics made available by the laying of hands and through the presence of the Holy Spirit for the salvation of the believers. In addition, when we speak of Sacrament in an eastern meaning, we speak of grace. The Sacraments are a means to offering Grace and at the same time a place where Grace operates the believer's deification: „Grace is the power of God: 'You will receive power when the Holy Spirit comes on you' (Acts 1:8) 'the Spirit of grace' (Heb 10:29) is the divine agent of this power. The Spirit's kenosis is resilient to any conceptual definition of grace, and school theology is preoccupied more with it's phenomenology, and less with it's ontology. *The Letter of the Eastern Patriarchs* differentiates between the preventive, lighting grace, which is given to any man and the sanctifying and justificatory grace. The later functions in the Sacraments and enacts the deification status."[45] (the underlying belongs to us) As we shall see later on, due tot he fact that the Sacraments are means of God's Grace, the Sacrament of priesthood becomes the supreme means through which the means of divine grace are administered. The grace that works in the Holy Sacraments is, under these conditions, managed by a ***double grace*** that works in the Sacrament of Priesthood and through which all the other Sacraments fill with graceful and heavenly presence those who partake to them.

Far from satisfying the desire for the supernatural, the miraculous, for some things mysterious, etc., the Sacrament of the priesthood is reality, the Reality that is completely present. The serving priesthood in eastern theology is not a *reality* of the presence of Christ, but the reality of the co present grace that enacts salvation from the Great Saviour through the bishops and priests. In addition, the Sacrament of the priesthood is considered a sacrament not because we can participate in it, but because it makes our participation to the mysterious sanctification possible through the priesthood, and also to the elements of uncreated energies.

The serving priesthood declares itself an indispensable part of the priestly office assumed by Christ. "Therefore, the intercession of the priest is not identical to the substitution of Christ; the priest did not become another Christ. The power of Christ works through the priest, actually through his act, which not

---

[45] Paul Evdokimov, *Ortodoxia*, p. 290.

properly his, but the Church's, without becoming the power of the priest. However, Christ's power does not come to through the priest as through a passive channel, but he must pray and participate through that which happens through prayer for the other. And because the priest's definition is given through the fact that he must bring prayers for the people to God, by transforming, somehow, their prayers into his prayer and sending them to the altar above, he is *a servant together with* Christ."[46] *He must pray and participate to that which takes place through prayer.* This, apparently secondary, declaration makes it known to us one of the deepest dogmatic truths in eastern theology on the sacrament of the priesthood and, respectively, about the priestly office in the Eastern Church: the Priest partakes nominally to the accomplishment in the believers of that which he requests in the prayer. "Serving together with Christ" does not express the meaning of this kind of expressions within the evangelical churches. Serving together with Christ suggests, in the eastern church, that the priest actively participates at that which must be accomplished in the being of those who seek God, he actively partakes at God's intention of bringing unity to all the members of his body in a deificatory communion. In other words, the priest becomes part in the action that Christ accomplishes in people, an action of sanctification, of cleansing and, why not, of forgiveness of sins. Probably this claim, at least from an evangelical perspective is outside the biblical context.

One of the most important aspects of the early Christian community, which Christ pointed out even before the cross, was that of unity. In John's Holy Gospel, we find this aspect as follows: "My prayer is not for them alone. I pray also for those who will believe in me through their message, that all of them may be one, Father, just as you are in me and I am in you. May they also be in us so that the world may believe that you have sent me. I have given them the glory that you gave me, that they might be one as we are one: I in them and you in me. May they be brought to complete unity to let the world know that you sent me and have loved them even as you have loved me." (Jn 17:20-23) This unity that Christ speaks of is not about an exterior constraint or about a self obligation on man's behalf. Christ, who dwells within us and among us, and especially through his love, is the One who calls us towards this unity. The Apostle Paul affirms that Christ's love is the one that ties us together (2Cor 5:14). Therefore, it is about something that attracts us, not something that forces us; it's about something that is inviting, not something that pushes us; we deal with a mysterious ministry that God accomplishes for our salvation. This godly disposition, through which we can be partakers to God's world, even though it has subjective aspects, it is accomplished through objective re-

---

[46] Dumitru Stăniloae, *Teologia dogmatică ortodoxă*, vol. 2, p. 160.

alities. The novelty of man in Christ consists in the fact that he communicates himself to God, uniting with people who strive towards the heavens in the theandric body, the Church. This is realised through the Sacraments. "This way, in the Baptising the new man in Christ is born, fully personalised and opens to communication with the Holy Trinity and with his neighbour. That is why, when the first step of true transcendence of man towards his neighbour is accomplished, or his unity with them through the brotherly communication within the Church, as a mysterious and living, multi-personal body of the Lord, trusting oneself at the same time to the others' accountability ..."[47]. However, this kind of communion is managed and enacted through the sacrament of the priesthood, which is by a double grace that intercessess grace. The unity towards which they strive and which is kept, at the same time, has a doxological, worshiping character. Through this manifestation, the priesthood as sacrament administers grace within the sacraments. The sacraments unite and include us. We become for the same moment the objects of Trinitarian communion, but also the subjects of Trinitarian communion and this reality takes place in the shape of grace, "I have given them the glory that you gave me, that they may be one as we are one..." (Jn 17:22). The Holy Spirits descent now of the priests prayer done at the Holy Eucharist protects the communion within the believers and the priestly grace intercessess the saving grace. All the exaltation that the Church brings to the Holy Trinity concurs around and in the self of the sacramental moments of the liturgy. We are no longer strangers here, we are not graded judicially here by God's requests, instead we reconstitute our salvation together with the One who gives it to us, and this salvation has graceful shades of cosmic dimensions. In the Sacrament of Priesthood, the tripersonal God reties himself through his love and through the Body of Christ to his creation, and then the entire Universe rejoices in the worshiping expression emitted from the communion of all the body's members.

When we pronounce Sacrament in eastern theology, we speak about a unity in Christ. This reality is mediated by the protruding spiritual living that is amplified through the administered sacraments by the priestly authority and subsumes the unity of the Church in a doxological manner. Nicolae Mladin mentions that this reality resided precisely in the way that sacraments follow one another. "Therefore – he says – the unity with Christ is not static (we do not simply receive an unchanged quantity of grace), but it is dynamic: it is birth and childhood (Baptising) [...] and it is a fulfilment until the age of Christ's fullness (Eucharist)."[48] We are attracted towards God in a growing force, the Sacraments give an ever growing objective depth of the changes that happen in

---

[47] Dumitru Stăniloae, *Chipul nemuritor al lui Dumnezeu*, vol. 1, p. 203.

[48] Nicolae Mladin, *Asceza și Mistica paulină*, p. 99.

us my making our subjective joy a concrete doxological eruption that expresses itself towards the heaven and the world that in Christ, the Church is one. "The Communion with Christ deepens more and more, the life of Christ is imparted to his members in a growing fullness, until Christ 'takes face' in His every member. However, if the unity with Christ is a unity in love, its intensification is a natural process: love knows no bounds; it is a force of spiritual unification between two persons that leads to complete resemblance. Between Christ and Christians everything becomes commune ..."[49] The unity that Christ accomplishes through the Sacraments is not one that answers the human egocentric needs and interests, we cannot compare it to any kind of human unity, even if it deals with the most noble purposes. The unity that the Sacraments produce and maintain is a mystical one, man finds himself as a carrier of God's image, and consequently as worshiper of this God, the reality that the world cannot understand. At the baptising of Christ, the cosmos is filled by the voice of the Father and by the universal whiteness of the Holy Spirit shown as a dove, and the Son expresses the divine universality, through his body tot he entire human nature. All this heavenly complexity is sacrament and doxology. When the reality anticipated in the upper room took place at the cross, the persons of the godhead moved in/towards the Great Self, the Holy Trinity; 'the universal white' turned it's face: "The sun stopped shining" (Lk 23:45), the Bread and Water of life gave itself: "Father, into your hands I commit my spirit" (Lk 23:46) and the silence was heard for the fist time in a doxological way expressing the universality and eternity of God: "Be silent before the Sovereign LORD [...] The LORD has prepared a sacrifice; he has consecrated those he has invited." (Zeph 1:7). In both cases everything was glory, the salvation that was born within the Holy Trinity rehearsed grace, love and communion in volcanic doxology. Nothing in this image is affected in the moment of the development of the sacraments in the Church. At each baptising, the universe is filled by the God's voice, with each baptising salvation that Christ has brought is amplified and at each baptising the Holy Spirit gives again the whiteness of righteousness to each soul that accomplishes this. At each Holy Eucharist, the communal meeting between Heaven and earth, between Head and Body, between the eternal reality and the eternalised reality rises above the tight boundaries of time and we deal with an ontology of things. The priest is the one through whom it is accomplished and he is the one through who accomplishes it; the complexity of this office receives extraordinary shades in eastern theology.

We find our salvation in the Sacraments as graceful and communal reality that eludes the control of reason. Something happens with us and in us that goes over the sentimental and psychological subjective aspect but at the same time it

---

[49] Nicolae Mladin, *Asceza și Mistica paulină*, p. 99.

transcends the pragmatic and objective aspect. We deal with a different kind of space in which the human nature perceives and is perceived outside the status of sin, it is about the world of God which falls back towards Itself extending in us, in other words, it is about our meeting and settling in Jesus Christ; we find the doxological unity between us and the unity between us and Christ. "This mystical unity with Christ, that became reality through the Holy Sacraments, does not belong to the psychological domain, it is a reality that transcends the meta-empirical, the meta-psychological and the metaphysical. 'This is not the essential thing, that something happens within the one who is baptised [psychological effects], but that he is transposed in the realm of Christ', who's life is unseen, because it is divine. The unity with Christ is an objective fact, that belongs to the ontological realm: it is a communication of divine life in the 'subconscious' or, better said, in the 'substance of the soul' or 'spirit', that is the root of the entire man. That is why it is a sacramental fact."[50] So, the doxological unity in which God places us through the Sacraments, is the our transmutation into another kind of spherical climate, as Mladin says, it is about the sphere of Christ. This sphere is something more than a simple location of the deandric body, the Church. This sphere presents now the salvation that had and still has a chronological development. The expressed unity in the sacraments under the shape of doxology gives us for that specific moment all that it was, is and will be, in their words, it anticipates eternity, it detaches us from time and space. For this reason, life cannot in Christ without the Sacraments. Our transfer into his sphere proves the doxological quality of the sacrament and expresses this doxology. When we unite sacramentally with Jesus, this unity revendicates eternity as beauty and exaltation given only to the Holy Trinity, and we can be united sacramentally with Jesus only when the Sacraments are administered. Due to this reason, in eastern theology the sacrament of priesthood has a special status, because through it God decided that the unity with the sacramental Jesus must be enacted.

The meaning of the Sacraments is also eschatological. At least, when we speak of the Sacrament of Holy Eucharist, we also speak of the end that is to come, meaning, we speak of the beginning of our existence as eternals. The return of the Lord Jesus Christ, the salvation as final determination, under the aspect of atonement as well as that of transfiguration, the restoration of the entire creation, all this phenomenology that is related to the eschaton reverberates gracefully and exultingly in the moment in which we commune. "Already in the book of the Didachy, at the end of the first century and the beginning of the second, the idea that in the Sacrament the Church experiences that which is promised for the Parusia, is clearly stated, that is the eschatological unity of all

---

[50] Nicolae Mladin, *Asceza și Mistica paulină*, p. 117.

in Christ: 'Just as this bread, once scattered over the mountains, now gathered became one, in the same way may your Church gather from the margins of the world into your Kingdom'."[51] We notice that when the priest administers the Sacraments, in this distribution of grace he also anticipates the eschatological unity. However, the final unity of all who are saved will consist in a never-ending exaltation of the Father, the Son and the Holy Spirit. This is why the unity of the members of Christ's body and, implicitly, of the Church is a problem of sacrament; of its administration as well as of the participation in it.

The entire church life finds its meaning and purpose only through Jesus Christ who prolongs himself towards us through the Sacraments. Through the Sacraments we enter the Church, through the Sacraments we grow in the Church, through the Sacraments we find meaning and connection between us and the Church, around them are gathered all who want to receive the saving grace for the glory of God. Man can enter in the Church only through baptising, man can become sacramentally one with Christ only at the moment of the Holy Eucharist, and, man, can grow in grace only through the Sacrament of repentance. Through that which we live in these Sacraments, to our salvation, Christ extends his body towards the world uncovering at the same time the participation at the recovery of our nature, of the Father as well as of the Holy Spirit and therefore making us partakers at the remaining in God as eternal worship. This communion, that is the communal partaking, that is accomplished now of the Sacraments, marks out the human persons in whom the divine has been extended towards the world and it gives birth to the doxological feeling and manifestation in them in which the Father, the Son and the Holy Spirit are above everything. The incarnation of Christ, his crucifixion, the saving work, and even his intercession before God for our expiation, all these have been left to us objectively in our subjective participation at the Church's sacraments. The priest is invested through the priestly grace offered by Christ and the Holy Apostles, through the laying of hands, to enact this holy ministry. That which objectifies again this subjectivity is the relation that is established between those who are members of the body and person of Christ. These are a note to the entire world. Before departing from the Apostles, Jesus Christ related to them through a sending off towards the entire world: "But you will receive power when the Holy Spirit comes on you; and you will be my witnesses in Jerusalem, and in all Judea and Samaria, and to the ends of the earth." (Acts 1:8) Through that which they were to accomplish, Christ was giving himself to the entire world for its salvation. They were fulfilling these sacraments evoking, in what Christ had already accomplished, the glory of the triune God, that the doxological expression oft he sacraments. The Apostles were going to-

---

[51] Ioannis Zizioulas, *Fiinţa Eclesială*, p. 161.

wards the world not with a *something*, but with a *someone*, the objects of their preaching that the people, did not find *something*, but were found by *someone*. "The disciples became the treasurers of our Saviour' sacraments, but without stealing for them this honour, nor making themselves called to this through themselves, but being given the task of apostleship and being ordered to fulfil the holy ministry of the saving preaching, that is of Christ's Gospel, to all who are under the skies. Because, he made them the enlightened teachers of the sacraments by saying, 'Go, teach all the nations'."[52] This grace, this adding of grace is the priestly grace and, maybe, the pastoral one. This sending does not have a character of selecting certain individuals, or of activism, through which someone is convinced to switch to another system of thought as a more valid option compared to all other, no, this sending is made as a unique chance of all the ontological problems of life. The objects of this sending will be filled with another nature; the solution of life will take place in those who will receive this filling, not an alternative. It is about the receiving of a body, of the entrance into a body, of the evoking in this body of the glory of God. This greatness, also given to us, and which rehearses Christ's doxological presence in us, is reflected in the participation at the Holy Sacraments, moment in which the sacrifice of Christ extends through the Sacraments towards us and through us into the world. The benediction that is delivered at each baptising extends the body of Christ doxologically towards other objects of his sending of the Lord Jesus Christ, all is Sacrament, all is grace and all is doxology. The body of Christ is broken and imparted towards the world is actually a presence of the Father through the Holy Spirit, a presence in which love anticipates worship, and worship brings out in a loving manner the objects of Christ's saving extension of his body.

In conclusion, the orthodox dogmatic perspective regarding the idea of sacrament is very complex, and, not always, based on human traditions, as evangelical theology negatively concludes. The issue of the sacraments is the issue of the unity in Christ, regardless of how we name it, it must exist in any Christian church. The key moments of worship are and will always remain those that are administered and enacted by the ordained one; the priest, the pastor, the elder or any other name we might give. The sacramental unity and power of the faith life cannot take place outside these Mysteries or Sacraments. "The unifying power of the Sacraments has at its roots the unifying power of the incarnation, the hypostatical or personal unity of the two natures in Jesus Christ. The general base of the Church's Sacraments is the faith that God can work over his creature in it's visible reality. In this sense, the general meaning of the Sacraments is the unity of God to his entire creation. This is a mystery that incorpo-

---

[52] Sf. Chiril al Alexandriei, *Scrieri partea a doua*, p. 378.

rates everything. There is not one part of reality that would not comprise this mystery."[53] Out of this declaration we necessarily deduce the value and implication of the priestly office. With us, among us and for us; like us, like Christ and for us and for Christ, the priest or pastor, in the sacramental office expresses Grace through which grace is given to us and expresses the Holiness through which sanctity is given to us. "Therefore the sacraments character is, to a great extent, anti-magical not only because it forms the manifestations of the a body, but also because each Sacrament is based on a natural fact or on a historical event."[54] However, in order for this super-physical event to take place in someone's life it must be administered by those whom this authority was given to, by those who have the Sacrament of ordination.

The Ordination

When talking about priesthood, from a biblical perspective, as well as from a Christian perspective, we are talking about ordination. Ordination is an event that detaches itself from the tradition of laying of hands. It is not only a laying of hands that the patriarchs would execute on the first born, as Abraham and Isaac had done, a patriarchal blessing that would assign the "priest" in the family. Ordination in the office of the priest is another kind of projection regarding God's choice, ordination in the priestly office is a choice that declares the universality of the job and its authority, an objective declaration of that which God does in order that man might be forgiven and saved. The first situation of this kind is met in the history of Jewish people, when God institutes the aaronic priesthood. "Have Aaron your brother brought to you from among the Israelites, with his sons Nadab and Abihu, Eleazar and Ithamar, so that they may serve me as priests. Make sacred garments for your brother Aaron, to give him dignity and honor. Tell all the skilled men to whom I have given wisdom in such matters that they are to make garments for Aaron, for his consecration, so that he may serve me as priest... *anoint and ordain them. Consecrate them* so they may serve me as priests." (Ex 28:1-3; 41) The one ordained as priest had the quality of being the tie between the people and God, he was the one who symbolised through his ministry and presence Christ himself, the one declared by God High Priest, through whom forgiveness of sins was fulfilled and, respectively, the declaring of salvation.

---

[53] Ştefan Buchiu, *Întrupare şi unitate*, p. 174.
[54] Nikolaos Matsoukas, *Teologia dogmatică şi simbolică*, vol. 2, p. 348.

Even though many forms of the liturgical manifestation of priesthood are taken over from the aaronic one[55], in eastern theology, the priesthood is something different. "... Aaron brings a blood soaked sacrifice, he sacrificed oxen and bulls, goats, calves and heifers, and the New Testament priest brings the sacrifice without the blood, the spiritual sacrifice of the Son and the Word of God, who sacrificed himself for the life and salvation of the world."[56] Due to this reason the priesthood in eastern theology must be seen as superior to the aaronic priesthood and, from a certain perspective, it's fulfilment. Ordination in the Eastern Church does not realise in any way the purpose of the aaronic liturgy, but it is the object of a purpose and of a superior liturgy, the one that is fulfilled and declared in Jesus Christ, the Son of God. The authority of the priesthood in the New Testament is one that works in the members of the body of Christ, it is not one that words only above them. This kind of authority validates the engaging of the godly Sacrament through which the priest is the identity and the method that God uses to change the natural man into a spiritual man. "The priests are the one to whom our spiritual birth was entrusted to; they are the one whom were given to give birth to us through baptising. Through the priests we are clothed in Christ (Gal 3:27); through the priests we are buried together with the Son of God (Rom 6:4; Col 2:12); through the priests we become the members of the exalted Head of Christ (Col 3:15)."[57] Ordination must be regarded as an act of supreme sacrament, an act through which the ordained one receives the divine investment and thus becomes a divine worker. The debate regarding the priesthood must not be determined by the priests' indecency who compromise the office, but this sublime subject and this biblical reality must acquire the hones place of evaluation in a theologically-biblical environment in which we discus the office, not the one who want to lift themselves at the level of this office or the one who in an interested way give another meaning to God's intention. When you say priest of pastor in the context of God's intention, this reality receives a superior order of approach and existence, different than when you say priest of pastor, in order to have a controversial debate on the difference between the traditional churches, on one hand, and the protestant and neo-protestant, on the other.

The ordination has a direct connection with the debate of apostolic succession or the descendence from Christ, and regarding the ministry that Christ desires to be fulfilled. The subject itself, to a lesser extent the debates, is of a unique

---

[55] The garments, the incense, certain liturgical behaviors, the organizing of the church building that corresponds, somehow, to the Temple because it include a compartment that is the equal of the Holy of Hollies, etc.

[56] Sfântul Nectarie de Eghina, *Despre preoție*, p. 18.

[57] Sfântul Ioan Gură de Aur, *Despre preoție*, p. 85.

seriousness and it tied directly to soteriology. The denial of the possibility to prove apostolic descendence in the Christian churches is most of the times reciprocal and interminable, but the denial of the need of ordination does not exist in any of the Christian churches, because it is a common and indispensable feeling, generated by the presence of the Holy Spirit and by the nominal mandate of Jesus Christ. Because of this fact in Christianity in general and in eastern theology in particular, we seek of the New Testament priesthood as a different succession from the Old Testament one, a succession that does not symbolise, but that is participative, the priest is a co-participant with Christ and from Christ at a graceful ministry of sanctification of those who make up the Holy Body, that is the Church. "The sanctification or ordination of these people is precisely the act through which Christ, under a visible form, chooses and invests these as organs through which, when they will enact the sacramental acts, he himself will enact them in an unseen way; and when they will teach the pastors in his name, he himself will teach them and pastor through them. Bu through sanctification he does not make them worthy only for this, but also compels them. This means that he invests them with a 'charism' or with a 'gist', so that they might enact with seriousness, with responsibility and as a duty of these ministries, so that what they enact might be enacted by Christ himself through them."[58] In eastern theology the subject of the priestly grace is the one who hold antinomically and dilemmaticaly together the difference between the ministry of Christ and of the priest, but at the same time the unique identity of these graceful works. That which the priest enacts is actually that which Christ enacts by making it possible for us to see that which cannot be seen.

The New Testament ordination implies a qualitative and existential difference in relation to the aaronic one. The New Testament ordination declares the ministry of the saving sacrifice of the Lord Jesus Christ as being accomplished, while the aaronic one was only pointing to the later one. Because of this, the ceremony at the Old Tent symbolised the Spotless Sacrifice that was to be brought, and the service that the church priest would enact declares the Spotless Sacrifice as being fulfilled and has the authority to impart it at the Eucharist to all the believers. In this spiritual image, the qualitative difference is underlined. When speaking about an existential difference we take into consideration the reality of the being on whom each of the two priesthoods are being fixed. "The priesthood of the old cult had Aaron as foundation, a man submitted to sin, shown by Moses as priest of God, and the New Testament priesthood has as foundation the Highest of Priests, the man-God himself, our Lord Jesus Christ, who has showed his apostles, through the descent of the Holy

---

[58] Dumitru Stăniloae, *Teologia Dogmatică Ortodoxă*, vol. 3, p. 100.

Spirit, mystagogue and liturgist bishops of his divine Sacraments."[59] The priesthood's descent in eastern theology is a Christological descent one and not an old testamentary, aaronic. The ordination of which we speak in eastern theology is not one that declares the aaronic succession, but it is one that declares the succession of Jesus Christ's authority and, respectively, the succession of the apostles' authority. "The ordination is the condition and the means to fulfil all the other Sacraments, even thought, it is and follows the other Sacraments, that is the initiation and the confession. In the beginning Christ was sent as Bishop, who, by becoming unseen through his ascendance to the heavens and into the glory at the right hand of God, left the apostles and his followers as visible bishops, his organs, strengthened by him with the Holy Spirit's power."[60] In other words, the aaronic priesthood symbolised that which Jesus Christ was to enact and the Christian priesthood enacts together with Christ a divine service.

The ordination must be seen and approached from the complex perspective of that which God bound himself to do and not what man plans to do. The liturgical and festive aspect of ordination is only that which reaches to us in a normal and visible way, as it happens at any of these kinds of celebrations. If ordination resumes only to this, we are dealing with a partinical investing of human origin for the offering of rights and authorities with the purpose of an orderly development of a human community's life. At the moment of ordination God bound himself to do some things completely different.

For this reason, in eastern theology, this act is called Sacrament and in neoprotestant theology, the behaviour is as that that takes place at the Sacrament, but it avoids the term. At the ordination, God introduces us into a over-physical phenomenon. The council of bishops who enact the laying of hands and the prayer for the descending of the Spirit, as well as the one over whom the hands are laid, and those who participate as witnesses at this event, that is all the above mentioned, over-physically live a reality in which they receive the certainty of the life of faith from the future to come and from the anticipated future when in a certain way, all will be priests of God: "Blessed and holy are those who have part in the first resurrection. The second death has no power over them, but they will be priests of God and of Christ and will reign with him for a thousand years." (Rev 20:6).

The event of ordination must surpass confessional delimitations. We have the habit of recognizing or denying reciprocally the ordained quality of the pastors or priests who are from other Christian churches. This attitude can be justifies

---

[59] Sfântul Nectarie de Eghina, *Despre preoție*, p. 18.
[60] Dumitru Radu, *Îndrumări misionare*, p. 566.

when we purse different administrative aspects that protect the functionality of the human part of each of the churches. If we assume the responsibility of looking in a plenary the problem of ordination, than this aspect receives a completely new perspective and makes us accountable in a different way. The confessional elegance is a politically religious issue and the pastoral elegance is a matter of repentance. In the old days, there were prophets who mocked at Jeremiah, but these were not the prophets of God, but of the emperor. The ordination gives us the certificate of belonging to the ministry of God and to God. Even if the Eastern Church speaks about the canonical ordination and the non-canonical one, through this aspect it attributes validity to the first and denial to the second, the setting aside for God of a man set aside for this ministry, must profit from another a thing; in the end God is the one who recognises his workers.

In the Eastern Church, the authority to ordain does not belong to all priests. The authority to transmit the priestly grace belongs only to the bishop. The bishop is considered the direct successor of the apostle and through them the successor of the Lord Jesus Christ. This competence is one that is recognised at a communitary level. The ordination always takes place within a Christian community; it is not a separate act from the Church or an isolated case. The ordination is the declaration of participation of the Body of Christ, a declaration through which in the communion of the churchly community the authority of the one called to the service of Christ and the Church, is validated. "… This special charism is activated only within the body of the Church in the entire community, as we might say, and in no way outside it. It cannot be evidenced as something autonomous because it is the central function of the body. This is why, the priestly charism, presupposes the presence of the body in order for it to come to fruition. Otherwise, the function is not fulfilled, and no Sacrament is enacted without the presence e of the entire body."[61] Consequently, the ordination must be regarded as enact through which the body of Christ is kept functioning. The ordination is not only the competence, but it is also the life in its function of keeping in the self consciousness of the body. It is about a self consciousness that takes the body towards a destiny and it declares this destiny. This thing happens in this way in order to bring out the responsibility that it is attributed to the ordained one regarding each member of the body. The ordination does not create leaders, it creates responsibility, a spiritual responsibility with eternal consequences. Referring to this accountability John Chrysostom makes the following remark: "If to the one who maddens only one man, and little one for that matter, it is useful to tie a millstone to his neck and be thrown into the sea (Mt 18:6), and if those who hit the conscience of their brethren sin

---

[61] Nikolas Matsoukas, *Teologia dogmatică și simbolică*, vol. 2, p. 365

towards Christ (1Cor 8:12), what will happen, I wonder, to the priests, what punishment will they receive when they lose not only one, two or three, but a large number of believers?"[62] The derivation of responsibility from the text of the Holy Scriptures that John Chrysostom made is not an artificial or forced one, but it is exactly the intention that God had regarding the ordained ones and the act of ordination itself. Ordination does not validate only a connection of succession through the Apostles, of the Lord Jesus Christ, but it validates or should validate the content as well. The priest must contain the same Spirit, the same purposes and attitudes towards the people that Jesus himself had.

In eastern theology, the ordination is tightly connected to the doctrine or the doctrines regarding grace. The event of ordination is an event of the grace of the Lord Jesus Christ and it is the grace of Christ. Therefore, when we speak of succession, besides the things mentioned above, we also speak about a realization of grace. The ordained one enjoys an addition of grace and keeps in himself the special grace. "The Church, the Scriptures, **the priesthood** (underlining is ours), the Sacraments we are named 'holy', both because they were holy in themselves and because they sanctified people through the holy grace which they carried."[63] The ordained priest becomes a grace carrier in the way in which Christ's Church is a carrier of grace, and, why not, in the way in which Christ was a carrier of grace by calling people full of sins to repentance. Because of this, the ordination is not just a celebration, but also a Sacrament. We deal with and also participate, at the same time, to a super-physical, surreal, and sur-rational reality. We partake in a time and at a space where God personally takes in his hands the natural common and institutes it, through the sacrifice of the Lord Christ and through the direct action of the Holy Spirit, as a reality that anticipates the transcendent context of God and the world of holiness and eternity that is to come.

The ordination is the specific measure that God enacts in order to make the ordained one capable of being a carrier of grace. Thus, the priest becomes a component of the spiritual Vessel that enacts the holy divine works and redirects with authority and responsibility the souls of the members of the Church towards the Kingdom of God. "The Sacrament of ordination or priesthood is the Sacrament in which, through the laying of hands by the bishop of the Church and through prayer, the specially trained individual is imparted continually, in the Church and for the Church, **the divine grace** from the levels of priesthood, giving him the power of teaching the word of God, to enact the holy Sacraments and to lead the believers towards salvation. Ordination means both the entrance into the clergy and the reception of the grace of priesthood in

---

[62] Sfântul Ioan Gură de Aur, *Despre preoție*, p. 170.
[63] Jaroslav Pelikan, *Tradiția creștină*, vol. 1, p. 173.

one of the three levels: deacon, priest, bishop. That is why it is also called the Sacrament of sacramental priesthood or of grace in the Church."[64] Through this divine measure, the priest becomes the carrier of grace, but at the same time, the grace of God shown to us. Due to this, in the east, seeing the priest by the laymen (and especially when he is dressed in the gown) is considered as a great privilege and quicken pious and self-examination attitudes. Without exaggerating, in a severe synthesis of eastern theology regarding the Sacrament of ordination or of the priesthood, we can argue that the priest is or should be an ***incarnation of grace***. Although, apparently, just one of the seven Sacraments, the ordination or priesthood, has precedence within the egalitarianism of Sacraments, because it is the only one that gives life to all the other Sacraments, and makes grace efficient in the other Sacraments. Just as without Christ all sacrifice in old Israel would have been identical to the heathen ones, the Sacraments in the Church would be, without the priest, emotional moments of a collectivity identical to those that celebrate birthdays or commemorations of similar events in our lives. Through the Sacrament of Ordination, the natural common is desperate and coagulates itself at the intervention of God into a heavenly reality. The event itself is no longer one that bears the heavenly or one in which the heavens are involved, but the event itself is a heavenly one.

"Ordination is one of the seven Holy Sacraments of the Church, that offer grace to a high degree ... ordination is enacted at the altar ... through the laying of the bishop's hands on the head of the one who receives the ordination."[65] These three specifications: "grace in a high degree", "is enacted at the altar" and "the laying of the bishop's hands" declare the spiritual triunity of the act. We are dealing here with a grace that is not common, *grace in a high degree*, we are dealing with a space that is not common, *the altar*, and we are dealing with an authority that is not common, *the bishop's hands*. Ordination separates therefore the priest from the common world and makes it forever. The priest is set aside for God. In the Sacrament of Ordination we do not deal with the pretences of certain people about themselves, that we are not interested from a theological, dogmatic and biblical perspective about what the priests say about themselves. However, if we are interested in this it is due only the appreciation that we must have towards the self-respect of any man. When we speak of the Sacrament of Ordination, we are interested or should be interested what God says about this act. "Those who ordain the unworthy are just as harshly punished as those who are ordained, even if they do not know the one who is ordained ... in order to see the truth, listen to what the blessed Paul to his disciple Timothy, the beloved and true spiritual son: 'Do not be hasty in the laying on

---

[64] Dumitru Radu, *Îndrumări misionare*, p. 567.
[65] Nicolae D. Necula, *Tradiție și înnoire în slujirea liturgică*, vol. 3, p. 234.

of hands, and do not share in the sins of others' (1Tim 5:22)."[66] Actually, Paul's words express God's attitude towards this reality. The ordination is an intervention of God not of the people, the ordination is a decision of God not of the people and, not least, the ordination is a divine grace, not human kindness.

As a conclusion, in eastern theology, the miracle of ordination, the Sacrament of Ordination represents a special place. Excluding the polemical and monopolising elements of enacting this act, elements that can make the object of inter-confessional dialogue, with the known success or failure, the evaluation of the ordination value and the theological dogmatic discourse, in the east, regarding this subject is one that forces us to pay attention and to an honest research. The ordination must not be seen as a church issue or as a sectarian one, the ordination must be considered as being divine. The ordination is the reality that God chose not to be dispensed of in the ministry of salvation for humanity.

The sacrament of ordination in eastern theology is grace itself. We are dealing with the given grace and the grace that is given. The given grace has a sense in a certain shade of religious and spiritual competence of which only a few people are worthy, namely those who accept God's calling. These persons who become accountable out of their own desire and who are held accountable by God, become an unmitigated part of what the Holy Scriptures call "the grace of God has been shown." The ordination is a showing of grace. The priest must be the one through whom God "It teaches us to say 'No' to ungodliness and worldly passions, and to live self-controlled, upright and godly lives in this present age, while we wait for the blessed hope the glorious appearing of our great God and Savior, Jesus Christ..." (Tit 2:12-13). "... The priest must never, just as silver or gold, sound fake, he must not have a sound of brass, wherever he finds himself, whatever life's circumstances are and regardless of the matters he needs to resolve; he must not have any bad thought or deed ..."[67].

Secondly, the ordination is the grace that is given. In other words, through the priests ordination he is given grace in a most high degree, but he can also offer it to those who truly seek God. "In the oldest formula of ordination that was kept in the *Apostolic tradition* of Hippolytus, there was a prayer that implored God to send the power of the Holy Spirit over the bishop, that Christ had given the Apostles, and to make him worthy to intercess on behalf of the people and to forgive their sins."[68] The above argument places eccentrically and almost shockingly the service of the priest. "To intercess in the name of the people" and "to forgive their sins" is a request which if God executes it means that the

---

[66] Sfântul Ioan Gură de Aur, *Despre preoție*, p. 133.
[67] Sfântul Grigorie din Nazianz, *Despre preoție*, p. 228.
[68] Jaroslav Pelikan, *Tradiția creștină*, vol. 1, p. 178.

Sacrament of Ordination is spiritual exercise of the same authority as the exercise of the existence of Christ as High Priest. Even if we cannot agree with the superior limit of these characteristics invoked in prayer for the ordination of the priest, we cannot ignore the fact that pastoring, regardless of how much we delineate it from the functions of Christ, it remains the duty of staying between the people and God with the meaning and purpose of bringing the former to reconciliation, through Jesus Christ, with God the Father. Pastoring also presupposes and administration and an offering of grace from which situations of forgiveness result for those who desire this, a forgiveness that does not place the priest in the stead of God, but make him co-forgiver with God in order to save souls.

The Sacrament of Ordination remains, therefore, the extreme manifestation and vulnerability of God's love reason for which each priest and each pastor should tremble.

The Priesthood as Means for the Enactment of Sacraments

Just as we have noted above, in eastern theology the Church's life is considered as gravitating around the Sacraments. Actually, without the Sacraments there is no Church life. In the Sacraments, and in their participation, the communion between the members of Christ's body takes place. In them our communion through Christ and the Holy Spirit with God the Father takes place, in them there is the offering of grace, in them there is our progress in and towards holiness. Partaking in the Sacraments is partaking in the divine nature, it is the argument that we are on the path towards deification. "There are seven concrete possibilities of integrating or reintegrating of our individual lives in the life of the ecclesial body. At the same time, these are just as many events (deeds) of realisation and manifestation of the Church, a charismatic constitution of the new creation that receives life from the Spirit."[69] The sacraments in the Eastern Church are the life of the Church, they are the reality that makes possible the existence of the Boundless in the limited, of the Eternal into the perishable and of the Omnipresent into the habitable. The sacraments can be understood as some uncreated *super-energies* of God through which He makes himself present and felt by those who participate in his charisms.

Even though to some of these Sacraments naturally correspond certain "civil"[70] manifestations, the theological dogmatic attitude of the Eastern Church offers

---

[69] Christos Yannaras, *Abecedar al credinţei*, p. 168.

[70] That is the Sacrament of Baptizing corresponds to the receiving of a birth certificate, the Sacrament of marriage corresponds to ceremony under the jurisdiction of the Cesar through which a man and a woman are united as husband and wife, the Sacrament of repentance corresponds to the family education and schooling that deals with the equipping of each child and mature man with a high morality.

an accentuated attention towards the quality that it has to have the one who administers these Sacraments when they are enacted in the context of church community. In this context we do not deal only with the enactment of certain confirmation acts, but those who are qualifies for the fulfilling of these divine sermons operate, for those for whom these are enacted, the Sacrament of God's grace. In other words, the priest are persons invested by God to work with the grace that comes from God, and respectively, grace that is in them.

Through Sacraments towards the great Sacrament, that then administers all the others, is the Sacrament of priesthood. Baptised and ointed with the Holy Spirit, communing in the Body and Blood from the Body and Blood of Christ, uniting with his wife in the Sacrament of Marriage and growing into deification through the Sacrament of Repentance, the priest is born through the laying of hands. He, who is from Sacraments, in great Mystery is set aside in order to enact the unity of the members in the Triune doxology when the Holy Spirit fills the communion of believer gathered at any of the Church's sacraments. "The priesthood is the power of graceful authority that breaks the deforming powers of impurity and renews man. This power of authority is that which places into a functional manifestation all other Sacraments in order to accomplish the rebirthing, the movement, the nourishment and a continuous, ever growing, fulfilling progress towards perfection."[71] All that the exalting atmosphere gathers and that which the exalting community declares while gathered together, capable and opened for the divine presence through the Sacraments, especially through the Sacrament of Baptising and of the Holy Eucharist, is the job of the priest. The pastoring of the church actually consists in the way the priest knows how to take those who were given to him to be pastored, towards these moments of complete liturgical manifestation. The grace and vocation must meet in a accomplished way with the authority of the laying of hands and with the lived righteousness, and the carrier of the above mentioned, that is the priest, is the only one in whom and through whom God fulfils a Christi like ministry, makes the observation of that which Christ enacts in the heavens possible with the purpose of cleansing and saving us. All this heavenly image, this entire divine manifesto enacted among the people, must make the priest responsible towards the sufficient and complex love through which God manifests himself in the moment when the believers live the ecstasy of the Sacraments. "The priest must try to conform himself as much as possible the reality of Christ's love, through an extremely accentuated responsibility of his as servant towards the Master who loves all, who has shown us the ways through which he wants to save us. This responsibility paints again the subordinate status of the human priesthood, but also the dependance of our salvation to

---

[71] Nikolaos Matsoukas, *Teologia dogmatică și simbolică*, vol. 2, p. 363.

Christ the Intercessor. Because Christ the Intercessor is quickened by the supreme responsibility for the souls before heavenly Father , and from this responsibility feeds the responsibility of Church's visible priest, because he is responsible of the fulfilling of the responsibility of Christ towards the Father for the believers, and through this fulfilling he brings out even more strongly his quality as Mediator of Christ towards the Father and towards us, but also the priests quality as Christ's intercessor."[72] In this context the administration of the Sacraments by the priest is not only a functional one, but also one of intercession. Through the Sacrament of priesthood, the possibility of participating at a liturgical sermon is not realised only at an administrative level, but each Sacrament is the means through which the priest mediates or mediates our approaching to God in a special, unique and unrepeatable way.

The priesthood, in eastern theology, is the means, method and authority that enacts a liturgical complex that brings the believers close to one another and together brings them closer to God. Normally, none of the seven Sacraments can be enacted by anybody else besides the priest. "The priesthood as Sacrament has the priest as an organ of the Holy Spirit, a mystagogue and liturgist of the divine blessing sermons; through the priesthood, a man from within men enacts for the people those that are to be towards God."[73] When we speak of the priest as an organ of the Holy Spirit, we speak of someone in whom God has enacted a different work than in other people and has paid in him a favour and a debt to administer the works that are foreign to the people that do not have the grace of priesthood. We must admit that this spiritual complexity presupposes a divine ministry in the priest which rises above a simple administrative validation and that is more profound than an emotion of religious nature. As a vessel of honour chosen by God the priest is validated as economist of the divine sacraments that also include immediate human realities and it is in now way a validation as economist of the secular human problems in which certain divine sacraments could be found. In the first case, the human problems are recovered in order to be overlapped with the divine ones and to make them integral to these, in the second case, all are part of secular life that deludes itself with emotions that it considers as coming from God. The priesthood as means for the enactment of Sacraments and as serving the believers, who approach God through the sacraments, is the super-physical reality that moves and gives life to the body and its members in accordance with the meaning and purpose that come from Christ, the Head of this body. In these conditions, the priest is not only the ambassador of Christ in the Church, but he is the *Christ* at the hand of all who trouble themselves in love towards the supreme Love that

---

[72] Dumitru Stăniloae, *Teologia dogmatică ortodoxă*, vol. 2, p. 160.
[73] Sfântul Nectarie de Eghina, *Despre preoție*, p. 19.

is Jesus who is hidden in God the Father. "The functionality of the church body has a power of grace that is central and axial, that guides or coordinates all the other graceful manifestations. This central power is the Sacrament of Priesthood."[74] That is why, in eastern theology it is quite improper or even impossible to speak about the approaching of God outside the Sacrament of priesthood or to estimate in any way the life of the Church without a priest. The unseen that is visible in the Sacraments, in the moment in which the priestly prayer invokes the descending of the Holy Spirit, makes it possible the transcending of the church body from the divine presence and from the divine light in such a way that the salvation to come is lived in the present. This universal and universalising engagement is due to the priestly sacrament and to the way this is expressed as means of enacting the Holy Sacraments. This cosmic engagement receives life through the Holy Spirit so that we can speak about a being of the Sacrament or a Sacrament as mystical-communion being. When the epiclesis takes place, when the priest's prayer that invokes the filling with the Holy Spirit is listened to through the fact that the Person of the godhead fills the church building, the gathered members of the body, and finally yet importantly, the Sacraments, then the liturgical event becomes the Sacrament of God.

The background purpose for the priest to be able to enact the Sacraments, that is, for him to be able to administer the grace of God, is of the Holy Spirit. "The unanimous patristic tradition of the East attributes the working power in all 'spiritual rituals' to the hypostatic intervention to the Third Person of the Trinity. Before the proper epiclesis, the Liturgy utilises preliminary 'epiclesis', progressively rising towards the final formula."[75] The final formula is a spiritually cosmic state, it's accomplishment is helped by the priest who has a plenary involvement that follows from the Sacrament of spiritual priesthood that "puts together" doxologically the entire atmosphere that carries on in the Church. "The Holy Spirit as hypostasis is active in different ways and in different grades in people, producing different effects in them. But through all of them he unites man with Christ and through this he makes man commune from the infinite holiness and deification that is in the body of Christ, or in the human nature of Christ."[76] Therefore, in eastern theology, the priesthood as means for the enactment of the Sacraments must be understood only through the ministry of the Holy Spirit. The gathering of the ones declared as being God's rises above a simple human gathering because of the Spirit's filling, a filling that is nominal and that operates the work of the divine grace at the same time with the accomplishment of the express prayer that the priest lifts to God.

---

[74] Nikolaos Matsoukas, *Teologia dogmatică și simbolică*, vol. 2, p. 363.
[75] Paul Evdokimov, *Prezența Duhului Sfânt în Tradiția Ortodoxă*, p. 121.
[76] Dumitru Stăniloae, *Teologia dogmatică ortodoxă*, vol. 2, p. 200.

A necessary aspect that needs to be mentioned regarding the debated theme is the importance of ecclesial interiority. Through the Sacrament of Priesthood the capacity, that the divine grace can be administered for those who strive to receive the righteousness given through the Sacrifice of our Lord Jesus Christ is declared, but this Sacrament cannot overpass the ecclesiastic interiority. The Sacrament of Priesthood that enacts the other Sacraments must be engaged in the interior communion of the Church, the *Sacrament of Sacraments*. "The enacting of the Sacraments outside the liturgical community is inconceivable in orthodox tradition. In essence, it is about a participation of the people at the priesthood of Christ, independently from the fact that it does not have the special charism of priesthood, that is irreplaceable in the midst of the functional variety of charisms. In this way the special priesthood is integrated functionally in the general priesthood of the entire body of the Church."[77] The administration of the divine grace through the enactment of the Sacraments is a problem of communion; it is a problem of participation at the love of God into holiness, not only for spiritual comfort. The Sacrament of priesthood, this co-operation with Christ in his own Body is the sacrament that opens the possibility of living a divine love in the Sacraments that are administered by the priest. This is possible only within the communitary love, in the ecclesial interiority that is spin off from the love of God and an expression of it. "Therefore the gathering in the Church is before all the Sacrament of love. We go to church for love, for the new love of Christ himself, who gives himself to us in our unity. We enter in the church in order for this divine love, 'might reverse in our hearts again', so that, again and again, we might 'clothe ourselves with love' (Col 3:14), so that by making up this Body of Christ we might stain in the Christ's love and show his love to the world."[78] In these conditions, the priesthood as means through which the Sacraments are enacted, must be understood in the context of the ecclesial body, of the church being that through Holy Spirit is transfigured in the way in which Christ himself was transfigured on mount Tabor. This entire divine picture is engaged by love and engages sacramentally the love of Christ for the people, the love of the priest for Christ and for those whom he serves and the love that allows the synergy between all the distributing sacraments of grace and the believers who receive this grace. At the ministry of Sacraments we take part at the way in which each human person is engaged communionally and declares the existence of the Church Being, that the complex Person of the Lord Jesus Christ who assumes our existence as his body by making us part of that which we can be through him. Due to this reason, the exercise of the priestly sacrament, as well as the other Sacraments cannot exist outside Church. "The Baptising, the Unction, the Priesthood and the Confes-

---

[77] Nikolaos Matsoukas, *Teologia dogmatică şi simbolică*, vol. 2, p. 365.
[78] Alexandre Schmemann, Euharistia Taina Împărăţiei, pp. 141-142.

sion are Sacraments before all in the virtues of this reference of theirs to the Eucharist. In other words, they regard not only the isolated individual, they do not share only a 'personal' grace, but they regard the individual in his relationship with the Church."[79] The priest must be the graceful nuance that by leading to the fulfilment of the unseen ministry of Christ and that becomes visible through him, might animate in a doxological and eschatological way the joy of those that have access to the divine grace.

As a conclusion, in eastern theology, the Sacraments must be seen as means of the graceful ministry of God and as means that work the grace of God in those who take part at them. Through them the super-physical and physical between God as the One who creates man and man as the one who seeks God, is kept uninterrupted, a cardinal and living bond that remains in the Lord Christ. "From Christ the power of God extends through the Sacrament over all people through gestures and matter."[80] The role as intercessor and enactor of this spiritual complex follows from the Sacrament of priesthood, from the ministry of the priest. He is the one who intercesses the given grace in the Sacraments and he is the one who through his ministry makes a heavenly activity visible, so that through faith the believer can become a participant, through the visible things, at the invisible, and through the symbolic, at the eternal. This ministry presupposes always and indispensably, from a dogmatic perspective as well as from a liturgical one, the nominal and plenary ministry of the Holy Spirit. "The Eucharist" – Serghei Bulgakov writes – "as all other church sacraments was possible only through the descent of the Holy Spirit"[81], nothing can take place outside the space of presence of the Trinity's third Person, and the space that liturgically outlines the Holy Spirit's presence is the Church, the Body of Christ. Consequently, the priestly office in eastern theology must be seen as an exercise of presence and ministry of the Holy Spirit in the Church, in the priest, in the Sacraments, and through them, in those who come near God.

The sacrament of priesthood validates the priest as nucleus that mystically coagulates the members of the church body on their journey towards deification. This happens in a superior order of human understanding in such a way that the incomprehensible and mysterious world of God becomes and is his world even more incomprehensible in the Church. "If all the Sacrament" – says Dumitru Stăniloae – "is a unity of the contrary, the Church is the ultimate Sacrament, because it is the shape of the supreme unity of God with all that is created. It will be in its completeness in the next life, God's way of being 'everything in

---

[79] Karl Christian Felmy, *Dogmatica experienței ecleziale*, p. 239.
[80] Dumitru Stăniloae, *Teologia Dogmatică Ortodoxă*, vol. 3, pp. 9-10.
[81] Serghei Bulgakov, *Dogma euharistică*, p. 35.

all'. Thus, the notions of Sacrament and Church coincide."[82] The coincidence of these notions become personified in exactly the priests ministry that because of the given priestly grace, can foreshadow the meeting of the Sacrament and the Church, that are in Christ the High Priest, in him the carriers of grace.

Beginning with Melchisedec and continuing with Aaron, the Holy Apostles and those who came after them, Jesus Christ lies under the incidence of the vulnerable and contestable realities of the great dedication in order to make accessible, legitimate and missionary, the law that expresses the capacity of forgiveness. To the churchly priesthood belongs this role of charismic equivalence through which it does not monopolize the capacity of forgiveness and salvation but dissipates it as a gesture that flows from the Great Lover of people and who, through the Sacrament of Ordination, was lit up in every priest. The priesthood in this case will not remain a canonical caste but a universalisation of the priestly way in which Jesus Christ wanted and enacted the opening of the gates of God's Kingdom. The priestly office, under these conditions, remains the Sacrament born out of Sacraments, having as purpose the bringing to everyone's disposal God's love.

IV. The Priesthood: The Sacerdocy through which the Members of the Body are Tied to the Head of the Church, Christ

In the east, the problem of the church priesthood is always approached starting from the priesthood of the Lord Jesus Christ. Usually, the relationship between Christ and Church is regarded through analogy with the relationship between God and creation through Jesus Christ. This discourse is usually done with great care not to misunderstand the church priest's authority and not to makes any confusion between the absolute and perfect priesthood of Christ and the human church priesthood. In spite of this, most of the times, the conclusions give a status slightly more significant to the church priesthood than it might usually be deduced after evidencing the importance of the priesthood of God's Son.

In eastern theology the unity and integrity of the Church constitutes the main subject in which God' work of salvation is assimilated. The unity and integrity of the church are regarded as supreme and final arguments in favor of the fact that it constitutes the body of Jesus Christ and that in it the works of grace operate the believers holiness through the active presence of the Holy Ghost. The Church, the instituted miracle of Jesus Christ proves its divine worth and divine descendence through the fact that it is complete and unitary. The com-

---

[82] Dumitru Stăniloae, *Teologia Dogmatică Ortodoxă*, vol. 3, p. 11.

munion of the people present at the moments of liturgical worship, the sense and written Word of the incarnated One, which objectify only in the Church and only through it, are just as many arguments that the Church must be united through grace and it's integrity cannot be questioned under any condition. Due to this, in the East the dominant metaphor, and respectively, favored regarding the Church is the metaphor of the Body. As we have mentioned before, the Church is seen as a divine-human organism that is declared, because Christ is the Head and because it is the body, as theandric "being". The being of the Church results precisely from the fact that Christ is the Head, it is the body, and in this "Mystery of Mysteries" that is the Church, its unity and integrity is confirmed by the ministry of the Unseen, Jesus Christ, through those who are visible, meaning the priests and the ministry of the inaccessible One, that the Holy Spirit, through the perceptible and accessible ones, that is the Holy Sacraments. The priestly sacerdocy cannot be separated from the Church and neither can the Church be separated from the priestly sacerdocy; the Church is where the priesthood is. The church can be only where Christ, the High Priest, is; and he is only there where his unseen ministry becomes visible through the ministry that the church priest officiates.

For the Eastern Church the existence of the New Testament priestly office is an intrinsic condition that operates the sense of the Church and confirms to the believers that fact that they belong to the real body of Christ. This reason determines us to debate and show, in what follows, the importance of the church priest's importance regarding the maintaining of Church unity and integrity and his role in the community of "members" with the purpose of perfecting the Body of Christ and implicitly of each single individual.

The Priesthood of Christ: Premises of Cosmic Unity

The cosmic unity of Christ is the central element of the meaning of salvation in eastern theology. Christ as High Priest is seen in a unilateral sense, the One in whom this unity can be achieved and the One who can accomplish it. Due to this reason in eastern Christianity, the self-deification promoted by the modern and postmodern world is not seen as a progress, but as a regress both from a social perspective as well as from a spiritual one. "Because of the conflict with the medieval inquisition, but owing to enlightment as well, contemporary man closed himself in his own autonomy and refuses any appeal to transcendence."[83] Resolving this situation receives a meaning only in Jesus Christ's double nature and who unifies in his own Being the divine nature with human nature and who through his Priestly ministry fulfills beforehand through the church priesthood the cosmic unity that is to be declared at the restoration of

---

[83] Dumitru Popescu, *Hristos biserică societate*, p. 15.

all things. Actually, nature is not seen outside communion. Whether we speak of nature as a non-ontological reality or of nature as a human and divine ontological reality, nature in the east is seen as the complexity of communion determined by the existence of God himself and his purpose. "... The meaning of 'nature'" – says Ioannis Zizioulas – "should be qualified immediately through that of communion: created 'nature', as well as divine 'nature' are truth not as 'natures' but as a communion of natures, the first as quality of communion through participation and the second as in itself, without participation."[84] The independence from God and God's independence are seen as foreign to God declares it to be. God brings forth his authority and superiority towards the created nature not through independence from it, even though he has it at an absolute level, but through communion with it. This eliminates the deistic orientation and reiterates God as source and content of love. The East offers God in a radical way all the action regarding our perfection, a reality that is to finalize out cosmic integration, and this can be achieved only in Christ, in the Christ of after the resurrection, the One who ascended to the Father and therefore was transfigured forever. In these acts of divine nature and not independent of the sense of the existence of the created nature, God warps the cosmic unity that is to be finalized through the perfect communion and the absolute and final elimination of sin.

The transfiguration of Mount Tabor is seen as an event and as an anticipated divine intervention through which the cosmic unity desired by God and accomplished by him might be foretasted through the Holy Apostles by the entire humanity that was to believe and follow Christ. Christ who was crossed by the divine light, brought forth on Mount Tabor the unity and the communion of the unblemished divine nature with the deified human nature, or, better said, glorified human nature. The premises of cosmic unity that results from the priesthood of Jesus Christ are actually the premises in which the model of the recreated man is proposed. "The transfiguration of the world cannot be enacted but through renouncing the self and ascetic endeavors."[85] The communion towards which God brings his cosmos is the one in which man as microcosms as well as planet Earth with is own macrocosms, become once more realities outside sin and God would in these not only the one who supports[86] their existence, but

---

[84] Ioannis Zizioulas, *Fiinţa eclesială*, pp. 97-98.
[85] Kallistos Ware, *Împărăţia lăuntrică*, p. 48.
[86] According to orthodox teaching, all the material and immaterial realities, the human beings and all that has life exists only because God acts in these through the uncreated energies. In other words, if God retreats from man or from the fallen angels or even Lucifer, all these would cease to exist. The redoing of the unity and cosmic communion through Christ presupposes in this case that God would not exist in the human being only through

the One who is in communion with them. The priesthood of Jesus Christ is the premise and method through which God finalizes this purpose of his love.

The fundamental element through which the "start" is given for the development of God's plan to bring his creation back into a perfect communion with himself is the event of the incarnation of the Son of God. The assuming of the fallen human body by the One in whom there is no sin to be found, becomes the official declaration according to which the price of unifying or the love from which this unification flows and which would show itself at the cross was very near. This loving act with salvation shades was undergoing in order to eliminate evil from the universe and the anticipation, when through the priestly office of Jesus; the cosmic unity could have been accomplished again. "The very Word of God, became through its incarnation the Priest of creation par excellence, or bringing it back to God, of the re-gathering of the scattered people from their primordial unity, in God. [...] He remains through this Priest forever, the unique divine Priest, the unique human in whom we have entrance and the capacity of sitting next to God. And because he is unseen following his Ascend, He, as unique and complete Priest, is the spring of the entire visible priesthood."[87] According to the notes of Dumitru Stăniloaie in this universal and divine measure one can notice in a kernel the birth of the church priesthood, birth that would exercise and in which the same universally conciliatory ministry will be exercised, through which the cosmic unity would be perfected in order to give over in conditions of sanctity the definitive restoration of the divine communion.

The priesthood of the Lord Jesus Christ redirects and universalizes God's love that through he aaronic priesthood received a nominal sense, restricted, taking into consideration only the people of Israel. When we speak about the priesthood of Christ we speak about the premises that first declare a universality of the divine love regarding all nations, and then this aspect is found in the way that these are recuperated and integrated in the cosmic unity and communion, of the entire creation that awaits salvation. Because, says the Holy Apostles Paul "...the whole creation has been groaning as in the pains of childbirth right up to the present time. Not only so, but we ourselves, who have the first fruits of the Spirit, groan inwardly as we wait eagerly for our adoption as sons, the redemption of our bodies" (Ro 8:22-23). This problem of passing from the particular to the universal, from planet Earth to the Great Cosmos, is evidenced in the way it passes from the aaronic priesthood to the priesthood of Christ. "...The law of salvation of a single nation will be replaced with the law of

---

the uncreated energies which supports his existence, but in the ones who are to be saved he might exist also at the level of communion.

[87] Dumitru Stăniloae, *Teologia Dogmatică Ortodoxă*, vol. 3, pp. 98-99.

love, that has in it qualitative intensities of justice. Therefore, after this law of love, the priesthood could not be comprised of only one nation, only one people, but all the nations, according to the words of the same Apostle, Paul, who presents Christ as Bishop and Savior of all people." (1Tim 4:10)[88] The priesthood of Christ the Lord presupposes forgiveness, forgiveness presupposes communion, and communion presupposes universalisation. Man as being is forgiven, the non-ontological cosmos is cleaned or restored and the communion towards whom God engages the direction of creation through the sacrifice and ministry as priest of his Son is that which raises above the way in which we propose the society's existence and the necessity of morals.

The role of Jesus Christ's priesthood or the choice of God for resolving this problem through the intercession and sacrificial activity brings forth an astonishing fact compared to our way of thinking. We notice from this kind of approach that God uses, that the intention and accomplishment of the cosmic communion is not an act of revenge, it does not presuppose a war strategy through which the Sovereign re-attach lost territories to his *empire*, but it is the expression of another behavioral quality, a quality foreign to the human realm. God accomplishes through Christ's universal priesthood a cosmic unity on the levels of love, with certain measures of sanguinic belonging. He is the Father and the humans are his children. Creation is the masterwork, which he restores by reinvesting himself esthetically and emotionally. The decision of reinvesting himself is not one that results from the pride of possessing power or from the certainty that totalitarian egocentrism offers, but the decision of reinvesting in the restoration of communion is born in his own love and expresses only love. The means in which such a overflow of divine feelings could touch the firmament of all that God wanted to happen was Christ, the God his Son. The plot in which he enacted apriorically the ministry of priesthood, in his own passions, in his own sacrifice and in the propitiation in his own blood, so that later he might be declared High Priest in his double nature and in the sublime priestly activity, declares universally and undoubtedly that the priesthood as legitimating of God's love expresses the end of the spear and the tip of the spear of unifying community through a love shown in Christ as irreducible. "Christ, Christ incarnate is Truth, because he represents the ultimate and unconditional will of God's ecstatic love, who wants to bring the created being into communion with his own live and to know it in this event of communion."[89]

As a conclusion the priesthood of Christ as premise of the cosmic union must be evaluated within God's love and as effect of this love. Also, in the church

---

[88] Ioan Mihălțan, *Preoția Mântuitorului Hristos și preoția bisericească*, p. 36.
[89] Ioannis Zizioulas, *Ființa eclesială*, pp. 101-102.

priesthood, as we shall see in what follows, we must find God in the same passionate manner, through which he gives birth to the argument from himself that we exist in the universal elements that God brings froth through the sacrifice and ministry of Christ as priest to the great and eternal communion of his holy love. The argumentation consists in the visible elements of the church priesthood that can be submitted to the arithmetical evidences and which fortify the certainty that our faith and our life in Christ have the sense and finality of our hope. This way of grafting found in the human life's liturgical patterns through communion with the entire cosmos, works on the mechanisms of divine love. The priesthood must be seen as a premise or as the only premise of love for this comunional unity.

The Serving Priesthood: the Premises of the Church's Unity in Christ

When we speak about the priesthood in the Eastern Church, we speak about an indissoluble tie between the priest or a becoming priest and the church. This results out of many ways of approaching the problem, but the most evident is mentioned at the end of theological studies where receiving the degree is strictly connected to the vow of faith towards the Church, that the graduate makes for his entire life. Under these conditions, the way in which the vow is connected to those who tend towards the priesthood creates the paradigm or the walls of human participation that solidifies and makes the Church unbreakable and undividable. The priestly vow becomes the sacerdotal communion in which the Sacrament of Ordination is officiated, and it's synergy, validated by the filling with the Holy Spirit, declares the unique and unifying existence of the Holy Church. The unity of the Church considered from the perspective of the priestly office is a unity that derives from God's very own way of being in general and from the perfecting ministry of Christ and the Holy Spirit in particular. "Eastern theology never considers the Church outside of Christ and the Holy Spirit."[90] In this paradigm, the priest is the arcade that connects the human elements to the divine ones. He, the priest, is the seeing of Christ the invisible and the visible work of the unseen work of Jesus and, at the same time, he is the administrator who determines and who is determined by the Holy Spirit through the authority that binds through the Sacraments the believers to the communion with the divine Grace. Through the churchly priesthood, the church does not gravitate around the leader who coagulates socially a category of people, through the church priesthood, the church is coagulates soteriologically around Christ; it is a perfect act only through the participation of the third person of the godhead, the Holy Spirit. "The church is the work of Christ on

---

[90] Vladimir Lossky, *Teologia mistică a bisericii de răsărit*, p. 206.

earth; it is the image and dwelling place of the Holy presence of earth in the world. And at the day of Pentecost, the Holy Spirit descended over the Church that was represented at that time by the twelve Apostles and those who were with them."[91] The church priesthood in the east is real only under the conditions of the Church, of a church that results from the sacred work of the Lord Jesus Christ and the descent of the Holy Spirit. The first coordinate is indirect or succesorial and it is offered through the apostles and bishops. The second coordinate is the direct one that takes place in the moment of the laying of hands and it is confirmed by the mysterious presence of Jesus Christ as well as by the filling with the Holy Spirit after the prayer. The complexity of the event that is finalized in the access to the invisible through the visible priesthood offers a real certainty of the church unity and management of its unity.

The liturgical dimension of the priest's work is one that is very loaded by this responsibility of uniting the body's members, that is the Church, with Christ who is it's head. The liturgy itself becomes in the moments of supreme manifestation a heavenly communion in which all that is worldly is recuperated in the world of God, a world through which the eternal existence is anticipated. "As a representative of the believers, he presents to God their proper offering – that is their gifts, the worship and their prayers, and as a chosen vessel of Grace, he transmits to the believers that which comes from God, that the divine Grace, the forgiveness of sins, the eternal life and, in general, all the spiritual gifts and the material goods that we receive from God. The serving priest is therefore the link between God and people, between heaven and earth."[92] In other words, the priest is the reality that comes from the hands of God towards the hands of people and it is the reality from people's souls towards the interiority of God. The priest underwrites and accomplishes the church unity through the fact that his office represents the love and the Trinitarian community in a double sense. In the priest we meet the love of God given to the people and which works among the people and still in the priest we meet God's love that return to himself and in himself with the answer of human love hidden in God's love. In the priest takes place the communion that comes from God towards the people in salvific sense and still in the priest we find the communion of God that resonates with himself, deifying the human nature as well, that is recuperated in this divine communion.

In the east, the problem of the church's unity is not seen as a party-minded. From the church unity or from it's possibility to fragment results the proof of it's authenticity. This offers new weight to the dogmatic appreciation regarding the priestly office and regarding the priest. The priest is the extension of the

---

[91] George Florovski, *Biserica, Scriptura, Tradiția – Trupul viu al lui Hristos*, p. 47.

[92] Ene Braniște, *Liturgica generală*, pp. 97-98.

glorified Christ's existence, which unites in Himself, that is, in Christ the fruit that the Word of God brings. Therefore the church is see in the context of Christ's sacrifice as a reality that continually contemporanises the Golgotha event and keeps alive the availability of Christ's sacrifice that results from God's love. This develops a special grace of the priest, because the sacrifice of Christ can be actualized or brought up to date in the believers who form the universal priesthood and, respectively, through the priest put aside for this. "The extension of this holy sacrifice throughout the ages needs the serving priesthood that is nourished by the bishopry and the Christ's sacrifice in order to make those from the general priesthood partakers to the sacrifice."[93] Therefore, the priest as a liturgical stander, as the one who enacts the spiritual sermon in its complexity, ties the members' humanness through which man is then to the transfigured humanness that is in Christ, the Son of God.

Because of this, only the church that is united can be the rightful saving church, only the church that is in an irreducible communion can be the church full of the Holy Spirit, only the church that is a stander on such a functionality represents the church that ties itself in Christ, its Head. For this reason it is also known as the Sinodal Church, that is a church whose way of being is founded on the ecumenical councils, on the synods' decisions, councils and synods that have always promoted the step towards the unity in Christ. "The church is the transfigured and regenerated humanity. The sense of this regeneration and transfiguration lies in the fact that in the Church humanity becomes a unity, 'in one body' (Eph 2:16). The life of the Church means unity and unification. The body is 'tied' and 'grows' (Col 2:19) in the Spirit's unity, in the unity of love. The Church's domain is unity. And, of course, this unity is not an exterior one, but an inner, organic one."[94] The serving priesthood constitutes the fundamental premise from the perspective of visible things, regarding the church's unity. The church hymns, sung by the priest, the administration of Sacraments, all the liturgical activity of the priest is one that paradigmatically declares the church's unity, it sustains and develops it. The priest, through the sermon that he accomplishes is organically tied to Jesus Christ, the accomplisher of this sermon. Due to the priestly grace and authority that derives from it, the priest is not organically tied only to Christ, but he is also tied organically to the believers and he ties the church's believers organically to Christ. This reality is a super-sensitive one that is declared by God. From Christ, who is the Head of the Church, the church receives its life that is each member that forms the body: "…Instead, speaking the truth in love, we will in all things grow up into him who is the Head, that is,

---

[93] Ioan Mihălțan, *Preoția Mântuitorului Hristos și preoția bisericească*, p. 84.

[94] George Florovski, *Biserica, Scriptura, Tradiția – Trupul viu al lui Hristos*, p. 49.

Christ. From him the whole body, joined and held together by every supporting ligament, grows and builds itself up in love, as each part does its work." (Eph 4:15-16) The Jewish people's unity mediated before God through the aaronic priesthood is one that prepared the reality that was to come: the birth, the life of holiness, the passions and death, the resurrection and the ascent of the Lord Jesus Christ in order that, in the end, he might take over, and forever the priesthood. The church's unity is mediated by a priesthood that serves an accomplished reality; Christ is not about to be, but Jesus Christ is. Therefore, the priestly office is the divine sacrament through which the ordained one consents that in him God might meet organically and anticipatively the glory of the transfigured cosmic unity, the Church, the reality that expresses the Kingdom of God, in its future fullness.

The priest is the one who, through his status and through his ministry, makes the vulnerability of the church unity impossible. In the priest, God recapitulates a kind of relationship that existed only at the level of the relationship expressed in the Holy Trinity. "As the Son of God came in a body to open in himself our entrance to the Father and thus the only man in whom we can unity with the Father and between us, in the same way he uses people in his body one man for each community of believers in order to keep us united with himself. An he must commune in His holiness, so that His holiness might be extended through, as unifying power. The believers must have in this man, taken from amongst them, just as His human nature was taken from within us, a chosen organ from above as means to unify them with Christ whom he represents. Through the priests Christ Himself works, as unique proper Priest, at the visible and invisible unity of people in him."[95] The priest represents, according to the things noted above, a model. When we speak of the priestly office in the East, we do not speak about a solution that God offers in order to solve the problem of sin and for solving the distance produced between him and man, but when we speak about the priesthood in the East, we speak about a model. God makes himself available for our communion and our salvation through the model of divine communion. In this case, the priesthood is not an appendix to that which God proposed to do, but it is the action in himself, it is the recapitulation in an a perceptible way of that which cannot be conceived, it is the recapitulation in a visible sense of that which cannot be seen, it is the interiorized recapitulation of that which is exteriorized and cosmic. The opening in Christ towards the Father, is recapitulated by the priest, that which is in Christ, towards Christ. This thing becomes even more serious and more important when in some situations the priestly presence must be seen and evaluated as presence of the personal Christ. "In the exercise of his liturgical

---

[95] Dumitru Stăniloae, *Teologia Dogmatică Ortodoxă*, vol. 3, p. 100.

function, that is during the sermon, the bishop represents the Savior himself, as High Priest or Bishop."[96]

In conclusion, we cannot speak about the Church of Christ outside the existence of the priest. Regardless of the terminology that we might use and regardless of the way, we develop the theology regarding the priestly office or the pastoral one, the Church of Christ does not exist outside it. He is the one ordained; "It was he who gave some to be apostles, some to be prophets, some to be evangelists, and some to be pastors and teachers, to prepare God's people for works of service, so that the body of Christ may be built up until we all reach unity in the faith and in the knowledge of the Son of God and become mature, attaining to the whole measure of the fullness of Christ." (Eph 4:11-13) Even if in certain situations we can speak about an overrated priestly office in the East, or even if sometimes it polemics about Sacrament of Priesthood becomes uncomfortable, we must observe that the unity of Christ's Church has as a premise the priest's or pastor's consecrated life and ministry. To this gift and grace of serving, God decided it's existence and He is the one who offers the special status in methodology and it fulfillment of the salvation plan. Out of this divine attitude derives our obligation towards God and towards those whom he puts aside for serving. "The gift of the priestly level exceeds both thought and word...The priesthood flies from earth to the heavens, bringing God with great haste our pleas. The priesthood mediates before the Master on behalf of the slaves."[97] This poetisation of the priestly office that Ephrem the Syriac makes allows a terminological interchangealibility and at the same time declares the unity of worship context in which Jesus the High Priest enacts our salvation, and, at the same time, the same Jesus recapitulates himself in that which he has ordered to do to those who pastor the church.

The General Priesthood: the Meaning of Divine Love and Communion

Alien to some protestant perspectives of appreciation regarding the priesthood in eastern theology, there is a place given also to the priesthood of all believers. Even if at the level of contradictions regarding the way in which the terms are evaluated (older, bishop, dean, etc.) there are still suspicions or meanings that seem to be induces in eastern exegesis, at the a general level of the subject there is still a considerable and honest amount of space that is given to this teaching in a strictly biblical sense. As we shall see later, the believers' priesthood or the general priesthood is not one that comes through the laying of

---

[96] Ene Braniște, *Liturgica generală*, p. 96.
[97] Sfântul Efrem Sirul, *Despre preoție*, p. 311.

hands as a special gift, but as one that is received through the administration of certain gifts by the priest[98] to the believer, and the receiving of the special priesthood must be necessarily preceded by the general priesthood because they have a common substance and common purpose; the cosmic communion with Christ. "An unbreakable bond that unites them presents us a factual reality of their fulfillment, because you cannot get to the special Priesthood without passing through the general priesthood. First one must baptized in the name of the Holy Trinity, to be strengthened through the unction of the Holy Chrism, to become strong the life-giving sap of the Holy Eucharist and then to clothe yourself in the fire power of the special priesthood."[99] In the general or universal priesthood we find the ultimate sense of divine love and communion, a love and communion that derive from the priesthood of the Lord Jesus Christ through the sacerdotium of special priesthood, but that expresses its spiritual splendor because it finds its destination and return back towards God in and through the universal priesthood. In eastern thought, the general priesthood does not substitute the special priesthood, but it is neither the other way round. In the general priesthood the new face that must be received by the one who has part of this "dedication" as well as the ties that he must have with God in this new state. "This general or public priesthood of the believers, or the *common sacerdotium* of God's people – as it is called in the west – is actually the state of the new being in Christ of those who, once incorporated in him through the baptizing, have also received the personal relationship of the Spirit, in the Sacrament of Unction, thus becoming not only 'christofors' but also 'pneumatofors', uniting themselves fully with Christ in the Holy Eucharist. The state of new being in Christ is the plenary quality of the Christian man."[100] The general priesthood is seen therefore as a result of the enacting of certain sacraments in the life of the one who believes and then as a way of life through which the believer is using himself before Christ to his glory. The general priesthood gives meaning to the divine communion and love because in it he finds fulfillment in God's purpose, purpose that is derived from his intention of saving humanity. This salvation is fulfilled by putting together in fellowship the earth and the heavens, the heavenly offices with the one from earth, and this does not happen at a negotiation level, but in the spiritual opening that the believer has in towards God's love proposal.

The general priesthood as meaning of the divine love and communion must be seen in the east from the perspective of sacrifice. Actually, at the base of the

---

[98] The Sacrament of Baptizing, the Sacrament of Unction or the receiving of the Holy Spirit and the Sacrament of Holy communion.

[99] Ioan Mihălţan, *Preoţia Mântuitorului Hristos şi preoţia bisericească*, pp. 140-141.

[100] Dumitru Radu, *Îndrumări misionare*, p. 583.

communion and love, or more correctly said, the divine love and communion derive and are exemplified in the sacrifice. Jesus Christ developed the divine love and made it possible to be seen, by us, through the sacrifice, and the participation beforehand at the Holy Dinner and later at the Holy Eucharist is a participation in a communion, a derivation of the supreme sacrifice, a derivation from the supreme sacrifice. Therefore, the universal or general priesthood has a meaning only as sacrifice and only in the sacrifice of Christ. Because only through Christ as sacrifice and only in the sacrifice of Christ. "... The sacrifice of the Christians, or they as sacrifices, must join the sacrifice of Christ. Because only through Christ as sacrifice may they enter as sacrifice to the Father."[101] The complexity of this profound ministry and of this profound love gives the state of beatitude in the human soul when this becomes useful for it self because the fact that it first became useful from God. The situation in which we become useful spiritually for God and respectively for ourselves is the situation in which we are priests, "a royal priesthood". In this case, the sacrificed Christ hides us with him in God as sacrifices. This fellowship, this mysterious fusion of love makes all the data unknown in this equation of our participation at the communion with God making it available to our spiritual experiences through which our sanctification is taken further. Man is sanctified only through the sacrifice brought by Christ, the High Priest, a sacrifice actualized in the Sacrament of Communion be the priest who finalizes the heavenly purpose and value only in those who, at their turn, belong to the universal priesthood. The general priesthood and the special priesthood must be seen as a mystical-synergic phenomenon. "We cannot speak about a clear separation between the special Priesthood and the general one, or about a separation of these from the priesthood of the Savior Christ, but neither from an identity. There is a balance regarding between these priesthood and the Church, because the Church is a universal sacramental community. Because as the priests depend on the bishops, the bishop depends on the bishopric collegiality of the whole Church through his ordination and through a communion with the church. Therefore, also the believers owe their spiritual goods to the communion with the whole Church."[102] It is about a synergy that denies the split and at the same time it denies the confusion of identities. This is not accomplished in order to make people depend on other people, but to allow the development of the way God wanted to forgive us of our sins and save us. Due to this fact in the general priesthood the heavenly love and communion have their sense and functionality. The divine grace, the universal value of God's love that have been shown in the crucifixion of Christ, meet and recuperate it's objects, that is the humans.

---

[101] Dumitru Stăniloae, *Teologia Dogmatică Ortodoxă*, vol. 3, p. 107.

[102] Ioan Mihălțan, *Preoția Mântuitorului Hristos și preoția bisericească*, p. 137.

The divine love and communion must be understood as sacramental feelings and attitudes. We cannot approach the divine attitude at discourse level or at the level of inter-human relation types. Between our existence and the existence of God, we deal with a reality towards which man cannot go. It is not in the power of man and it is not our initiative to overtake the space and time in which we live in order to enter the communion with God. His existence is a transcendental one, only he is able through his uncreated energies to come towards us, and we can resonate to all these through moments and attitudes of sacrality: prayers, participation at the Holy Sacraments, etc. Due tot his fact we must regard the general priesthood as a reality realized by God and with a sacramental sense. "From baptizing to the Eucharist, the believer makes a qualitative jump as from image to likeness or comparable with the advancing into the pneumatisation of Christ's human nature, that took place between birth and resurrection. This advancing of the baptized one into an ever increasing unity with Christ is the advancing from the 'first resurrection' (the Baptizing) towards the anticipation of the second resurrection, the sacrament of Holy Eucharist."[103] The general priesthood is a pneumatological act that assumes the individual through baptizing and develops him communionally towards that which God desired him to become. In the body of Christ, the baptized one receives the characteristic of personhood; he exists towards the communion and only with this purpose. In him, in the believers, with a final and recuperating sense, the divine love and communion declares the purposes of Jesus Christ's sacrifice as being accomplished and fulfilled. The grandeur of these liturgical-sacramental statuses can no longer be the object of that which is human and secular. Everything develops beyond the intellectual and rational. "Through this sacramental aspect , any form of sociological nature is completely obsolete, through the fact of the birth of a *new being*. The Church preaches and teaches, it heralds and confesses, but its primordial task is the *conversion of people*, and this in the powerful meaning of a transformation that goes far beyond any intellectual or simple faith adhesion."[104] As we have already seen, in the east, that which makes the general priesthood to declare the meaning of divine love and communion is its sacramental aspect, the involvement of God's grace in this becoming. Also, this grace is involved through the priest, he is the one who received the sacramental grace of ordination and in virtue of this becomes capable to express the involvement of God through the administration of Sacraments as the one who desires to become a member in the body of Christ. And once one has become a member of the pneumatised Body, he also belongs to the priestly community in all its complexity.

---

[103] Ştefan Buchiu, *Întrupare şi unitate*, p. 185.

[104] Paul Evdokimov, *Ortodoxia*, p. 140.

Even though the community of lay members is made conscious only in a smart part at an informative level, of the status that each believer has, at a behavioral and communitary level, the general priesthood massively declares its existence. The faith regarding salvation, the certainty of salvation, the peace that derives from the sentiment of belonging to the Orthodox Church, the cult of the dead, etc., all these declare the common substance of the priesthood in which they believe and of the priesthood, they belong to. Actually, this communitary complexity, through the Christ's priesthood, becomes cosmic as well. "Man is a member of a communitary body and saves his integrity in relation with the godly enlightment through his participation at divine works."[105] Liturgically, sacramentally and doxologically, the entire Church ties the earth to the heavens and becomes inhabited by God in the ministry of the Holy Spirit. The participation at the divine things cannot be an isolated one, that takes place somewhere on earth and in an individual way. The participation at the divine works is one made through communion, a communion that transcends time and space and makes us contemporary with God. This aspect requests a participation at the offering, a consummation of it and the communion with God through it. The authority of this action belonged only to the priest; due to this no one can participate at the Holy Eucharist unless one is a priest, because we are dealing with the sacrifice, the body and the blood of the Lord Jesus Christ. "Orthodox theology through the general priesthood understands their right to commune with the graceful life of the Church through the Holy Sacraments, by participating at the Eucharistic offering, not alone, but only together with the priest or the bishop who is their point of convergence."[106] This right is received not through a human untying but through a descendence that derives from the priestly office of the Lord Jesus Christ and which is exercised in an unseen way by the serving priesthood. "...The eucharistical gathering also becomes and is from now on, from Eucharist to Eucharist, body and blood of Christ; man accomplishes his primordial and ultimate vocation of being co-bodily and co-bloodily with the risen Christ."[107] "Man" this apparent generalization is in fact a very severe particularization and a nominalization. It is only about the man who communes and only the one who belongs to the general priesthood communes, that is the one who is a priest in a specific way. The divine love and communion declare their accomplishment when the body of Christ is complete, and this body is complete only in the moment of filing with the Holy Spirit, a filling that takes place only when the general priesthood participates. The moment with the highest degree of representation of the general priesthood, a moment in which the love and communion are lived in a divine sense,

---

[105] Nikolaos Matsoukas, *Teologia dogmatică și simbolică*, p. 372.

[106] Ștefan Buchiu, *Întrupare și unitate*, p. 200.

[107] Boris Bobrinskoy, *Împărtășirea Sfântului Duh*, p. 283.

is the moment of the Holy Eucharist. Here all the *presences* are whole. God the Father, the Lord Jesus Christ, the Holy Spirit and the Church, represent the cosmic love and universal communion served in an unseen way by Christ, as High Priest, who brings his own offering, by the serving priesthood who in a visible way brings the Savior's offering in the bread and whine over which the Holy Spirit is called, by the general priesthood who communes, in faith, with the seen offering in the Sacrament of the Eucharist, as well as in that brought by Christ, which is unseen, and the entire heavenly atmosphere reaches it's climax of the representation of God's Kingdom through the filling with the Holy Spirit.

In eastern theology, the meaning of the love that comes from God and the meaning of the communion in God must not be seen as belonging only to the Church as hierarchy and only to the priesthood as sacerdotium. The meaning of the love that comes from God must be expressed by the entire body of Christ in the flowing through of the Spirit and it must express the entire body in the complexity of the diversity of each person that participates in a general or sinodal way at the declaring of the Church's universality. The communion is not the unilateral sense that the priest accomplishes because he does not administer the Sacraments towards himself, but he administers through participation, through the communion towards Christ, in which he finds the entire unity. The priest places in the complexity of his graceful being the multitude of believers whom he represents and communalizes. Then, together with it makes the entire church to be full of Christ. Due to this reason the divine love and communion must not be seen as unilateral actions of the serving priesthood because the Lord Christ himself did not declare the love and communion as being exclusively his actions, but the declared them and offered them through participation. "To the continuous deepening of the Church unity the contributes the personal work of each member based on the general priesthood, conferred to the believers by their ecclesial identity or their belonging to the Church of Christ."[108] All this action must be seen and evaluated in a spiritual way and with spiritual purposes. In the east, the love and communion cannot be lowered to the level of a club, regardless of the positive meaning that might be given to this term. The general priesthood is the meaning of godly love and communion, because the final meaning of all these is the salvation of man, not the forming of spiritual casts, and the action and divinization of all that happens is the nominal and heavenly action of God.

The divine love and communion is accomplished in three ways: the way on which Jesus Christ walks through his incarnation, the life of holiness, passions and death, resurrection and ascendance to the right hand of God; the way of

---

[108] Ștefan Buchiu, *Întrupare și unitate*, p. 200.

sacerdotal ministry of the serving or church priest and the way that each secular man walks in order to become priest. From the ascendance of Christ, each converted person had the grace of becoming, through participation at the things requested by Jesus, a member of the Church, a member of the Holy Body. "The neophyte would walk step by step through each of the three stages of a single act that would make him a member of the people of God, recapitulated in Christ, that would sanctify him a s priest, prophet and king. However, the Eucharist that fulfills this gradual initiation is not only a simple Sacrament among other sacraments, but it is their perfection. It is the Sacrament of Sacraments and, depending on the integration, it is the most adequate expression of the Church. The Church is the eucharistical *koinonia* continued and perpetuated."[109] This is the complete and complex sense in which the general priesthood must be seen as a sense of divine love and communion. This priesthood is considered as coming from God, but it can never be confounded with the sacramental priesthood or with the priesthood as sacrament, even though, in the ensemble of the cosmic communion it belongs to sacramentality and, without exaggerating, it also belongs to the sacrament.

In conclusion, the general priesthood in eastern theology is not treated only with the meaning of counteracting and annulling the protestant and evangelical declarations regarding the priesthood. The general priesthood in eastern theology is debated in a responsible discourse and recognized as an element with a separate and necessary identity in the complexity of the Salvation Plan's development. Without attributing it irreverent qualities, thing that does not take place at the protestants or evangelicals, the general priesthood is regarded in the east as being the background itself of the Church. It is the winning and the fruit of Christ's sacrifice and behaves through the Sacraments administered by the priest as the fruit of divine grace and as a priesthood in which doxological worship and glory represent the sky in a state of maximal ecstasy and joy.

The Priestly Sacerdotium: the Means and Method of the Theandric Expression of the Church in which the Kingdom of God is Anticipated

The priesthood theology, as we have already seen until now, is essential in the orthodox dogma, both by it's prerogatives that is has, as well as through the fact that it determines theologically and dogmatically which these are. The priesthood in the east is a Sacrament, a Sacrament that administers the Sacraments, a Sacrament through which the Church exists, a Sacrament that makes

---

[109] Paul Evdokimov, *Ortodoxia*, pp. 140-141.

the welding at a communional level of Christ, the Head, with the other members of the body, that is the general priesthood.

This reality we shall develop in what follows through the perspective of the double nature of the Church. Jesus Christ through his incarnation and through the glorification of the human nature chose to be the transcendent and divine part of the Church. In the miracle of his humanization, as well as through the miracle of the glorification of the assumed human body, Jesus declared himself the creator of a cosmic organism through which to take to himself and into himself those who accept his love and his intention regarding salvation. The complementary element of this divine act and which was hidden in him is the Church. The Church, that is Christ the High Priest and the Church, that is the human serving priests and general priests, must be seen from this perspective of a double nature, not to embellish the ecclesiological discourse, but to be truthful to the biblical text. "After all, no-one ever hated his own body, but he feeds and cares for it, just as Christ does the church – *for we are members of his body.*" (Eph 5:29-30) The interior element of this divine complex in which and which expresses the existence of this double nature and in which the unity of these two natures is expressed is the priestly or pastoral office. The ministry of the priest declares Christ among the church's believers and the church's believers in Christ.

When we speak about the priesthood in the context of a double nature of the Church, we must take into consideration the problem of hierarchy. The hierarchy has a very important place in the ecclesiological theology and, respectively, in the theology of the Sacrament of Priesthood. However, we cannot honestly research the problem of the priesthood outside the writings on the hierarchy. The theandrical expression of the Church through the priestly sacerdotium requests the underlining of the priestly stages because only this way we can observe how this type of expression anticipates the Kingdom of God. The three stages of the priesthood – bishop, priest, deacon – even though they are conferred through the laying of hands and are all part of the Ordination Sacrament, not all represent the succession through which the priestly grace can be passed on further. The priest and the deacon cannot ordain other priests. This task of high spiritual status belongs to the bishops competency. "The bishop is the complete representative of Christ, the unique and unifying Bishop. Each bishop is the head of the local church, 'the head of the fullness of Christ'. Because Christ invests him not only with the charism and responsibility of enacting the Sacraments, accomplished by the priest, but also the Sacrament of Ordination, so that all priests might have the priesthood and be obedient to him."[110] We notice, therefore, that only in the bishop we find the means and

---

[110] Dumitru Stăniloae, *Teologia Dogmatică Ortodoxă*, vol. 3, p. 101.

method through which the Church, in its double nature, can be expressed. The bishop is part of the "unbroken chain", that is of the succession that comes directly from Christ. He creates "branches" in the priests and deacons, but the grace that leads further in the sacerdotal existence of the double nature of the church is conferred only to the one who follows him, that means another bishop.

When we speak about the bishop, we do not speak only about an administrative stage. Even if administratively the bishop has authorities that the priest does not have, the superior quality of the bishop derives from that which he represents in himself. In the east, the bishop overlaps with certain divine features, he brings from Christ that which can coagulate the believers in a single body and leads towards Christ, in a fulfilled way, the human and communitary unity of those who form the church and believe in the coming Kingdom of God. Due to this fact, the bishop must be seen as a means and a method through which the double nature of the Church is expressed. "The dignity of the bishop is, therefore, very necessary to the Church, so much so that without it neither the Church nor the Christian can be and can be deemed as such. Because the one made worthy of being bishop as an apostolic successor, is the living icon of God on earth, he is the spring of divine Sacraments and of the Holy Spirit's gifts..."[111] Regard what harsh definition regarding the radicalism of this office and regarding it's profoundness. When we say bishop, we implicitly refer to the church and Christian, and outside the bishop or without him, the declaration regarding the existence of the church or of the Christian is a declaration empty of content, it is nonsense. In the same way, when we speak of the bishop, we refer to the living icon or the living representation of God that is without the bishop the people cannot participate relationally in God, without him we speak only about an intellectual adhesion or a concept. This kind of thinking is completely foreign to the thinking and practice of the Orthodox Church. The bishop in the consensus of the above mentioned, represents the means through which God gives a functional and existential unity to the being of the church, to this organism that is organized in a double nature and which in it's universal dimension makes possible the assimilation of all the persons, of the Holy Trinity as well as of the believers, into a communion that anticipates the glorified world to come. In spite of this, in eastern thinking the bishop doe not presuppose, and we cannot find this anywhere, the lack of Christ. "The Church is the body of Christ, the fulfillment of the One who fulfills everything in all. The fulfillment exists at once in Christ and then it becomes differentiated in its arranged elements, canonical in time: 'From him the whole body, joined and held together by every supporting ligament, grows and builds itself up in love, as each part does its work' (Eph 4:16) The priesthood, the Sacraments,

---

[111] Dumitru Radu, *Îndrumări misionare*, p. 577.

the dogmas, the cannon of the biblical books, the cult, all institutional forms are established gradually and they form the visible form of the Body, but everything in these forms is assured by ***The Absolute Priest – Christ.*** Christ does not transmit his own powers to the apostles, which would mean his absence. The Icon of the Pentecost underlines the presence of the Leader, the Head of the Body in place reserved to Christ leading the apostles."[112] The priestly sacerdotium does not in any way exercise a kind of liturgics or a salvation with a missing Christ, the Son of God is always present. Actually, outside of Christ or without his presence there is no bishop. This reality does not suggest confusions regarding nature, it does not suggest a hierachization that derives from the difference of natures (the superior divine one, the inferior deified nature), this reality represents a means decided by God through which he desires to respect the love towards his own creature and which he wants to assimilate in a divine communion. The are no policies to be paid and there are no ranks to be established, but the divine happiness is declared in the unity and holiness of the redeemed ones.

In the priestly office of Christ there was laid as a totality of divine measures to accomplish once again the edenic charm of the unhindered meeting between Adam and God in an unmediated way. Due to this, the priestly office, as we underlines above, does not intend to form a cast, which would force and impose its necessity. The job of the priest is superior to this corrupt way of thinking. "As a main purpose, this ministry try to re-establish a tighter communion between us and the Most Holy Trinity through the dynamism of divine energies, because Christ in his sacrifice is not a passive Christ, but forever full of a great love towards the Father, but at the same time also towards the others. The sacrifice of Jesus for us was brought in order to lift us from our state of egotism."[113] The theandric expression of the Church must be a communitarian one, not an egocentrically individual one. Due to this, the priestly ministry is the one that must be seen as a means and as a method that expresses in a communitarian way and through communion the double nature of the church. If this is not the case, the human community would lack the presence of Christ and the fullness of the Holy Spirit, and, consequently, we would not deal with the Church. The sacrifice of Christ lifts us from our egotism of our individuality and forces the priesthood to a ministry in a communitarian sense and consensus. The priest is tied through him to Christ, at the same time and with the same ministry, all the members.

Salvation is a divine problem that assimilates in it dilematically and in the shape of sacrament the eternal nature and the perishable nature, but eternified

---

[112] Paul Evdokimov, *Ortodoxia*, p. 179.

[113] Ioan Mihălțan, *Preoția Mântuitorului Hristos și preoția bisericească*, p. 85.

in Christ. Because of this, the Church established by Christ comports in itself the dilemma and the sacrament, outside the Church, or without the Church there is no salvation. Regardless of how embarrassing this affirmation sometimes is, it is a finding imposed by the complexity of the Salvation Plan and in no way b the arrogant expression of certain Christian churches to the detriment or as a reply to other churches. We shall note now the affirmation and the explanations that follow from it: "Outside the Church there is no salvation. All the force and the categorical idea of this aphorism lies in its tautology. Outside the church the is no salvation, because *the Church is salvation*. Because salvation is the discovery of the way for anybody who believes in the name of Christ. Revelation can be found only in the Church. In the Church, as Body of Christ, in his divine-human organism, the mystery of incarnation, the mystery of the 'two natures', indissolubly united, it fulfilled continually."[114] There is no salvation outside God and there is no salvation outside the space in which God extends himself soteriologically. The pace where God extends soteriologically is the Unceasing Sacrifice brought by Christ through his own crucifixion. Through this sacrifice God extends further creating the Church both as a space for the salvation of those who seek it as well as a space in which God can be found and glorified. The links that ties the Sacrifice to the Church and due to which we can speak about a theandric unity is the priestly sacerdotium. As a means and method, the priestly grace animates the common denominator in which the church expresses itself theandrically and makes it possible the anticipation of the God's Kingdom.

Conclusions

In eastern theology, it is quite complicated or even impossible to debate on central subjects of dogmatics outside the priestly office. Even though to the subject itself it is not given an extensive space, most of the dogmatic subjects are developed in relation to the priesthood. Ecclesiology, pneumatology, soteriology, christology, triadology, etc., all these as well as others encompass in the dogmatic debate different aspects of the priesthood as well as it's importance.

Starting from the writings of the Church Fathers and with a rich use of the New Testament, especially, orthodox dogmatics proposes a priestly sacerdocy from a patristic and biblical perspective, which is quite honest. The origin of the priesthood in the Christian Church, is seen as being in the priesthood of Christ and superior aaronic priesthood of the Old Testament. From the perspective of eastern dogmatics, the Church cannot exist outside the priesthood, reason for

---

[114] George Florovski, *Biserica, Scriptura, Tradiția – Trupul viu al lui Hristos*, pp. 47-48.

which the sense and the authenticity of the priesthood in the contemporary Christian society is justified and requested by Christ.

In the church's Sacraments that the priest administers, eastern theology sees the extension of the ministry of Christ in such a way that the priest expresses the perspective of the unseen ministry of the God's Son. Due tot his fact the priest, through his ministry, extends towards the believers and in the Church the priestly ministry of the Lord Christ. In these conditions the priest and the church are the realities in which Christ transcends history and the perishability and ties in anticipated way the earth to the sky. "The Church is a pyre, composed from the lit candles, representatives of the believers, not only when the public prayers are said with the believers gathered together (at the Holy Liturgy and the other sermons), but it is also a lit pyre extended into all the believers, even when they pray individually, through the fact that they hold to the Church, being warmed by the same Spirit of Christ, received through the Sacraments of the Church, therefore having the same Christ in themselves."[115] This atmosphere is kept lit and alive by the ministry that the priest accomplishes as economist of divine grace. Only under these conditions the presence of Jesus is found in the Church and only under these condition the Church does not lose its purpose and being.

In eastern thought, the priesthood is superior to a certain type of socio-human administration. The priesthood is the complexity of the ministry that has as purpose the unity of the entire body of the Lord Jesus Christ who is the Head that is the Son of God. In the declaration and safekeeping of this unity, the priesthood plays a very important role, but not one of a mediator, but in the priesthood lies the unity itself. The divine-human character of the Church is accessible in the works that the priest enacts. The priesthood at the level of Christ in complementarity with the priesthood at the level of the ministry in the church and with the general priesthood affirm in a divine way the universality of the communion between believers and Christ, that is between the human dimension of the Church and its divine dimension that is hidden in the Son of God, the High Priest as mediator of the human race. The priesthood administers a divine-human organism and exists in this organism with a soteriological and worshiping purpose.

---

[115] Dumitru Stăniloae, *Iisus Hristos lumina lumii și îndumnezeitorul omului*, pp. 214-215.

Selective Bibliography:

Alexe Ștefan, Sfinții Trei Ierarhi și actualitatea gândirii lor despre preoție, [f.d] [f.l]

Andruțos Hr., Simbolica, Editura Centrului Mitropolitan al Olteniei, Craiova 1955

Bălan Ioanichie, Convorbiri Duhovnicești, Vol. II, Editura Episcopia Romanului și Hușilor, 1990 [f.l.]

Braniște Ene, Liturgica generală, Editura Institutului Biblic și de Misiune al Biserici Ortodoxe Române, București, 1993

Bria Ion, Dicționar de teologie ortodoxă, Editura Institutului Biblic și de Misiune al Biserici Ortodoxe Române, București, 1994

Buchiu Ștefan, Întrupare și unitate, Editura Libra, București, 1997

Bulgakov Serghei, Dogma euharistică, Editura Paideia, București, 2000

Chiril al Alexandriei, Scrieri partea a doua, Editura Institutului Biblic și de Misiune al Bisericii Ortodoxe, București, 1992

Clement Oliver, Trupul morții și al slavei, Editura Cristiana, București, 1998

Coman Iacob, Theo – Doxa – Logia, Editura Episteimon, București, 1999

Corneanu Nicolae, Credință și viață, Editura Dacia, Cluj – Napoca, 2001

Credința ortodoxă, Editura Mitropoliei Moldovei și Bucovinei, Iași, 2000

Crouzel Henri, Origen – Personajul, exegetul, omul duhovnicesc, teologul, Editura Deisis, Sibiu, 1999

Evdokimov Paul, Ortodoxia, Editura Institutului Biblic și de Misiune al Biserici Ortodoxe Române, București, 1996

Evdokimov Paul, Prezența Duhului Sfânt în Tradiția Ortodoxă, Editura Anastasia, București, 1995

Felmy Karl Christian, Dogmatica experienței ecleziale, Editura Deisis, Sibiu, 1999

Florenski Pavel, Dogmatică și dogmatism, Editura Anastasia, București, 1998

Florovski George, Biserica, Scriptura, Tradiția – Trupul viu al lui Hristos, Editura Platytera, București 2005

Lossky Vladimir, Teologia mistică a bisericii de răsărit, Editura Anastasia, [f.l, f.a]

Luther Martin, Scrieri, vol. 1, Editura Logos, Cluj-Napoca, 2003

_____, Scrieri, vol. 2, Editura Logos, Cluj-Napoca, 2003

Matsoukas Nikolaos, Teologia dogmatică și simbolică, vol. II, Editura Bizantină, București, 2006

Mihălțan Ioan, Preoția Mântuitorului Hristos și preoția bisericească, Editura Episcopiei Oradea, Oradea, 1992

Mladin Nicolae, Asceza și Mistica paulină, Editura Deisis, Sibiu, 1996

Necula D. Nicolae, Tradiție și înnoire în slujirea liturgică, vol. 3, Editura Institutului Biblic și de Misiune al Biserici Ortodoxe Române, București, 2004

Origen, Omilii și adnotări la Levitic, Editura Polirom, București, 2006

_____, Omilii și adnotări la Exod, Editura Polirom, București, 2006

Pelikan Jaroslav, Tradiția creștină, Vol. I, Editura Polirom, București, 2004

Popescu Dumitru, Hristos biserică societate, Editura Institutului Biblic și de Misiune al Biserici Ortodoxe Române, București, 1998

Radu Dumitru, Îndrumări misionare, Editura Institutului Biblic și de Misiune al Biserici Ortodoxe Române, București, 1986

Sfântul Ioan Gură de Aur – Sfântul Grigore de Nazians – Sfântul Efrem Sirul, Despre Preoție, Editura Institutului Biblic și de Misiune al Biserici Ortodoxe Române, București, 2007

Sfântul Nectarie de Eghina, Despre preoție, Editura Sofia, București, 2008

Schmemann Alexandre, Euharistia taina împărăției, Editura Anastasia, 1993

Stăniloae Dumitru, Ortodoxie și românism, Editura Albatros, București, 1998

_____, Teologia dogmatică ortodoxă, vol. 2, Editura Institutului Biblic și de Misiune al Biserici Ortodoxe Române, București, 1997

_____, Teologia dogmatică ortodoxă, vol. 3, Editura Institutului Biblic și de Misiune al Biserici Ortodoxe Române, București, 1997

_____, Chipul nemuritor al lui Dumnezeu vol. I, Editura Cristal, București, 1995

_____, Iisus Hristos lumina lumii și îndumnezeitorul omului, Editura Anastasia, București, 1993

Vintilescu Petre, Preotul în fața chemării sale de păstor al sufletelor, Editura Mitropolia Olteniei, Craiova, 2007

Ware Kallistos, Împărăția lăuntrică, Editura Christiana, București, 1996

Yannaras Christos, Abecedar al credinței, Editura Bizantină, București, 1996

Zizioulas Ioannis, Ființa Eclesială, Editura Bizantină, București 1996

General Bibliography:

Aurelian Augustin, *Mărturisiri*, Editura. Institutului Biblic și de Misiune al Bisericii Ortodoxe Române, București, 1994

Bălan Ioanichie, *Convorbiri Duhovnicești I*, Editura. Episcopia Romanului și Hușilor 1993.

Bălan Ioanichie, *Convorbiri Duhovnicești II*, Editura. Episcopia Romanului și Hușilor 1990

Bielawski Maciej, *Părintele Dumitru Stăniloae, o viziune filocalică despre lume*, Editura Deisis. Sibiu 1998.

Bria Ion, *Tratat de teologie dogmatică și ecumenică*, Editura. România Creștină, București, 1999.

_____, *Iisus Hristos*, Editura. Enciclopedică, Buc. 1992

Cabasila Nicolae, *Despre viața în Hristos*, Editura. Institutului Biblic și de Misiune al Bisericii Ortodoxe Române, București, 1997.

Clement Olivier, *Trupul morții și al slavei*, Editura. Christiana, Buc. 1996

_____, *Întrebări asupra omului*, Alba-Iulia, 1997

Cireșeanu Badea, *Tezaurul Liturgic al Sfintei Biserici Creștine Ortodoxe de Răsărit*, vol. 1, București 1911

Cireșeanu Badea, *Tezaurul Liturgic al Sfintei Biserici Creștine Ortodoxe de Răsărit*, vol. 2, București 1911

Cireșeanu Badea, *Tezaurul Liturgic al Sfintei Biserici Creștine Ortodoxe de Răsărit*, vol. 3, București 1912

Chiril al Alexandriei, *Scrieri partea întâia*, Editura. Institutului Biblic și de Misiune al Bisericii Ortodoxe Române, București. 1991.

Chiril al Alexandriei, *Scrieri partea a doua*, Editura. Institutului Biblic și de Misiune al Bisericii Ortodoxe Române, București. 1992

Evdokimov Paul, *Taina Iubirii – Sfințenia vieții conjugale în lumina tradiției ortodoxe*. Editura Asociația Cristiana. Buc. 1994.

_____, *Femeia și mântuirea lumii*, Editura Cristiana 1995

_____, *Cunoașterea lui Dumnezeu în tradiția răsăriteană*, Editura Christiana. Buc. 1995.

_____, *Rugăciunea în Biserica de Răsărit*, Editura Polirom, Iași, 1996.

Eusebiu de Cezareea, *Scrieri partea a doua*, Editura Institutului Biblic și de Misiune al Bisericii Ortodoxe Române, București. 1991.

Grigore de Nyssa, *Scrieri exegetice, dogmatico-polemice și morale*, Editura Institutului Biblic și de Misiune al Bisericii Ortodoxe Române, București. 1998.

Grigoraș Aurel, *Dogmă și cult privite interconfesional și problema intercomuniunii*, în Ortodoxia Nr. 3-4 Iulie-Decembrie 1977 București

Houston James, *Alive to God-Studies in Spirituality*, 1992 by Regent College. Illinois.

Ică I. Ioan, *Dumnezeu – Unul în ființă și întreit în Persoane*, în *Credință ortodoxă și viață creștină*, Sibiu, 1992.

_____, *Modurile prezenței personale a lui Iisus Hristos și ale comuniunii cu El în Sf. Liturghie și Spiritualitatea ortodoxă*, în Persoană și comuniune, Editura și tiparul Arhiepiscopiei ortodoxe Sibiu, Sibiu, 1993.

Ică I. Ioan jr, *Persoană sau/și Ontologie în gândirea ortodoxă contemporană*, în Persoană și comuniune, Editura și tiparul Arhiepiscopiei ortodoxe Sibiu, Sibiu, 1993.

Jan van Ruusbroec, *Podoaba nunții spirituale sau întâlnirea interioară cu Cristos*, Editura Humanitas, 1995.

Lossky Vladimir, *Introducere în Teologia Ortodoxă*. Editura Enciclopedică București 1993.

Louth Andrew, *Deslușirea Tainei – Despre natura teologiei*, Editura Deisis, Sibiu 1999.

Negruț Paul, *Revelație, Scriptură, Comuniune*, Editura Cartea Creștină, Oradea 1996.

Simeon Noul Teolog, *Discursuri teologice și etice Scrieri I*, Editura Deisis, Sibiu 1998.

Soloviov Vladimir, *Fundamentele spirituale ale vieții*, Editura Deisis. Alba-Iulia 1994

Spidlik Tomas, *Spiritualitatea Răsăritului Creștin – manual sistematic* vol. 1, Editura Deisis, Sibiu 1997.

Spidlik Tomas, *Spiritualitatea Răsăritului Creștin – manual sistematic* vol. 2, Editura Deisis, Sibiu 1998.

Stăniloae Dumitru, *Chipul nemuritor al lui Dumnezeu*, vol. 1, Editura Cristal, București, 1995.

_____, *Chipul nemuritor al lui Dumnezeu*, vol. 2, Editura Cristal, București, 1995.

_____, *Spiritualitatea Ortodoxă – Ascetica și Mistica*, Editura Institutului Biblic și de Misiune al Bisericii Ortodoxe Române, București, 1992.

_____, *Trăirea lui Dumnezeu în Ortodoxie*, Editura Dacia, Cluj-Napoca. 1993.

_____, *Teologia Morală Ortodoxă* vol 3, Editura Institutului Biblic și de Misiune al Bisericii Ortodoxe Române, București. 1981.

White G. Ellen, *Hristos lumina lumii*, Editura Viață și Sănătate, București, 1997.

_____, *Marea Luptă*, Editura Viață și sănătate, București 1998

Abstract

By the present study we offer a non-polemical approach to the priestly office in the Eastern Orthodox Church. The perspective is a dogmatic-patristic-biblical one and is based on the research at doctorate level conducted by this author on the writings of the most representative Eastern Church Fathers and famous theologians of this church. We tried to positively evaluate the elements of Eastern dogma and, at the same time, to free ourselves of any haze and prejudice in our declarations and conclusions.

The main parts of this research are the following: 1. *The priesthood in the Eastern Church: Origin and Relevance*, 2. *Church Priesthood – The Extension of the Priestly Office Assumed by Christ*, 3. *The sacrament of the priesthood, method of administration of the divine grace* and 4. *The Priesthood – The sacerdocy through which the members of the body are tied to the Head of the Church, Christ*.

Although apparently there is a primacy of philosophical and patristic dogmatical discourse, the present research is based on the biblical foundations regarding the work of Lord Jesus Christ (His priesthood in heaven and in the Church, His priesthood as means to pass His grace and the mystery of forming Christ's body, whose head is Himself). Even though the priestly office in the traditional churches might wrongly assume some priestly prerogatives that belong only to Christ, those respective prerogative of Christ still stay.

Without any claim to an exhaustive study which has said the last word on the subject, we would be satisfied to know that it was received as a proposal to theological dialogue in the contemporary Christian context at the beginning of a new millennium. It is also our hope that this study will meet the expectations of any reader.

Christian Krumbacher
Priestertum aller Gläubigen: Eine evangelikale Perspektive
Ein Beitrag zur Ekklesiologie

Einleitung

In der **Ekklesiologie** (der biblischen Lehre von der Gemeinde) beschäftigen wir uns mit der göttlichen Schau Seiner Gemeinde. Gebaut wird sie mit wiedergeborenen Menschen, die Teilhaber wurden der göttlichen Natur (2Petr 1,4), die aber noch ihre menschliche Natur behalten haben. Es scheint fast unmöglich, aus diesem unbefriedigenden Material jemals eine Gemeinde zu bauen, die den biblischen Maßstäben entspricht. Das Idealbild ist uns jedoch nicht vorgegeben, um uns beim Bauen zu entmutigen, sondern zu ermutigen! Wir brauchen Pläne, nach denen wir uns richten können. So leben wir im Gemeindebau in einer Spannung: einerseits das hohe, von der Bibel vorgegebene Ziel, und andererseits die oft kläglichen Resultate. Fehlentwicklungen, die es zu korrigieren galt, finden wir schon im NT (z.B.: in Korinth, in den Gemeinden der Sendschreiben Offenbarung 2 und 3). Gott nimmt falsche Entwicklungen ernst. Doch sollen sie uns nicht in die Resignation führen, sondern uns zu vermehrtem Einsatz motivieren.

In der evangelikalen Theologie ist die Ekklesiologie ein unterentwickeltes Thema. Die Evangelikalen waren und sind sehr zögerlich bei der Entwicklung einer Ekklesiologie. Die Gründe dafür können sehr verschieden sein: Zuerst kann es daran liegen, dass sie eher praxisorientiert sind; manche denken an einen pragmatischen Hang der Evangelikalen; wieder andere meinen, es liegt an ihrem missionarischen Drang; Donald Carson beschreibt die evangelikale Einstellung wie folgt: *„We are too busy winning people to Christ to engage in something which seems too much like navel gazing."*[1] Aber der Drang zu missionieren rechtfertigt eine zögerliche Haltung zur Ekklesiologie nicht. Ich glaube eher, dass einer der Gründe dafür darin liegt, dass die Freikirchen aus verschiedenen Strömungen hervorgingen und lange Zeit keine gemeinsame Stimme hatten. (Wie z.B. in Deutschland zurzeit die VeF). Die VeF (‚Vereinigung Evangelischer Freikirchen') wurde am 29. April 1926 in Leipzig konsti-

---

[1] Evangelical Review of Theology. Bd. 27, Nr. 1, Januar 2003. S. 4. [Timothy George. Towards an Evangelical Theology. Downers Grove: InterVarsity, 2000, S. 123].

tuiert.² Auch der Individualismus hat einen verzögernden Effekt auf die Entstehung einer evangelikalen Ekklesiologie gehabt.

In diesem Artikel möchte ich mich nur auf einen Aspekt der Ekklesiologie beschränken, nämlich auf *‚das Priestertum aller Gläubigen'*. Es wird aber nötig sein, etwas zur Begrifflichkeit, zur Begriffsproblematik, zur biblischen Begründung und Begriffsgeschichte der 'Gemeinde' zu sagen.

1. Begrifflichkeit

Die Gemeinde ist eine ‚Erfindung' der Liebe Gottes. Sie ist von Ewigkeit her im Herzen Gottes als ein Geheimnis verborgen gewesen. Eph 3,9 *‚und für alle ans Licht zu bringen, wie Gott seinen geheimen Ratschluss ausführt, der von Ewigkeit her verborgen war in ihm, der alles geschaffen hat.'*

1.1 Begriff

Wenn wir auf Deutsch das Wort ‚Gemeinde', ‚Kirche' oder ‚Versammlung' gebrauchen, dann ist das die Übersetzung von dem griechischen Wort ἐκκλησία (ekklesia). Das Wort ‚ekklesia' kommt von ‚ek' = aus und ‚kaleo' = rufen, zusammenrufen.³ Die ‚Herausgerufenen' waren ursprünglich die wehrfähigen Männer einer politischen Gemeinde, die Versammlung der Israeliten, besonders wenn sie zu heiligen Zwecken zusammentritt (5Mo 31,30; Ri 20,2; 1Kön 17,47); von der christlichen Gemeinde (1Kor 11,18; 14,4f).⁴ Der *‚ekklesia'*-Begriff, ist außerbiblisch seit dem 5.Jh. v. Chr. als ‚Vollversammlung der rechtsfähigen Vollbürger der *polis*' *‚Stadt, Bürgerschaft'* belegt.⁵

Ein Beispiel finden wir in Apg 19,39: ‚*... in der gesetzlichen Versammlung'*. D.h.: Die Menschen der Stadt wurden zusammengerufen, um etwas zu besprechen.⁶ In Apg 7,38 wird es benutzt für Israel und in 19,32 und 41 für eine verwirrte Menge von Menschen. Etymologisch⁷ bedeutet das Wort Ekklesia **‚die Herausgerufene'**. So verstanden sich auch die ersten Christen als Herausgeru-

---

² Freikirchenhandbuch. Informationen, Anschriften, Texte, Berichte. Hrsg. Vereinigung Evangelischer Freikirchen, Brockhaus Verlag, Wuppertal: 2004. Klaus Peter Voß. S. 12.
³ Duffield, Guy P. & Nathaniel M. Van Cleave. Grundlagen pfingstlicher Theologie. Solingen: 2003. S. 504.
⁴ Bauer, Walter. Griechisch-Deutsches Wörterbuch zu den Schriften des Neuen Testaments und den übrigen urchristlichen Literatur. Gießen: 1928. S. 374.
⁵ Coenen, L. Theologisches Begriffslexikon zum Neuen Testament. Theologischer Verlag Rolf Brockhaus, Wuppertal: 1972. S. 784.
⁶ Grenz, Stanley. J. Created for Community. Connecting Christian Belief with Christian Living. 2. Ed. Baker Book House, Grand Michigan: 1998. S. 208.
⁷ Etymologisch bed. Wortherkunft; von der Geschichte des Wortes her.

fene: aus der Welt, aus der Sünde, aus dem Verderben – zu Gott, zur Befreiung, zum ewigen Leben.[8]

Die christliche Gemeinde ist die durch Gottes Schöpferisches Wort ins Dasein gerufene Versammlung von Menschen, die sich durch Jesus Christus im Heiligen Geist zum Dienst aneinander und zur Sendung an die Welt erwählt wissen.[9] Zwei Wesenselemente begründen den *Begriff*: der versammelnde Aufruf Gottes (im Wort Gottes) und die den Ruf verwirklichende Antwort (der Glaube) der sich Versammelnden. Beide Elemente – das theologische (convocatio) und das morphologische (contio) sind einander nicht im Verhältnis von Ursache und Wirkung, sondern von Wahrheit und Wirklichkeit zugeordnet.[10] Im Ereignis des göttlichen Rufes und der menschlichen Antwort gewinnt die Gemeinde greifbare Gestalt.

1.2 Begriffsproblematik

Die *Problematik* des Begriffs ‚Gemeinde' ergibt sich aus der Spannung zwischen *Begriff* und *Bezeichnung*: Einmal lassen sich die Begriffsmerkmale gesondert ausdrücken (z.B. im AT (5Mo 9,10): übersetzt die Septuaginta (LXX) das hebräische Wort ‚*qahal*' und ‚*'edā*', mit dem im AT das auserwählte Volk Israel bezeichnet wird. Die Ekklesia Gottes war der ‚*qahal Jahwe*', die Versammlung, die von Gott zusammengerufen wurde.[11] Der *eine* Begriff *ekklesia* kann durch verschiedene gleichwertige Wörter austauschweise umrissen werden (z.B. im deutschen Sprachgebrauch: Gemeinde und Kirche); umgekehrt kann *eine* Bezeichnung verschiedene ungleichwertige Begriffsinhalte meinen. Das geschichtlich wandelbare *qahal* meint den „*Aufruf*" der Männer zu Kultfeier, Gerichtssitzung oder Kriegszug.

Das Wort *'edā,* eine spätere Prägung der Priesterschrift, bezeichnet die um das heilige Zelt sich scharende Gemeinde und wird auf die Gemeinde des ersten Passa in Ägypten übertragen, *'edā* meint die Volks-, Rechts- oder Kult-Gemeinde.[12] Als kultisch reine Gottes-Gemeinde gliedert sie sich unter Moses Führung in Stämme, Sippen und Vaterhäuser, die durch Amtsträger (Fürsten,

---

[8] Weber, Heinz. Notizen zum Theologie-Unterricht. Was lehrt das Wort Gottes über die Gemeinde? (Ekklesiologie). Lemgo: 1993. S. 22.

[9] Die Religion in Geschichte und Gegenwart. RGG Bd. 2, S. 1325 [Gemeinde]. J.C.B. Mohr (Paul Siebeck). Digitale-Bibliothek/Band 12. 3. Auflage, Tübingen: 2006.

[10] Fallbusch, E. Jan M. Lochman u.a. Hrsg. Evangelisches Kirchenlexikon, Bd. 2/4, S. 48-49. Gemeinde. 3. Auflage. Digitale-Bibliothek Bd. 98. Göttingen, Vandenhoeck & Ruprecht 1985-1997.

[11] Grenz, Stanley. J. Created for Community. S. 208.

[12] Die Religion in Geschichte und Gegenwart. RGG Bd. 2, S. 1326 [Gemeinde]. J.C.B. Mohr (Paul Siebeck). Digitale-Bibliothek/Bd. 12. 2006]

Älteste, Häupter) geleitet werden. Die kultische Reorganisation unter Esra machte die Zugehörigkeit zur Gemeinde nicht von objektiven Kriterien (5Mo 23), sondern von der subjektiven Stellungnahme zum absolut verstandenen ‚Gesetz' abhängig.

Die LXX übersetzt *qahal* meist mit *ekklesia*. Mit der Zeit formt sich in der Apokalyptik der neue Begriff der *eschatologischen Gemeinde* aus. ‚Israel' wird zur endzeitlichen Heils-Gemeinde der Frommen, als ‚Überrest' (Amos 5,15; Jes 7,3).

Schließlich können neue geschichtliche Lagen dazu nötigen, den ursprünglichen Sinn durch Anreicherung oder Verkümmerung abzuwandeln. So hat sich in der Neuzeit durch die Formveränderung der Wörter die Unterscheidung von Kirche (für Gesamt-Gemeinde) und Gemeinde (für Einzel-Gemeinde) entgegen dem neutestamentlichen Gebrauch in der historischen Forschung durchgesetzt und die Begriffe beeinflusst.[13]

1.3 Biblische Begründung

Im *AT* tritt die Gemeinde zuerst als sakraler Verband der Stämme Israels in Erscheinung, d. h. als Gottes- und Volks-Gemeinde zugleich. Ausgegrenzt aus der Völkerwelt (durch die Erwählung), sammelt sich ‚Israel' unter der Führung Gottes um das zentrale Heiligtum der Lade Jahwes. Das NT sieht bereits die Ur-Gemeinde als die messianische Gemeinde der Endzeit an. Paulus übernimmt die Formel ‚Gemeinde Gottes' (1Kor 10,32; 11,22; 15,9; Gal 1,13) aus dem AT und verbindet sie mit der pneumatologischen Vorstellung vom ‚Leib Christi' (1Kor 12). Als ‚Israel Gottes' (Gal 6,16), als ‚neuer Bund' (1Kor 11,25) ist die Gemeinde Rechtsnachfolgerin des alttestamentlichen Gottesvolkes, jedoch zugleich durch Kreuz und Auferstehung Jesu Christi die *‚Gemeinde der Erstgeborenen, die im Himmel aufgeschrieben sind'*, (Hebr 12,23).

1.4 Begriffsgeschichte

Die historische Entwicklung lässt die ‚Gemeinde' als Orts-Gemeinde und die ‚Kirche' (als Verband dieser Gemeinden) auseinandertreten. Eine Erkenntnis der *Reformation* war: ‚Gottes Wort und Gottes Volk gehören wesenhaft zusammen.' (ecclesiola *in* ecclesia). Luthers Abneigung gegen das Wort ‚Kirche' im Unterschied zur ‚Gemeinde' ist aus seinen Schriften bekannt. Seine Übersetzung der Bibel benutzt es nie für Gemeinde. Auch auf reformatorischem Boden bleibt der Begriff ‚Gemeinde' (bei Bucer und Calvin) wirksam. Der Pietismus (Brüderunität) versucht noch einmal, die Kirche geistlich und orga-

---

[13] Die Religion in Geschichte und Gegenwart. RGG Bd. 2, S. 984. J.C.B. Mohr (Paul Siebeck). Digitale-Bibliothek/Bd. 12. 3. Auflage, Tübingen 2006.

nisatorisch von der Gemeinde her zu prägen, ehe die Aufklärung diese zum religiösen Verein entleert.[14] Im 19. Jahrhundert wurde durch die romantisierende Theologie, angetrieben von Schleiermacher, Ritschl, Kähler, Schlatter u.a., der Gemeindebegriff gewandelt. Die Proklamierung des 20. Jahrhunderts zum ‚Jahrhundert der Kirche' neutralisiert den Gemeindebegriff vollends. Erst im Kampf der ‚Bekennenden Kirche' begegnen sich wieder Gemeinde und Theologie. Die gegenwärtige systematische Theologie ist im Zuge der Ökumenischen Bewegung wie der kirchlichen Einigungsbestrebungen stärker an der Wirklichkeit der Kirche als an der Wahrheit des Gemeindebegriffs orientiert.[15] Das Wort ‚Kirche' muss vor der Abwanderung der Angelsachsen (449) schon bei ihnen gewesen sein, denn sie nahmen es mit.[16] Wir sollten bedenken: dem Wort Kirche haftet noch viel von seiner mittelalterlichen Bedeutung an, es meint eine sichtbare Organisation mit Machtanspruch. Emil Brunner schrieb über das Missverständnis der Kirche. Er fragt: Was ist Kirche? Diese Frage ist das ungelöste Problem des Protestantismus. Von den Tagen der Reformation bis auf unsere Zeit hat nie Klarheit darüber bestanden.[17] Die Ekklesia war nach E. Brunner *‚die gottesdienstlich versammelte Christusgemeinde, das gottesdienstlich versammelte Volk Gottes.'*

1.5 Ergebnis

‚Kirche' und ‚Gemeinde' haben im Verlauf der Geschichte ihre Begriffsinhalte weitgehend vertauscht. Der Vorzug des Gemeindebegriffs gegenüber dem der Kirche leuchtet ein.[18] Er ermöglicht es, folgende Sachverhalte klarer herauszuheben: a) den Zusammenhang zwischen AT, nachbiblischem Judentum und Urchristentum; b) den geistlichen Charakter des neutestamentlichen Begriffs *ekklesia* in seiner Realität, Totalität und Universalität; c) die Gemeinde als zentralen Haftpunkt der reformatorischen Grunderkenntnisse und Denkstrukturen; d) die Verbindung der ‚vertikalen' Gemeinschaft zwischen Mensch und Gott mit der ‚horizontalen' Bruderschaft der Glieder untereinander.

Das heute geläufige, aber sehr missverständliche Wort *‚Kirche'* leitete Luther von dem griechischen Wort *‚Kyriakos'* (= dem Herrn gehörig) ab. Es hätte im

---

[14] Die Religion in Geschichte und Gegenwart. RGG Bd. 2, S. 1328 [Gemeinde]. J.C.B. Mohr (Paul Siebeck). Digitale-Bibliothek/Band12. 2006]

[15] Die Religion in Geschichte und Gegenwart. RGG Bd. 2, S. 1328 [Gemeinde]. J.C.B. Mohr (Paul Siebeck). Digitale-Bibliothek/Band12. 2006]

[16] Melzer, Friso. Das Wort in den Wörtern. Die deutsche Sprache im Dienst der Christus-Nachfolge. Ein theo-philologisches Wörterbuch. Tübingen 1965. S. 238.

[17] Brunner, Emil. Das Mißverständnis der Kirche. Evangelische Verlagswerk, Stuttgart: 1959. S. 7. 59.

[18] Die Religion in Geschichte und Gegenwart. RGG Bd. 2, S. 1329 [Gemeinde]. J.C.B. Mohr (Paul Siebeck). Digitale-Bibliothek/Bd. 12. 2006.

Grunde genommen eine sehr treffende Bedeutung. Die Gemeinde ist nämlich eine Gruppe von Menschen, die dem Herrn gehört.[19] H.D. Wendland behauptet, es wäre unangebracht, wenn wir den Begriff Kirche zugunsten der Gemeinde streichen. *„Fehlentwicklungen lassen sich nicht durch terminologische Entscheidungen rückgängig machen."* [20] Wohl aber lässt sich der Begriff Kirche durch den der Gemeinde inhaltlich füllen. Es gilt, ihn aus dem Gesamt der biblischen Verkündigung neu zu entwickeln und auszulegen.

Aus der freikirchlichen Perspektive ist Gemeinde nicht da, wo Menschen zusammenkommen, um sich als Gemeinde zu bezeichnen, sondern: ***Gemeinde ist da, wo sich Gläubige unter die Herrschaft Christi und unter die Leitung und Autorität des Heiligen Geistes stellen.*** ER bringt die Glieder zu einem Leib zusammen (1Kor 12,13). ER lässt den Leib funktionieren vom Haupt her (Eph 4,15-16). Glieder bestimmen nicht über Glieder. Deshalb kann nie ein Mensch Grundlage einer Gemeinde sein (1Kor 3,4-8). Heute betrachten viele Menschen die Kirche als *‚Hörsaal'*, in dem sich die Gläubigen Bibelauslegung vortragen lassen. Andere sehen sie als *‚sozialen Club'*, dem sich verschiedene Leute anschließen, damit ihre Probleme gelöst werden; genauso wie man sich irgendeiner anderen Organisation anschließt, um daraus Nutzen zu ziehen.

Die Kenntnis über die Gemeinde ist selbst bei bibeltreuen Christen oft sehr mangelhaft. Viele christliche Gemeinden wissen nicht genau, wer sie eigentlich sind und was sie wollen. Deshalb ist die Frage nach der ‚Gemeinde' sehr aktuell geworden. Selbst in der Volkskirche ist die Frage nach echter Gemeinde aufgebrochen. Die landeskirchlichen Gemeinschaften müssen sich mehr und mehr die Frage nach biblischer Gemeinde stellen lassen. Sogar in der Katholischen Kirche ist seit dem Vaticanum II das Thema ‚Gemeinde' aktuell. Ausdrücklich werden die geweihten Hirten ermahnt, die Würde der Laien anzuerkennen und ihren Initiativen Raum zu geben.[21] Allerdings wurde dadurch der grundsätzliche Unterschied zwischen Priester und Laie nicht aufgehoben. Es wurde dort in den letzten Jahrzehnten mehr über Gemeinde nachgedacht als in den vergangenen Jahrhunderten. Die Gemeinde ist nach dem NT *ein ‚Geheimnis'*, das zur Zeit des AT ‚verborgen' gewesen ist, nun aber ‚offenbar' (Röm 16,25-26).

Das Wort, das Luther mit ‚Gemeinde' übersetzt, kommt im NT 114 mal vor. Im NT finden wir fünfmal das Wort Ekklesia im Sinne einer politischen Grup-

---

[19] Weber, Heinz. Notizen zum Theologie-Unterricht. Was lehrt das Wort Gottes über die Gemeinde? (Ekklesiologie). Lemgo: 1993. S. 23.

[20] Wendland, H.-D. Die Kirche in der modernen Gesellschaft. J.C.B. Mohr 1956. EKL II, S. 608 ff.

[21] Kreck, Walter. Grundfragen der Ekklesiologie. Chr. Kaiser Verl. München: 1981. S. 188.

pe oder für das Volk Israel![22] Gemeinde ist keine Denomination. Denominationen sind Schalen, Formen, die bei der Entrückung der Gemeinde zurückbleiben. In diesen verschiedenen Schalen mögen nun einzelne Gläubige sein, in der einen mehr, in der anderen weniger, die zur wahren Gemeinde Jesu gehören. Die Gemeinde ist die **Ekklesia** (= ‚Gemeinde') Gottes, damit das **Volk Gottes.**

2. Allgemeines Priestertum

Dieses Thema ist für die Gemeinde Jesu von großer Bedeutung und Relevanz. Es zwingt uns dazu, uns mit Kirchengeschichte zu beschäftigen. Es hilft uns zu sehen, warum die Freikirchen ihre Berechtigung haben. Es nötigt uns dazu, die Entstehung des Priestertums in der Bibel zu betrachten. Es vermittelt uns einen notwendigen Einblick in das Alte Testament, jenen Teil der Bibel, der so vielen heutzutage leider unbekannt ist. Es gewährt uns einen wunderbaren Blick auf das Priestertum Christi. Es zeigt uns unser Vorrecht und unsere Stellung und Verantwortung als Christen. Es bringt uns näher zu Gott. Es bekräftigt die Wichtigkeit jedes einzelnen Christen, ungeachtet seines Alters, Geschlechts oder Hintergrunds.

Das Thema ‚*Priestertum aller Gläubigen*' ist einer der Beiträge der protestantischen Reformation des 16. Jahrhunderts. Martin *Luther* hat in seinen reformatorischen Hauptschriften von 1520-1523 die Lehre vom allgemeinen Priestertum der Christen dargelegt.[23] Erwin Mülhaupt nennt Luther einen Gegner des Klerikalismus, der klerikalen Unbelehrbarkeit und Unfehlbarkeit, der Entmündigung des christlichen Laien, auch einen Gegner klerikaler Politik und alles klerikalen Dünkels und pfäffischer Arroganz. Gleichzeitig ist Luther für ihn ein Freund des allgemeinen Priestertums aller Christen, die sich von der Bibel allezeit etwas sagen lassen.[24] Luthers Verständnis vom ‚allgemeinen Priestertum' oder, wie es auch genannt wird, vom ‚Priestertum aller Gläubigen' wurde richtungweisend für genuin protestantische Ekklesiologie überhaupt.[25] Eine eigene Schrift für das allgemeine Priestertum gibt es von Luther jedoch nicht, weshalb konstruierend vorgegangen werden muss. Nicht die Entwicklung der Lehre Luthers, sondern die Kontinuität seiner Aussagen im Verlauf seiner Wirkung sind dabei von Interesse. Im Folgenden können natür-

---

[22] Weber, Heinz. Notizen zum Theologie-Unterricht. Was lehrt das Wort Gottes über die Gemeinde? (Ekklesiologie). Lemgo: 1993. S. 22.

[23] Luther, Martin: Werke. Kritische Gesamtausgabe (Waimarer Ausgabe). An den christlichen Adel deutscher Nation von des christlichen Standes Besserung, Bd. 6, S. 248ff; De captivitate Baylonica ecclesia praeludium. (WA Bd. 6), S. 497-573.

[24] Mülhaupt, Erwin. Allgemeines Priestertum oder Klerikalismus? Calwer Verl. Stuttgart: 1963. S. 41.

[25] Liebelt, Markus. Allgemeines Priestertum, Charisma und Struktur. Wuppertal: 2000. S. 24.

lich nur Grundzüge dieses Verhältnisses betrachtet werden, die für die Herleitung des allgemeinen Priestertums und des ordinierten Amtes wichtig sind. Luthers Auffassung vom Priestertum aller Getauften ist *nicht* in die lutherischen Bekenntnisschriften und somit in die offizielle Lehrauffassung der lutherischen Kirche eingegangen (vgl. Apologie des Augsburger Bekenntnisses Artikel 13).

Die Reformation[26] war eine Bewegung, die gewisse Lehren und Praktiken der Kirche von Rom reformieren wollte und die zur Etablierung der protestantischen Kirchen führte.[27] Im Vergleich zu Luther bildet für **Calvin** der Gedanke von der *‚Gemeinde als Leib Christi'* gewissermaßen den theologischen Rahmen, in welchem er seine Lehre vom Priestertum der Gemeinde entfaltet.[28] Die Gemeinde (als Leib Christi) partizipiert nun ihrerseits durch den Heiligen Geist am Priestertum Christi und hat damit auch Anteil an dessen besonderer priesterlichen Würde.[29] Für Calvin hat *‚das Amt'* das allgemeine Priestertum zur Voraussetzung. Deshalb kann Calvin sagen: *„Weder das Licht und die Wärme der Sonne noch auch Speis und Trank sind zur Ernährung und Erhaltung des gegenwärtigen Lebens so notwendig wie das Amt der Apostel und Hirten zur Bewahrung der Kirche auf Erden."*[30]

Ich möchte betonen, dass sich Geist und Recht, allgemeines Priestertum und geordnete Dienste in der Gemeinde nicht widersprechen. **Aber leider besteht auch in Freikirchen die Gefahr, dass man das Amt über das allgemeine Priestertum erhebt, dass das Recht über den Geist triumphiert und der Herrschaftsgedanke den Dienstgedanken verdrängt.** Wenn aber der Heilige Geist in unseren Gemeinden regiert, dann muss alles was in der Gemeinde geschieht, ihre Lehre und Ordnung, dem dienen, dafür offen sein, ihm den Weg bereiten, anstatt ihn zu versperren. So wenig Wort und Geist im Gegensatz zu einander stehen, so wenig darf das Charisma gegen das Amt oder das Amt gegen Charisma ausgespielt werden. Die Amtsträger und Diener am Wort sind nicht Her-

---

[26] Von ‚Reformieren': Besser machen durch Beseitigung oder Abstellen von Mängeln oder Fehlern.

[27] Die Lehren der Reformation kann wie folgt zusammengefasst werden: a) **Sola scriptura** (allein die Schrift), mit der Betonung auf der Bibel als der alleinigen Grundlage für Glaube, Lehre und Praxis der Kirche. (b) **Sola fide** (allein der Glaube), mit der Betonung auf Rechtfertigung allein aufgrund des Glaubens – nicht aufgrund von Werken. (c) **Sola gratia** (allein die Gnade), wobei die Betonung hauptsächlich auf Christi stellvertretendem Werk am Kreuz und auf der Lehre von der Prädestination liegt.

[28] Markus Liebelt. Allgemeines Priestertum, Charisma und Struktur. Wuppertal: 2000. S. 57.

[29] Calvin, J. Institutio Christianae Religionis (Unterricht in der christlichen Religion), nach der letzten Ausgabe übersetzt und bearbeitet von Otto Weber. 5. Aufl. Neukirchen-Vluyn: 1988. Teil 4, S. 19, 28.

[30] Kreck, Walter. Grundfragen der Ekklesiologie. Chr. Kaiser Verl. München: 1981. S. 167.

ren der Gemeinde, sondern auch sie stehen, wie jedes andere Glied am Leibe Christi, unter der Verheißung und Zucht des Wortes Gottes, das – wie der Gemeinde – auch ihnen immer wieder gegenübersteht. Grundlegend ist, Amt und Gemeinde gehören unlöslich zusammen.

In vielen Freikirchen besteht die Gefahr, dass die Ordnung den Geist erstickt und das wirkliche Leben der Gemeinde verhindert. Nach Paulus soll das ganze Leben des Christen und der Gemeinde ein ‚vernünftiger Gottesdienst'(Röm 12,1) sein. Dann würde das Zeugnisleben der Gemeinde im Gottesdienst und darüber hinaus wieder zu einem Zeugnis für die Welt. Die Freikirchen (Gemeinden) schulden der Welt ein Zeugnis durch ihre Gottesdienst- und Gemeindeordnung. *Wir müssen uns als Freikirchen fragen, wieweit es wirklich das Ärgernis der Kreuzesbotschaft (1Kor 1,18ff) ist, das den heutigen Menschen oft vom Gottesdienst und der Gemeinde abschreckt, und wieweit wir selbst den Weg versperren, sei es durch starre, traditionelle Formen des gemeindlichen Lebens, sei es durch eigenwillige Experimente und Tricks, die zu deutlich eine propagandistische Absicht verspüren lassen.*

Wir müssen wie unsere Väter alles daran setzen, damit die Voraussetzungen dafür geschaffen werden, dass unsere Lokalgemeinde eine Stätte wird, die für das Wirken des Heiligen Geistes offen ist, in der jeder seine Gaben einbringen kann. Damit bin ich wieder beim Thema: Priestertum aller Gläubigen besagt, dass der einzelne Gläubige unmittelbar und direkt – ohne einen irdischen Mittler – Gemeinschaft mit Gott hat (Röm 5,1-2).

2.1 Begriff

Im Neuen Testament wird der Begriff ‚Priester' mit dem Wort ‚hierateus' ausgedrückt. Sucht man nun im Neuen Testament nach dem Begriff ‚hierateus' oder ‚hierateuma', so fällt auf, dass dieser Begriff *nie auf einzelne Angehörige* der christlichen Gemeinden angewandt wird. Die theologische Übertragung des ‚hierateus'- und ‚hierateuma'-Begriffs auf die Gemeinde des Neuen Bundes ist von großer Bedeutung. ‚Hierateuma' erscheint im NT nur in 1Petr 2,5 und 2,9, wo alle Christen der ‚ekklesia', Gemeinde, als ein heiliges Priestertum bezeichnet werden.[31] In Kultreligionen steht oft eine gesonderte Kaste von Priestern kraft ritueller Handlungen, die allein sie vollziehen können oder dürfen, als Mittler zwischen dem Volk und den Göttern. Der Priester ist eine Art ‚pontifex' (der die Brücke schlägt zwischen Gott und Menschen). *Vom allgemeinen Priestertum wird gesprochen, wenn jedes Mitglied des Volkes ganz oder zum Teil priesterliche Rechte und Funktionen ausüben kann.*

---

[31] Bauer, Walter. Griechisch-Deutsches Wörterbuch zu den Schriften des Neuen Testaments und den übrigen urchristlichen Literatur. Gießen: 1928. S. 579.

Der Begriff ‚*hierateuma*' hat im Neuen Testament drei verschiedene Bedeutungen: (a) Er bezeichnet die Priester des alten Bundes. (b) Er bezeichnet das einzigartige eschatologische Hohepriestertum Jesu Christi. Diese Bedeutung findet sich vor allem im Hebräerbrief. (c) Schließlich wird der Begriff ‚*hierateuma*' verwendet, um das gemeinsame Priestertum aller Glaubenden zu bezeichnen.

2.2 Heils- und kirchengeschichtliche Entwicklungen

Das Alte Testament sieht im Bundesschluss am Sinai (2Mo 19,6; 23,22 LXX.) Israels Erwählung zu einem ‚Königreich von Priestern'. Priesterlich wirkt Israel auch als Mittler der Völker zu Jahwe.

2.2.1 Das Priestertum geht auf das Alte Testament zurück.

Das Wort Priester kommt über 700 mal im Alten Testament vor. Das hebräische Wort ist ‚*kohen*'. Es wird manchmal durch das Adjektiv oberster oder höher qualifiziert. Der Priester stand ‚*als ein Diener*' vor Gott. Die Position ‚*des Stehens*', im Gegensatz zum Sitzen, ist im Hebräischen impliziert: Kohen ist abgeleitet von kahan, und hat dieselbe Bedeutung wie ‚*kur*', ‚*stehen*'. Die Aufgabe des Priesters im AT bestand darin, **vor Gott zu stehen**. Überdies gab es eine dreigliedrige Hierarchie von hauptamtlichen Dienern Gottes: (1) Oberster Priester; (2) Priester; (3) Leviten. Jeder Stand war von den anderen unterschieden und hatte seine eigenen spezifischen Aufgaben und Privilegien. Die Priesterschaft setzte sich aus Männern vom Stamm Levi zusammen. Dies scheint eine Art Belohnung für den Stamm Levi gewesen zu sein; dafür, wie sie auf Mose reagiert haben, nachdem die Israeliten das goldene Kalb angebetet hatten (2Mo 32). Damals ‚*... stellte sich Mose unter das Tor des Lagers und sprach: Her zu mir, wer dem Herrn angehört! Da sammelten sich zu ihm alle Kinder Levis.*' (2Mo 32,26). ‚*Dann sagte Mose: Ihr seid heute dem Herrn geheiligt worden, denn ihr habt euch gegen eure eigenen Söhne und Brüder gestellt, und er hat euch heute gesegnet.*' (2Mo 32,29). ‚*Zu jener Zeit sonderte der Herr den Stamm Levi aus, um die Lade des Bundes des Herrn zu tragen, vor dem Herrn zu stehen, ihm zu dienen und in seinem Namen zu segnen, bis auf diesen Tag.*' (5Mo 10,8).

Gott belohnte die Treue der Leviten. Auch Mose vergaß dies nie und gab den Leviten besondere Anerkennung, als er seinen letzten Segen über die Stämme Israels ausprach (5Mo 33,8-11). Obwohl sie kein Erbteil in Form von Landbesitz erhielten, waren sie doch der Stamm mit dem höchsten Prestige in Israel (5Mo 18,1-2).

Das Priestertum repräsentierte die Verbundenheit des Volkes Israel mit Gott. Unter dem Mosaischen Bund sollte die ganze Nation sein: ‚*Ein Königreich von*

Priestern' (2Mo 19,6). *„Eine heilige Nation'* (2Mo 19,6; 3Mo 11,44ff; 4Mo 15,40). Das Priestertum wurde zum Mittler des Bundes. Es hatte daher repräsentativen Charakter. Diejenigen, die Gott dienten, mussten in ihrem Charakter ihm ähnlich sein. Dieser Stand der Heiligkeit war im levitischen Priestertum symbolisiert. Die Priester sollen Heiligkeit auch durch ihren eigenen besonderen Gehorsam gegenüber dem Gesetz demonstrieren.[32] Der Tod von Nadab und Abihu nach ihrem eigenmächtigen Opfer (3Mo 10,2) zeigt, dass die besondere Weihe ein besonders strenges Gesetz (V. 8-15) und einen besonders strengen Gehorsam erforderlich macht.

Die Priester hatten auch Pflichten. Auch wenn sie hauptsächlich mit dem Dienst an der Stiftshütte, dem Opferdienst im Tempel und dem Gottesdienst zu tun hatten, hatten sie auch andere Aufgaben. Eine Gruppe Männer aus jeder der drei levitischen Sippen bildete den Tempelchor; sie haben möglicherweise eine Reihe von Psalmen komponiert (z.B. die Psalmen 85 und 87). Dann mussten sie auch im Namen Gottes Fragen beantworten, die auf andere Weise nicht entschieden werden konnten (z.B. wann der richtige Zeitpunkt sei, um in den Kampf zu ziehen); sie gebrauchten heilige Steine, Urim und Thummim genannt, die in der Brusttasche des Hohen Priesters aufbewahrt wurden (2Mo 28,30; 5Mo 33,8-11). Wenn der Priester den Urim-Stein herauszog, war die Antwort ein Nein. Wenn der Priester den Thummim-Stein herauszog, war die Antwort ein Ja. Nicht nur durch ihr Leben als Modell sollen die Priester Jahwe verherrlichen (3Mo 10,3), sondern auch durch die Lehre (3Mo 10,11), die ebenfalls zu ihren Aufgaben gehörte (Mal 2,7). Leider mussten die Propheten die Priester und Leviten oft zur Rede stellen, weil sie diese Pflichten vernachlässigt hatten (Hes 34).

2.2.2 Das Priestertum im Neuen Testament

Am priesterlichen Opfer- und Zeugendienst nehmen kraft des allgemeinen Priestertums alle Gläubigen teil (1Petr 2,5+9).[33] Der Gedanke vom Priestertum aller Gläubigen hat seine biblischen Wurzeln in der Berufung und Erwählung der Gemeinde zum Gottesvolk des Neuen Bundes (1Petr 2,5.9; Offb 1,6; 5,10; 20,6). Im NT werden die Amtsträger nie Priester genannt. Alle Glieder der neutestamentlichen Gemeinde werden ein ‚**königliches Priestertum**' genannt. Könige kamen aus Juda; Priester aus dem Stamm Levi. Hier ist ein Gipfel (Klimax), Zustand und Schlussfolgerung für das Volk! Unter Berufung auf das

---

[32] Rieker, Siegbert. SBB. Ein Priestervolk für alle Völker. Stuttgart: 2007. S. 249.

[33] *„Laßt euch auch selbst als lebendige Steine aufbauen, als ein geistliches Haus, ein heiliges Priestertum, um geistliche Schlachtopfer darzubringen, Gott wohlannehmbar durch Jesus Christus! ... Ihr aber seid ein auserwähltes Geschlecht, ein königliches Priestertum, eine heilige Nation, ein Volk zum Besitztum, damit ihr die Tugenden dessen verkündigt, der euch aus der Finsternis zu seinem wunderbaren Licht berufen hat."*

Neue Testament hebt Luther hervor, dass priesterliche und kultische Begriffe und Merkmale in der römischen Kirche illegitimerweise auf kirchliche Ämter übertragen worden sind.[34] Sie können darum auch nicht die Grundlage für eine besondere herrschaftsbegründende Rechts- und Vollmachtstellung der Kleriker innerhalb der Gemeinde abgeben. Christus allein ist der einzige und wahre Priester, dessen Mittlerstellung und Opferhandeln durch Menschen nicht fortzuführen ist. Neben ihm, dem einen messianischen Priester, ist kein Platz für andere priesterliche Mittler- und Machtstellungen in der neutestamentlichen Gemeinde.

Im NT sind wir alle Priester (1Petr 2,5.9). Alles, was über die Beziehung der Leviten zu Gott gesagt ist, lässt sich im Großen und Ganzen auf uns übertragen. *Wir lassen nicht jemand anders stellvertretend für uns ein heiliges Leben führen; wir müssen selbst ein heiliges Leben führen (1Petr 1,16). Wir lassen nicht jemand anders für uns Anbetung machen; wir müssen selbst Gott anbeten (Heb 13,15). Wir bitten nicht jemand anders, Gottes Willen in Bezug auf unsere persönliche Führung zu bekommen; wir müssen Gottes Führung selbst suchen (Eph 5,17).* Dies bedeutet nicht, dass es keine besonderen Aufgaben oder Dienste gibt, die zum größten Teil von denen wahrgenommen werden müssen, die zu einem bestimmten Dienst berufen sind (1Kor 12,28; Eph 4,11).

Das Christentum beinhaltet eine radikale Weiterentwicklung des Konzepts von Priestertum. Die Lehre vom Priestertum Christi ist ein bedeutender Beitrag des Briefes an die Hebräer. *„Da wir nun einen großen Hohen Priester haben, der durch den Himmel gegangen ist „Jesus, den Sohn Gottes, wollen wir an unserem Bekenntnis zu ihm festhalten.'* (Heb 4,14). Er wird als die vollkommene Erfüllung des alttestamentlichen Priestertums verstanden. Er brachte das levitische Priestertum an ein definitives geschichtliches Ende. Er stiftete eine ein- für allemal gültige ewige Mittlerschaft zwischen Gott und den Menschen. Der Schreiber des Hebräerbriefes wusste, dass er sein Werk auf ihn zugeschnitten hatte. *„Unser Herr kam ja aus dem Stamm Juda, doch Mose hat Juda nie in Verbindung mit dem Priestertum erwähnt.'* (Heb 7,14). Aber es war das Priestertum Melchisedeks, das durch Jesus erfüllt wurde (Ps 110; Heb 7,1-25). Weil Jesus selbst nicht aus dem priesterlichem Geschlecht war, fragten einige: Kommt der Christus etwa aus Galiläa? (Joh 7,41). Jesus wurde von der sadduzäischen Priesterschaft allgemein gehasst, besonders aber von den Hohen Priestern (Mt 22,23-33; 27,1).

Die neutestamentliche Gemeinde ist eine heilige Priesterschaft. Sie wird mit der Priesterschaft des Alten Testamentes verglichen: (1Petr 2,5.9.10; Offb 1,6).

---

[34] Die Religion in Geschichte und Gegenwart. RGG Bd. 5, S. 581 [Priestertum]. Digitale-Bibliothek/Bd. 12. 2006.

Christen sind Priester im Tempel der Gemeinde. Wir könnten die Frage stellen: *„Was ist das Neue am Neuen Testament?"* Enthält das Neue Testament etwas, das dem Alten noch fremd war, an das dort noch nicht gedacht war? Viele Christen haben eine anscheinend sehr einfache Antwort auf diese Frage: „Die Zeit des Alten Bundes war eine Zeit der Furcht, die Zeit des Neuen Bundes ist die Zeit der Liebe." Diese Antwort enthält viele Missverständnisse, vor allem aus der Sicht der paulinischen Theologie. Und er ist einfach falsch. Denn schon in der Tora nimmt das Gebot der Liebe einen zentralen Platz ein (5Mo 6,4f; Joel 2,13; Hos 6,6; Phil 2,12). Josef Ratzinger hat in einem seiner Vorträge gesagt: *„Das Neue am Neuen Testament ist die Person Jesu."*[35] Er fügte noch hinzu: Das Neue ist außerdem die ‚Figur der Zwölf.' Jesus hat tatsächlich die Schwelle überschritten. Lukas (4,21) berichtet von Jesus erstem Auftritt in der Synagoge von Nazareth. Nach der Schriftlesung aus Jes 60,1ff sagte er: *„Heute hat sich das Schriftwort, das ihr eben gehört habt, erfüllt."* Das jesuanische „Heute" besagt: Du hast keine Zeit mehr. Denn die Welt brennt. Du musst jetzt handeln. Denn du bist der Sache Gottes begegnet. Du musst noch heute deine ganze Existenz einsetzen. Denn die Einladung Gottes ist an dich ergangen. Allerdings zielt Jesus mit dem ‚Heute' nicht auf die Pflicht, den Imperativ, das moralische „Muß", sondern auf den Jubel über das angebotene Fest, die Freude über den Schatz und die Perle, die man jetzt schon finden kann.

Das Neue am Neuen Testament ist: Jeder tut in diesem Tempel Priesterdienst. Dieser Dienst ist ein von den Menschen zu Gott und ein von Gott zu den Menschen hingewandter. Wenn der Hohepriester in den Tempel ging, vor Gott trat, hatte er die Menschen im Rücken. Er vertrat sie vor Gott. Die Namen der Stämme Israels trug er zweimal auf seinem Leibe: zum einen auf zwei Steinen (auf jeder Schulter einen, je sechs Namen auf jedem Stein), zum anderen auf der Brust, auf dem Ephod (12 Steine, je ein Name der Stämme Israels pro Stein). So treten auch wir vor den Herrn und legen Fürbitte ein für Mitchristen und Verlorene. Auch wir bringen Opfer dar: unseren Leib (Röm 12,1), das Lob der Lippen (Hebr 13,15), Wohltätigkeit (Hebr 13,16) und Teilnahme an der Gewinnung von Menschen für Christus (Röm 15,16).

Als Priester werden wir dann von Gott zu diesen Menschen gesandt. Gott steht hinter uns als ein Sendender; die Menschen sind vor uns, damit wir ihnen dienen. (Mal 2,1.6.7). Aus dem Missverständnis heraus ist z.B. in der Katholischen Kirche das ‚levitische Priestertum' zu finden. Die Messe ist eine Art Opferung. Vom Opfer Christi heißt es 'ein-für-allemal'. (Hebr 9,25f). Der einfache Versammlungsraum der ersten Christen ist zum pompösen Altarraum, mit Gold verziert, geworden. Das Ritual wurde an Stelle der freien Geistesleitung

---

[35] Ratzinger, Josef. Zur Gemeinschaft gerufen. Kirche heute verstehen. Freiburg, i.Br.: 1991. S. 104-109.

eingesetzt. Leider sind von der Evangelischen Kirche viele Riten übernommen worden (z.B. gewisse Liturgien, Sakramente usw.). Eine wichtige Erkenntnis der **freikirchlichen Ekklesiologie** kommt in einem alten Erweckungslied zum Ausdruck: *„Keine schönen Kirchen und Altäre; ... keine toten Formen, Menschenlehre, sondern Gottes Kraft erfüllte sie. ..."*[36] In Gemeinschaften wo der Heilige Geist wirken kann, erkennen die Gläubigen ihre priesterliche Stellung vor Gott für andere Menschen. Es war immer der Geist Gottes selbst, der in der Gemeinde neue Aufbrüche gewirkt hat, oft völlig überraschend und gegen alle Erwartungen. Nirgends beschäftigt sich die Bibel mit Pastoralplänen und Seelsorgestrategien. Stattdessen zeigt sie auf fast jeder Seite: Gott handelt nicht überall, sondern an einem konkreten Ort. Dieses alte Prinzip der Heilsgeschichte gilt auch heute. Man denke nur an jene Szene in Betlehem zur Zeit des Königs Saul. Der Prophet Samuel soll auf Gottes Wort hin für Israel einen neuen König salben und er sucht deshalb Isai. So geht es in der Bibel ständig zu. Gott bringt seine Geschichte auf andere Weise voran, als wir es uns ausdenken und planen. Dass da einer aus Nazareth kam, aus einem der unbedeutenden Dörfer Israels, und anfing, Jünger zu berufen, ist eine völlig unwahrscheinliche und im Grunde ‚unmögliche' Geschichte. Mit Sicherheit haben damals viele die Prognose abgegeben: „Aus dieser Geschichte wird nichts." Sie täuschten sich. In den folgenden Jahrzehnten entstanden rund um das Mittelmeer Hunderte von christlichen Gemeinden. Die Geschichte, die sich um Jesus abgespielt hat, ist zur heiligen Geschichte geworden. Wohl dir, wenn du ein Teil davon bist.

2.3 Priestertum Jesu Christi

Aus freikirchlicher Perspektive ist das allgemeine Priestertum (oder das Priestertum aller Gläubigen) im Priestertum Jesu Christi verwurzelt. Durch seine vollkommene Offenbarung und Verwirklichung des göttlichen Willens mit dem Menschen hat er das alttestamentliche Priestertum erfüllt und abgetan. Durch seine Verkündigung des Gottesreiches und durch sein Kreuzesopfer für die Sünde der Welt ist er der einzige Priester und Mittler zwischen Gott und den Menschen geworden (1Tim 2,4-5). In ihm und durch ihn haben alle, die an ihn glauben, Zutritt zu Gott und sind dazu berufen, der Welt gegenüber von Gott zu zeugen und im Dienst an der Welt ihr Leben zu opfern. Die Gemeinde Jesu Christi ist ein ‚Volk' von Priestern und Königen (entsprechend 2Mo 19,6: 1Petr 2,9; Offb 1,6; 5,10; 20,6), die kraft ihres Seins in ihm, dem Hohen Priester, als Licht der Welt (Mt 5,14; Phil 2,15; 1Thess 5,5) dieser den Willen Gottes vor Augen stellen und ihr eigenes Leben als Opfer für die Welt darbringen (Röm 12,1; Hebr 13,15-16; 1Petr 2,5). Dem alttestamentlichen Israel wurde gesagt: *„Dich hat der Herr, dein Gott, erwählt,* damit du ihm *als Eigentums-*

---

[36] Preist Ihn. Lied Nr. 124, Strophe 2. Stiwa Druck und Verlag. Urbach: 1978.

volk gehörst aus allen Völkern, die auf dem Erdboden sind." (5Mo 7,6). Im Hinblick auf die neutestamentliche Gemeinde wird eine ähnliche Aussage gemacht: *"Ihr aber seid ein auserwähltes Volk, ein königliches Priestertum, eine heilige Nation, Gottes eigenes Volk."* (1Petr 2,9). Der griechische Satz lautet: *‚laos eis Peripoiesin'*, wörtlich: *"ein Volk zum Besitztum"*. Dieser priesterliche Dienst geschieht in der Welt, hat aber im Gottesdienst der Gemeinde seinen Ursprung (1Kor 10,17, vgl. Röm 12,5) und tritt in der Anbetung des gegenwärtigen Herrn in Erscheinung (1Petr 2,4-6; Apk 5,8-14). In Hebräer 12,15 werden alle Gläubigen aufgefordert: *‚und **seht darauf**, dass nicht jemand Gottes Gnade versäume; dass nicht etwa eine bittere Wurzel aufwachse und Unfrieden anrichte und viele durch sie unrein werden.'* Diese – und noch mehr – Verantwortungen gehören zum **‚königlichen Priestertum'**.

2.4 Kirchengeschichtliche Entwicklungen

Kirchengeschichtlich gehört der Begriff *‚allgemeines Priestertum'* wesentlich zum Selbstverständnis der **Reformation**. In der katholischen Kirche setzte sich von Anfang an das episkopale Modell[37] von Gemeindeleitung durch, das dann auch (trotz Luthers Betonung des allgemeinen Priestertums) von der Kirche der Reformation übernommen wurde. Es gibt einen hierarchischen Apparat mit dem Bischof an der Spitze. Dabei wird übersehen, dass ‚Bischof' und ‚Ältester' im NT austauschbar verwendet wird.

Damit war aber auch die Institutionalisierung der großen Volkskirchen vorprogrammiert. Das andere Extrem ist das kongregationalistische Modell[38] der Gemeindeleitung. Die Gemeinde versteht sich als Demokratie. Älteste sind eher Vollzugsorgane der Gemeindebeschlüsse. Es geht um Mehrheitsbeschlüsse. Hier findet die moderne ‚Mitbestimmung' – gewerkschaftliches Denken – ihre Verwirklichung.

Das Aufkommen eines *‚Stellvertreter Priestertums'* im Verlauf der Kirchengeschichte, war ein Abweichen von der neutestamentlichen Norm, die sich bereits seit dem Ende des ersten Jahrhunderts abzeichnete.[39] Clemens (ca. 95)

---

[37] Kennzeichen der episkopalen (bischöflichen) Gemeindeleitungsstruktur ist die hierarchische Aufbau. Das NT kennt nur Älteste und Diakone. Bischof ist nur eine andere Bezeichnung für den Dienst des Ältesten (Apg 20,17+28).

[38] Kennzeichen der kongregationalistische Gemeindeleitungsstruktur: Die örtliche Versammlung hat alle Autorität und trifft alle Entscheidungen selbst (nach demokratischen Prinzipien). Diese Struktur hat viele gute Elemente; leider vernachlässigt sie das Ältestenprinzip, und Demokratie (Volksherrschaft) ist dem NT fremd. Unreife Gläubige haben das gleiche Stimmrecht wie geistliche Christen.

[39] Kendall, R.T. Theologie leicht gemacht. Lernen worauf es ankommt. Holzgerlingen: 2002. S. 414.

übernahm die alttestamentliche dreigliedrige Hierarchie von Hoher Priester, Priester und Leviten als einen analogen (ähnlichen) Typus des christlichen Dienstes. Die Didache (ca. 90-ca. 150) bezeichnete Propheten als ‚eure Hohen Priester' und sprach von der Eucharistie als ‚Opfer'. Tertullian (ca. 200) gebrauchte die Begriffe ‚Priester' und ‚Hoher Priester' für die Vorsteher der Gemeinde. Hieronymus (345-419) übersetzte in der Vulgata das Griechische ‚mysterion' mit ‚Sacramentum' (Sakrament). Augustinus (354-430) definierte den Begriff Sakrament als ‚ein sichtbares Zeichen einer göttlichen Sache'.

Wo der Heilige Geist wirkt, geschieht auch Berufung für die verschiedenen Dienste in der Gemeinde. *Die Erweckungsbewegung und **die Entstehung der Freikirchen** sind Beweise dafür, wie Gott Menschen beruft und befähigt für den Dienst.*

Seit der Verfassung des deutschen Reiches vom März 1849 gab es erstmals Glaubens- und Gewissensfreiheiten und die Erlaubnis zur Gründung von neuen Religionsgemeinschaften in Deutschland.[40] Ab 1849 war es einfacher, Vereine zu gründen. Die gesellschaftlichen Umbrüche der Zeit führten zur Gründung verschiedener Freikirchen in Deutschland. Die Freikirchengründungen in Deutschland hingen oft mit ausländischen, bereits bestehenden Freikirchen zusammen. Der Begriff ‚Freikirche' steht im Kontrast zu Volks-, Teritorial-, und Staatskirchen, und ist somit kontextuell bedingt. Dabei sind die Freikirchen geschichtliche als ‚Protestbewegung' aufzufassen, die sich aus verschiedenen Gründen von dem „Staats- oder Landeskirchentum und gegen eine Volkskirche" absetzen.[41]

Dank der verbesserten Kommunikationsmöglichkeiten des 19. Jahrhunderts waren Reisen in anderen Ländern unproblematischer geworden. *Es waren die Freikirchen, die nach der Wiederherstellung der neutestamentlichen Ekklesiologie gestrebt haben, und das gegen erhebliche Opposition von Seiten des Staates und der Kirche.* Man war bereit, für seine ‚ekklesiologischen Überzeugungen' auch erhebliche Nachteile in Kauf zu nehmen. Aber auch Freikirchen haben sich in ihrer Struktur von gesellschaftlichen Entwicklungen bestimmen lassen und müssen sich neu auf die biblische Ekklesiologie besinnen. Wir müssen lernen, dass wir eine Verantwortung für das Volk haben und uns nicht auf den individualisierten Privatglauben zurückziehen.

---

[40] Stadelmann, Helge. Bausteine zur Erneuerung der Kirche. Gemeindeaufbau auf der Basis einer biblisch erneuerten Ekklesiologie. Brunnen Verl. Gießen: 1998. [Stephan Holthaus. Die Entstehung der Freikirchen in Deutschland.] S. 19-39.

[41] Geldbach, Erich. Freikirchen. Erbe, Gestalt und Wirkung. Bensheimer Hefte 70. Vandenhoeck & Ruprecht, Göttingen: 2005. S. 36.

Die Entwicklung des allgemeinen Priestertums in den letzten 300 Jahren in den Freikirchen, kann wie folgt zusammengefasst werden: (1) Aus *‚freikirchlicher Perspektive'* haben alle Glieder des Leibes Christi (alle Gläubigen) im Heiligen Geist Anteil am einzigartigen Priestertum Jesu Christi. Diese Teilhabe am Priestertum wird durch das sakrale Handeln der Gemeinde an den Glaubenden dargestellt und vermittelt, vor allem durch die Taufe in den Tod Jesu und die Teilnahme am Herrenmahl; (aus pfingstlicher Perspektive auch die Erfüllung (Taufe) mit dem Heiligen Geist). (2) Das gemeinsame Priestertum verwirklicht sich in einem Leben in der Heiligung und der Jesusähnlichkeit. Dadurch wird erst ein geistliches Leben ermöglicht und ‚geistliche Opfer', die Gott wohlgefällig sind (1.Petr 2,5) dargebracht. (3) Das allgemeine Priestertum steht nicht in der Konkurrenz zum geistlichen Amt in der Gemeinde. Dieses ‚gemeinsame Priestertum' und das besondere *‚Priestertum des Dienstes'* (sacerdotium ministeriale) unterscheiden sich dem Wesen, nicht bloß dem Grade nach. Kann die Kirche im Ganzen als priesterliches Volk Gottes bezeichnet werden, so unterscheidet sich doch das Amt *(‚essentia et non gradu')* – dem Wesen und nicht nur dem Rang nach – vom allgemeinen Priestertum der Gläubigen.[42] Die Freikirchen haben versucht, die Menschen von einem *‚Staats- und Volkskirchentum, das durch Tradition und Kindertaufe große Teile einer Bevölkerung von Geburt an umfasst'* zu befreien, und Gemeinde von Brüdern und Schwestern im Sinne des Neuen Testaments zu sein. Bruderschaft bedeutet eine Verbundenheit unter dem gemeinsamen Vater, die Gleichgültigkeit ausschließt.[43] Obwohl alle in der Gemeinde Priester und Heilige sind, so sind dennoch die Charismen, die den einzelnen gegeben sind, verschieden, und es bedarf des geordneten Dienstes. Die Beauftragten (Amtsträger) bedürfen der Berufung Gottes und auch der Anerkennung der Gemeinde. Das priesterliche Leben geht in der Familie, im Gebet und im Liebesdienst über die Grenzen des geistlichen Amtes hinaus in das gesellschaftliche Leben, wo keine Grenze zwischen Amtsträgern und Laien existiert.[44] (4) So blieb das Priestertum aller Gläubigen lange Zeit eine weitgehend uneingelöste Entdeckung der lutherischen Reformation. Nach meiner persönlichen Sicht und Verständnis der Kirchengeschichte hat sich das Priestertum aller Gläubigen erst in freikirchlichen Kreisen zu seiner besonderen Ideelle und kirchenreformerischer Wirkungsgeschichte entfaltet. Dabei hat das Priestertum aller Gläubigen durchaus unterschiedlichen kirchlichen Erneuerungs- und Reformansätzen als Leitbegriff gedient. Verstärkt aufgegriffen wurde es von Ph.J. Spener (um 1680) in seinen Bemühungen um eine geistliche Erneuerung der Kirche (‚collegia pietatis'), dann von ‚Laien' im Rahmen

---

[42] Hünermann, Peter. Ekklesiologie im Präsens. Perspektiven. Münster: 1995. S. 191.
[43] Kreck, Walter. Grundfragen der Ekklesiologie. Chr. Kaiser Verl. München: 1981. S. 193.
[44] G. Niedermeyer. Das allgemeine Priestertum und das geistliche Amt. (ZSTh 7, 1930, S. 337-362).

der Inneren Mission durch ‚Johann H. Wichern' (um 1850). (5) Besonders aber im Raum der freikirchlichen Gemeindebewegungen (Methodisten, Baptisten, Pfingstgemeinden u.a.) wurde das Postulat zum Ausgangspunkt für Gemeindebildungen, die weniger amtszentriert waren und die Fülle und Gleichwertigkeit gemeindlicher Dienste und Funktionen betonten. Die Betonung lag darauf: „Jeder Christ ist mit den Rechten und Vollmachten des Priesters ausgestattet. Jeder Christ ein Missionar. An die Stelle des Verdienstgedankens (der Kirche Roms) tritt der Dienstgedanke. Gerettet sein gibt Rettersinn. Wesentliche Züge der neutestamentlichen Gemeinde wurden dadurch wieder auf den Leuchter gestellt. Jeremia 31,33 hat sich wirklich erfüllt.[45] Gerhard Lohfink bemerkt richtig: In der Heimkehr vom Exil hat sich zweifellos die Verheißung von Jeremia 30-31 in einem ersten Sinn recht bald erfüllt. Ein solches Herz hat es gegeben. Es war das Herz Jesu. Und alle, die sich im Glauben mit ihm verbinden, werden Anteil bekommen an seiner Kraft der ‚Tora-Treue' und an seiner in innerster Tiefe eingewurzelten Gotteserkenntnis.[46]

(6) Aus freikirchlicher Sicht gilt es, auf allen Ebenen kirchlichen Lebens Hierarchien abzubauen und Charismen der Einzelnen in der Gemeinde zu fördern und zu entfalten.

(7) Strömungen innerhalb der heutigen charismatischen Bewegung und auch Ansätze innerhalb der katholischen Basisgemeinden (L. Boff) berühren sich in dem gemeinsamen Interesse am Priestertum aller Gläubigen und in dem Bemühen, seiner theologischen Wiederentdeckung und seiner vielschichtigen kirchlichen, strukturellen Umsetzung neuen Nachdruck zu verleihen.[47]

2.5 Priestertum der Gläubigen und geistliches Amt

Die Übertragung des Priestertums allgemein auf alle Gläubigen. Die Übertragung eines ausschließlich Männern vorbehaltenen Priestertums auf beide Geschlechter:[48] *‚Und so seid ihr alle Kinder (Söhne) Gottes durch den Glauben an Jesus Christus. Denn ihr alle, die ihr auf Christus getauft worden seid, gehört nun zu Christus. Nun gibt es nicht mehr Juden oder Nichtjuden, Sklaven*

---

[45] Jeremia 31,33 *„Sondern das ist der Bund, den ich mit dem Haus Israel nach jenen Tagen schließen werde, spricht der HERR: Ich werde mein Gesetz in ihr Inneres legen und werde es auf ihr Herz schreiben. Und ich werde ihr Gott sein, und sie werden mein Volk sein."*

[46] Lohfink, Gerhard. Der niemals gekündigte Bund. Exegetische Gedanken zum christlich-jüdischen Dialog. Herder Verlag, Freiburg im Breisgau: 1998. S. 70f.

[47] Brandt, E.: Das allgemeine Priestertum im Leben der Baptistengemeinden. Una Sancta 1989. S. 91ff.

[48] Kendall, R.T. Theologie leicht gemacht. Lernen worauf es ankommt. Holzgerlingen: 2002. S. 411.

oder Freie, Männer oder Frauen. Denn ihr seid alle gleich, ihr seid eins in Jesus Christus.' (Gal 3,26-28).

Durch die Taufe in den Leib Christi sind die Gläubigen selbst zum priesterlichen Dienst berufen und ‚Geistliche' (pneumatikoi) geworden.[49] Ihr geistliches Priestertum erfüllen sie durch die Verkündigung des Evangeliums (Röm 15,16; Mission), in der Fürbitte (1Tim 2,1ff), in gegenseitiger Ermahnung und Stärkung (Kol 3,16; Gal 6,1f) und Werken der Liebe (1Kor 13; Gal 5). In solcher Hingabe bringen sie ein gottesdienstliches Opfer dar, Dank und Lob für die Versöhnung mit Gott.

Durch die Wiedergeburt sind alle Christen Glieder des geistlichen Standes und somit aller Funktionen des Amtes fähig geworden. Jedoch gilt auch dem neutestamentlichen Volk Gottes: *‚Und dient einander,* **ein jeder mit der Gabe, die er empfangen hat,** *als die guten Haushalter der mancherlei Gnade Gottes: wenn jemand predigt, dass er's rede als Gottes Wort; wenn jemand dient, dass er's tue aus der Kraft, die Gott gewährt, damit in allen Dingen Gott gepriesen werde durch Jesus Christus. Sein ist die Ehre und Gewalt von Ewigkeit zu Ewigkeit! Amen.' 1Petr 4,10-11.*

3. Textanalyse und Exegese über 1Petrus 2,5+9.

Nicht nur die Ekklesiologie des ersten Petrusbriefes und des Hebräerbriefes weist eine Ähnlichkeit auf (z.B. im Pilgermotiv), sondern der erste Petrusbrief nimmt gewisse urgemeindliche Gedanken auf und verbindet sie mit Paulinischem (vgl. 1Petr 2,4-10; Eph 2,20-22; Eph 4,12-16).[50]

Auf den Lasterkatalog (2,1) folgt eine Aufforderung, als Wiedergeborene nach der Grundnahrung, der ‚Milch' des Wortes, zu verlangen (V.2), wobei der Verfasser an die Erfahrung der Leser appelliert (V.3). Sie sollen zum auferstandenen Christus, dem ‚lebendigen Stein', herantreten (V.4), sich als ‚lebendige Steine' in das ‚geistliche Haus' der Gemeinde einfügen lassen und Gott ‚geistliche Opfer' darbringen (V.5). Das NT setzt diese Lehre vom wahren Opfer fort (Phil 2,17; Röm 12,1; Hebr 13,15; Röm 15,16; 2Tim 4,6; Offb 8,3).[51] V.6-8 folgt ein ausgedehnter ‚Schriftbeweis' für die doppelte Funktion des ‚Ecksteins' Christus, der Gottes Gnade und Gericht in einem offenbart: Jes 28,16

---

[49] Evangelisches Kirchenlexikon. [Priestertum]. EKL Bd. 3/9, S. 1326. Digitale-bibliothek/ Bd. 98.
[50] Schnackenburg, Rudolf. Die Kirche im Neuen Testament. [Questiones Disputatae]. Herder Verl. Freiburg: 1961. S. 78.
[51] Schelkle, Karl Hermann. Die Petrusbriefe; Der Judasbrief. Herders theologischer Kommentar zum Neuen Testament, Hrsg. Anton Vögtle and Rudolf Schnackenburg, Bd. 13:2. Freiburg: Herder, 1967. S. 59.

bringt zunächst die Heilsbedeutung (V.6-7a), Ps 118,22 und Jes 8,14 die Unheilsbedeutung zum Ausdruck (V.7b-8a). Zu dieser Unheilswirkung kommt es in der Begegnung mit dem Wort (V.8b). Im Unterschied zu den Ungehorsamen werden die Christen dann, und zwar vor allem mit LXX-Wendungen, als das Gottesvolk gekennzeichnet (V.9-10). Als ‚lebendiger Stein' hat Christus auch die Christen lebendig gemacht und von der Macht des Todes befreit. Als solche ‚lebendigen Steine' sollen sie sich (allerdings ist auch eine indikativische Fassung des griechischen Wortes möglich)[52] ‚aufbauen lassen' zu einem ‚geistlichen Haus', zum ‚Haus Gottes' (4,17). Nur durch Christus, und in Gemeinschaft mit ihm sind Christen lebendige Steine.[53]

Die Hoffnung auf den endzeitlichen Tempel Gottes, dessen wunderbare Errichtung vor allem die Apokalyptik erwartete, galt in der Urchristenheit als erfüllt (1Kor 3,16; wahrscheinlich auch Mk 14,58). Die christliche Gemeinde ist das endzeitliche Haus Gottes, in dem als dem ‚geistlichen Haus' der Geist Gottes herrscht (vgl. 1Kor 3,16). So gewiss dieses Haus nicht durch den Zusammenschluss der Glaubenden, sondern vom Geist geschaffen wird, so gewiss sollen sie sich in den auf Christus gegründeten Bau (vgl. V.7) einfügen lassen und an ihm die Funktion der Priester ausüben. Da alle angesprochen sind, ist die Unterscheidung zwischen ‚Priestern' und ‚Laien' aufgehoben. Alle Christen sind ‚Priester', die ‚geistliche Opfer' darbringen. Als ‚Priester' hat jeder direkten Zugang zu Gott, auch wenn wir verschiedene Aufgaben haben. ‚Geistliche Schlachtopfer' – keine wirklichen (vgl. Röm 12,1-2) (unsere eigenen Leiber Gott darbringen).

Die schon im Alten Testament begonnene ‚Spiritualisierung' des Kultes, wonach Gebet, Lob, Dank und Buße die wahren Opfer sind (Ps 50,14; 51,19; Hos 6,6; Mi 6,6ff), ist hier konsequent zu Ende geführt. Die geforderten ‚geistlichen Opfer' meinen aber nicht nur innerliche geistige Wirklichkeiten, sondern das Opfer der gesamten Existenz (Röm 12,1; Phil 4,18; Hebr 13,15f). Gott ‚wohlgefällig' werden sie ‚durch Jesus Christus', erst durch sein Eintreten erhalten sie Sinn und Wert.

---

[52] Schweizer, Eduard. Der erste Petrusbrief. Zürcher Bibelkommentare, Hrsg. Hans Heinrich Schmid, Hermann Spieckermann, und Hans Weder, Bd. 15. Zürich: Theologischer Verlag, 1998. S. 82.
[53] Schelkle, Karl Hermann. Die Petrusbriefe; Der Judasbrief. Bd. 13:2. Freiburg: Herder, 1967. S. 58.

(1.Petr 2,5) lasst euch auch selbst als lebendige Steine *(lithoi zōntes)* aufbauen, [54]
als ein geistliches Haus,[55] *(oikos pneumatikos) (eis)*
ein heiliges Priestertum, *(hierateuma hagion)* um
geistliche Schlachtopfer *(pneumatkias thusias)* darzubringen,
Gott wohlannehmbar durch Jesus Christus.

(2,9) **Ihr aber** seid ein auserwähltes *(eklekton)* Geschlecht,
ein königliches Priestertum *(herateuma)*,eine heilige *(hagion)* Nation,
ein Volk *(laos)* zum Besitztum,
damit *(hopōs)* ihr die Tugenden *(tas aretas)* dessen verkündigt, der euch aus
(ek) der Finsternis zu *(eis)* seinem wunderbaren Licht berufen hat.

Das ‚aber' steht im Gegensatz zu den Ungläubigen aus V.7 die verworfen sind; die nicht glauben; ungehorsam sind; sich über Jesus ärgern, stoßen; Was ist geschehen? Manchmal denken wir: Vielleicht ist es besser zurück zur Welt zu gehen. Aber nein! Hier ist ein Gipfel. Zustand und Schlussfolgerung für das Volk.

In den Versen 5 und 9 geht es vor allem um die Frage: Was heißt es, zu Christus zu gehören?

(1) Unsere Zugehörigkeit zu Jesus bedeutet einen neuen Lebensstil.

(2) Unsere Zugehörigkeit zu Jesus bedeutet einen neuen Standort.

Die Gemeinde Jesu, ein geistliches Haus: (a) Gebaut worauf? – Auf Christus als Grundstein. (b) Gebaut woraus? – Aus lebendigen Steinen. (c) Gebaut wofür? – Für den Dienst des Volkes von Priestern.

(3) Unsere Zugehörigkeit zu Jesus bedeutet eine neue Aufgabe.

Alle Christen sind Priester: (a) Sie kommen; (b) sie opfern; (c) sie verkündigen.

Es ist bedeutsam, dass der Apostel Petrus in V.5 das Bild vom Säugling verlassen hat. Es geht um das geistliche Haus und damit um Gottes Ehre und seinen Dienst. Das geistliche Haus umfasst die ganze Gemeinde aller Jahrhunderte auf der ganzen Erde. Wozu Gott selbst den Grund gelegt hat (V.6). Das heißt auch, dass er den geistlichen Bau geplant hat und nun ausführt. So viele Jesus als Herrn aufgenommen haben, sind lebendige Steine. Es liegt an ihnen, sich in das geistliche Haus einbauen zu lassen (Eph 2,21f). Geistlich bezeichnet nicht nur den Gegensatz zu einem stofflichen Gebäude, sondern weist auf den göttlichen Geist, der dieses Haus erfüllt (1Kor 3,16). Alle, die diesem Haus Gottes

---

[54] Feldmeier, Reinhard. Theologische Handkommentar zum NT. Der erste Brief des Petrus. Bd. 15,1. Leipzig 2005. S. 90. *„Lasst euch aufbauen'*. Die Aufforderung ist im Imperativ Passiv, macht deutlich, dass diese Gemeinschaft nicht aus ihren eigenen Beziehungen lebt, sondern durch das Wirken des Geistes in ihr gegründet und erhalten wird. (Mt 16,18).

[55] Oder: "ihr seid [zu] einem geistlichen Haus aufgebaut".

eingefügt sind, haben ihre verschiedenen und besonderen Aufgaben an dem jeweiligen Platz, an dem sie wie Steine getragen werden und gleichzeitig selber tragen. Aber nicht nur ein geistliches Haus sind sie, sondern auch – und damit wird das Bild phrasenhafter – eine heilige Priesterschaft. Wir heutigen Heidenchristen haben im Allgemeinen zu wenig Verständnis für die Größe des von Gott selbst verordneten alttestamentlichen Priestertums. Wir sind sehr oberflächlich in unserer theologischen Erkenntnis. Darum können wir so schwer die Bedeutung dieser Verse begreifen. Alttestamentliche Ämter hatten ihre Herrlichkeit, aber sie waren doch begrenzt und vorläufig (vgl. 2Kö 3,11). Die eigentliche Herrlichkeit leuchtet jetzt erst auf in Christus, im Neuen Bund an der Gemeinde. Jedes lebendige Glied in ihr ist jetzt zum Priester berufen. Im Opferdienst geht es um Gott. Er ist der Mittelpunkt allen Priestertums. Theozentrisch denkt die ganze Bibel. Von dieser Sicht her kann man auch den Menschen richtig sehen. Geistliche Opfer bedeuten: vom Geist gewirkte Opfer. Damit ist wohl angedeutet: echte geistliche Opfer können nur da gebracht werden, wo gestorben wird. Der Heilige Geist wirkt, dass jeder seinen Leib zur Verfügung stellt als ein Opfer, das da lebendig, heilig und Gott wohlgefällig ist (Röm 12,1). Unter geistlichem Opfer ist das Gebet zu verstehen (Ps 141,2; 119, 108; Offb 5,8; 8,3f) ebenso wie der Dank (Ps 50,14; V.23; 116,17), Lob und Bekenntnis des Namens Jesu (Hebr 13,15; Ps 27,6), wie auch das Wohltun und Mitteilen (Hebr 13,16; Phil 4,18); wo dem Herrn priesterlich gedient wird, kommt es stets auch zu diakonischer Verantwortung. Ebenso ist der priesterliche Dienst am Evangelium (Rö 15,16; Phil 2,17) ein Darbringen geistlicher Opfer. Die alttestamentlichen Opfer dagegen, wenn sie als Werkfrömmigkeit verstanden werden, gefallen Gott nicht, denn so spricht der Herr: *„Und wenn ihr mir auch Brandopfer und Speisopfer darbringt, so habe ich kein Wohlgefallen daran"* (Am 5,22f). Von den geistlichen Opfern aber darf man wissen, dass sie Gott wohlgefällig sind. Was alle Religionen mit großen Mühen – und dabei doch vergeblich – zu erreichen suchen, das besitzt die Gemeinde des Herrn![56] Sie kann Gott wohlgefälliges Opfer darbringen, und zwar durch Jesus Christus. Damit ist durch Jesus etwas errungen, was keine Religion kennt, nicht einmal der Alte Bund in voller Wirklichkeit.

Im starken Kontrast zu den ‚Ungehorsamen' überträgt der Verfasser im V.9 traditionelle Aussagen und Ehrentitel, die ursprünglich Israel galten, auf die Gemeinde und betont damit deren Kontinuität zum Bundesvolk des Alten Testamentes. *‚Auserwähltes Geschlecht'* zu sein – das zugrunde liegende hebräische Wort für ‚Geschlecht' wird in der Septuaginta meist mit *‚Volk'* übersetzt – war der besondere Stolz Israels. Diese Auszeichnung verdankt es nicht eigenen

---

[56] Holmer, Uwe & Werner de Boor, Wuppertaler Studienbibel: Neues Testament. Die Briefe des Petrus und der Brief des Judas, Wuppertal: 1976, 6. Auflage, R. Brockhaus Verlag, 2000. S. 83.

Vorzügen, sondern Gottes unbegreiflicher Liebe (5Mo 7,6ff; Hos 1,6.9). Auch im 1. Petrusbrief ist der Erwählungs- und Gottesvolkgedanke nicht mit dem Verdienstgedanken verbunden. In V.10 wird der Gottesvolkgedanke im Anschluss an Hos 2,25 durch den der Barmherzigkeit interpretiert: Die Glieder des Gottesvolkes sind die, die Gottes Erbarmen aus dem ‚Nicht-Volk' zum ‚Volk Gottes' verwandelte.[57]

Entscheidend aber ist das christologische und eschatologische Vorzeichen: Vom ‚erwählten Geschlecht' kann nur gesprochen werden, weil es den ‚erwählten Eckstein' (V.6) gibt, den endzeitlich ‚lebendigen Stein', der ‚bei Gott erwählt' ist (V.4). Nur darum ist dieses Geschlecht auch das ‚heilige', durch Christus geheiligte ‚Volk' (vgl. zu 1,15), dessen Eigentümer Gott ist. Dass das ganze Gottesvolk in allen seinen Gliedern aus Priestern besteht, sagte schon V.5. Hier heißt es ‚königliche Priesterschaft' – das ist die Septuaginta-Übersetzung von ‚Königreich von Priestern' (2Mo 19,6; 23,22 LXX) –, während im Anschluss an eine andere Tradition in Offb 1,6 und 5,10 beides koordiniert wird (vgl. auch Offb 20,6) und so auch die Teilhabe an der Machtausübung (in Offb 5,10 und 20,6 als Verheißung für die Zukunft) betont wird.

Wie die Welt aussieht, in die dieser Ruf ergehen soll, lässt sich aus den folgenden Abschnitten erschließen, die zur Bewährung des Christen in der Alltagswirklichkeit dieser Welt mahnen 1Petr 2,11-25.

4. Fazit

Im Gottesdienstsystem Israels wurden Priester als solche geboren, nicht dazu gemacht. Sie hatten dieses Vorrecht, weil sie zum Stamm Levi gehörten. Im neuen Bund jedoch ist Jesus der Hohe Priester und alle Gläubigen sind Priester aufgrund ihres Glaubens an ihn. Gläubige brauchen immer noch Jesus als den Mittler, der allein diese Aufgabe erfüllt. Weil sie Priester sind, können alle Gläubigen die gleiche innige Beziehung mit Gott haben. Wie Paulus an die Römer schreibt: *„Da wir nun gerechtfertigt worden sind aus Glauben, so haben wir Frieden mit Gott durch unseren Herrn Jesus Christus, durch den wir im Glauben auch Zugang erhalten haben zu dieser Gnade, in der wir stehen, ..."* (Röm 5,1-2a).

D.h. alle Gläubigen können so viel von Gott haben wie sie wollen.

Wenn wir den Herausforderungen der endzeitlichen gesellschaftlichen Umbrüche begegnen wollen, müssen wir uns als Freikirchen neu auf die biblische Ekklesiologie besinnen.

---

[57] Schweizer, Eduard. Der erste Petrusbrief. Zürcher Bibelkommentare, Hrsg. Hans Heinrich Schmid, Hermann Spieckermann und Hans Weder, Bd. 15. Zürich: Theologischer Verlag, 1998. S. 86.

Die Entwicklung einer robusten und vitalen evangelikalen Ekklesiologie ist vonnöten und würde die Integrität, das Zeugnis und die Ganzheitlichkeit der Freikirchen stärken. In kritischen Interaktionen mit bestehenden Ekklesiologien könnte die freikirchliche Theologie einen fruchtbaren Beitrag leisten. Wir müssen lernen, dass wir eine Verantwortung für das Volk haben und uns nicht auf den individualisierten Privatglauben zurückziehen. Gottes Volk lebt nicht zur Kultivierung der eigenen Frömmigkeit und kann sich nicht in selbstgenügsamer Isolierung gegen die Welt einigeln[58] (1Petr 3,15). Sonst werden wir in der Zukunft den Herausforderungen der Moderne nicht Stand halten können. Gott hat die Christen darum zu seinem Volk gemacht, damit sie seine ‚Macht- und Wundertaten öffentlich verkündigen' (Jes 43,21 ‚erzählen'). Auch sie selbst sind ja durch die Verkündigung aus der ‚Finsternis', d.h. aus Gottesferne und Unheil, aus Sünde, Irrtum und Tod, in ‚sein wunderbares Licht' gerufen worden (Eph 5,8; 1Thess 5,4f; Apg 26,18). Dieser wirksame Ruf aber soll zu allen Menschen weitergetragen werden.

Heute dürfen wir alle Menschen einladen, wie es einst Philippus im Johannesevangelium (1,35-41) gemacht hat. ‚Komm und sieh' – den geistlichen Reichtum, die rettende, befreiende und heilende Kraft die von ihr ausgeht, die Kostbarkeit ihrer Botschaft, die Schönheit der Gemeinde Jesu und die Einzigartigkeit des Volkes Gottes.

Bibliographie

Bauer, Walter, *Griechisch-deutsches Wörterbuch zu den Schriften des Neuen Testaments und der frühchristlichen Literatur*, Hrg. Kurt u. Barbara Aland, 6. völlig neu bearbeitete Aufl., Berlin, New York: Walter de Gruyter, 1988.

Brunner, Emil. *Das Mißverständnis der Kirche*. Evangelisches Verlagswerk, Stuttgart 1959.

Coenen, L. *Theologisches Begriffslexikon zum Neuen Testament* Wuppertal, Theologischer Verlag R. Brockhaus 1972.

Calvin, J. *Institutio Christianae Religionis* (Unterricht in der christlichen Religion), nach der letzten Ausgabe übersetzt und bearbeitet von Otto Weber. 5. Aufl. Neukirchen-Vluyn, 1988.

Die Heilige Schrift. *Elberfelder Bibel*. Wuppertal: R. Brockhaus Verlag, 2007.

Die Religion in Geschichte und Gegenwart. *RGG*. [Gemeinde]. J.C.B. Mohr (Paul Siebeck). Digitale-Bibliothek/Band 12. 3. Auflage, Tübingen 2006.

---

[58] Schweizer, Eduard. Der erste Petrusbrief. Zürcher Bibelkommentare, Hrsg. Hans Heinrich Schmid, Hermann Spieckermann und Hans Weder, Bd. 15. Zürich: Theologischer Verlag, 1998. S. 82

Dietzfelbinger, Ernst, *Das Neue Testament: Interlinearübersetzung Griechisch-Deutsch*, Neuhausen-Stuttgart: Hänssler Verlag, 1986.

Elberfelder Studienbibel mit Sprachschlüssel: Das Neue Testament: Wuppertal 1994. 4. Aufl., Wuppertal: R. Brockhaus Verlag, 2000. Elektronische Ausgabe.

Fallbusch, E. Jan M. Lochman u.a. Hrsg. *Evangelisches Kirchenlexikon*, Gemeinde. 3. Aufl. Digitale-Bibliothek Band 98. Göttingen, Vandenhoeck & Ruprecht 1985-1997.

Feldmeier, Reinhard. *Theologischer Handkommentar zum NT. Der erste Brief des Petrus*. Bd. 15,1. Leipzig 2005.

Freikirchenhandbuch. Informationen, Anschriften, Texte, Berichte. Hrg. Vereinigung Evangelischer Freikirchen, Brockhaus Verl. Wuppertal 2004. Klaus Peter Voß.

Geldbach, Erich. *Freikirchen. Erbe, Gestalt und Wirkung*. Bensheimer Hefte 70. Göttingen, Vandenhoeck & Ruprecht, 2005.

Goppelt, Leonhard, *Der erste Petrusbrief*, Hrg. Ferdinand Hahn, Meyers Kritisch-Exegetischer Kommentar über das Neue Testament, Bd. 7, 1. Aufl. dieser Neubearbeitung, Göttingen: Vandenhoeck & Ruprecht.

Grenz, Stanley. J. *Created for Community. Connecting Christian Belief with Christian Living*. 2. Aufl. Baker Book House, Grand Michigan 1998.

Haubeck, Wilfried / Heinrich von Siebenthal. *Neuer sprachlicher Schlüssel zum griechischen Neuen Testament*, Bd. 2: Römer – Offenbarung, Gießen: Brunnen Verlag, 1994. Elektronische Ausgabe.

Holmer, Uwe & Werner de Boor, Wuppertaler Studienbibel: Neues Testament. *Die Briefe des Petrus und der Brief des Judas*, Hrg. Werner DeBoor & Adolf Pohl, Wuppertal: 1976, 6. Aufl., R. Brockhaus Verlag, 2000.

Hünermann, Peter. *Ekklesiologie im Präsens. Perspektiven*. Münster 1995.

Kreck, Walter. *Grundfragen der Ekklesiologie*. Chr. Kaiser Verl. München 1981.

Lohfink, Gerhard. *Der niemals gekündigte Bund. Exegetische Gedanken zum christlich-jüdischen Dialog*. Herder Verlag Freiburg im Breisgau 1998.

Luther, Martin. *Kritische Gesamtausgabe*. Weimar 1883ff.

Markus, Liebelt. *Allgemeines Priestertum, Charisma und Struktur*. Wuppertal 2000.

Melzer, Friso. *Das Wort in den Wörtern. Die deutsche Sprache im Dienst der Christus-Nachfolge. Ein theo-philologisches Wörterbuch*. Tübingen 1965.

Mülhaupt, Erwin. *Allgemeines Priestertum oder Klerikalismus?* Stuttgart 1963.

Niedermeyer, G. *Das allgemeine Priestertum und das geistliche Amt*. (ZSTh 7, 1930, Zeitschrift für systematische Theologie (7/1930), (Gütersloh) Berlin 1923-1957.

Ratzinger, Josef. *Zur Gemeinschaft gerufen. Kirche heute verstehen.* Freiburg, i. Br. 1991.

Rieker, Siegbert. SBB. *Ein Priestervolk für alle Völker. Der Segensauftrag Israels für alle Nationen in der Tora und den vorderen Propheten.* Stuttgart 2007.

Schlatter, A., *Erläuterungen zum Neuen Testament: Die Briefe des Petrus, Judas und Johannes ausgelegt für Bibelleser*, 4. Aufl., Stuttgart: Calwer Vereinsbuchhandlung, 1923.

Schelkle, Karl Hermann. *Die Petrusbriefe; Der Judasbrief.* 5. Aufl. Herders theologischer Kommentar zum Neuen Testament, Hrg. Anton Vögtle and Rudolf Schnackenburg, Bd. 13:2. Freiburg: Herder, 1967.

Schnackenburg, Rudolf. *Die Kirche im Neuen Testament.* [Questiones Disputatae]. Herder Verl. Freiburg 1961.

Umwelt des Urchristentums, Hrg. Johannes Leipoldt / Walter Grundmann, Bd. 1: Darstellung des neutestamentlichen Zeitalters, 1966, 8. Aufl., Berlin: Evangelische Verlagsanstalt, 1990.

Voss, Klaus Peter: *Der Gedanke des allgemeinen Priester- und Prophetentums. Seine gemeindetheologische Aktualisierung in der Reformationszeit.* R. Brockhaus, Wuppertal 1990.

Abstract

Priesthood of All Believers – An Evangelical Perspective

In this article I want to focus on one aspect of ecclesiology, e.g. *"the priesthood of all believers."* As a first step I want to discuss the terms "church" and "fellowship" by looking at Scripture and their use in church history. The church is the community of men and women that was called into existence by the word of God and are called out by Jesus Christ and the Holy Spirit in order to minister in this world. From the *perspective of the "free churches"* we do not constitute a church simply because of the fact that people have assembled together, but: *a church is constituted wherever believers surrender to the authority of Christ and the leading and the authority of the Holy Spirit.* He brings together the members of the body (1Cor 12:13). He coordinates its functions from the head down (Eph 4:15-16). Members must not dominate each other and man can never be the foundation of the church (1Cor 3:4-8).

The topic **Priesthood of All Believers** calls upon us to take a look into church history. It reveals to us the reason for the existence of free churches as we study in particular the development of the priesthood in the Bible. For this purpose we do have to undertake a study of the OT, which at times has been overlooked in the past. This gives us a new perspective on the priesthood of Christ and the position and responsibility of every individual believer. This is important, because also in the free churches there is the danger that the emphasis on formal issues quenches the spiritual life in the church. According to Paul the life of a Christian and the church has to be a "reasonable service" (Rom 12:1). We have to remain open that the local church is a place that is open for the Holy Spirit and that everybody can share his gifts. The priesthood of all believers shows the connection of God to his people. They are a *"Royal Priesthood"* (Ex 19:6) and a *"Holy Nation"* (Ex 19:6; Lev 11:44ff; Num 15:40; 1Pet 2:4-9). Unfortunately, the prophets had to challenge the Priests and Levites at times, however, because they did not fulfill their duties (Isa 34).

It was always the Spirit of God that brought revival to the church. At times such an awakening came as a surprise and unexpectedly. This principle is still true today. Just think of the visit of Samuel to Bethlehem. He was supposed to anoint a new king and had thus only eyes for Isai. This is what frequently happened in the Word of God. But God moves in different ways than what we expect and plan for. The History of Jesus has become salvation history. If we want to stand the challenges and changes in our society we do have to emphasize a Biblical ecclesiology as free churches. A solid and developed ecclesiology will strengthen the integrity of the free churches.

Eugen Jugaru

A Comparative Study of the Orthodox and the Evangelical Perspective in Light of Historical and Biblical Teaching on Priesthood

Introduction

The priestly office, regardless of its religious tradition, has held an important position in the history of the Christian church throughout the ages. Even today, the Orthodox priest in his black robe or the Evangelical pastor in his "civil garment" is a public figure who is often invited to present his opinion regarding moral or social affairs. In spite of priest and pastor gathering together around the table or around the microphone, there is still an invisible dividing wall between Orthodox and Evangelical. I noticed this reserved attitude in my own country of Romania, which previously was a communist country. It is true that after the Revolution of 1989, things appeared to change, at least at the academic level. For example, some Evangelicals with a Bachelor or Master degree are continuing their studies for a Doctorate degree in Orthodox Universities. The question is: will the ecumenical force pull down that dividing wall, sometime in the future, or will the distance between them remain or increase?

In this article, I will present a comparative study of two different approaches in perspectives concerning the priestly office: Eastern Orthodoxy and Evangelical. As a starting point, I found that the Orthodox priest has a historical advantage due to the length of Orthodox Church history, while the Evangelical priest, who has been molded by a democratic society, seeks to understand and strives to better fit in our postmodern time. The Evangelical priest can relate in a more personal way toward people and toward the needs of the people, since he experienced the double conversion: from the world to the Lord, and then from the Lord to the world's needs. Evangelicals are speaking more often about universal priesthood rather than of the office of the priest, in contrast, the Orthodox traditional views are opposite. The universal priesthood proved its power when it was clearly explained by Christian preachers and released for Christian service. The practical aspect of universal priesthood teaching can be seen during the history of the spiritual awakening or in the numerous Evangelical movements as Anabaptists, Quakers, Puritans, Methodists, Baptists, Pentecostals or independent Charismatic churches.

The debate in the Christian world surrounding the concept of priesthood is an important issue, for it can provide a bridge of communication between different Christian traditions and can open the door for ecumenical understanding. Only when we can grasp a clear understanding about this subject, will we be able to better understand what new issues develop in communication, or contrarily, what new obstacles hinder the dialogue between different Christian churches or organizations.

> *The next great revival of Christendom will not come through the minister, the professional servants of God, but through the laity.*
>
> E. Stanley Jones

1. The Importance of the Study of Priesthood

Today, in the new socio-political and theological environment and in a global and a postmodern culture, the concept of priesthood, whether the individual priest or the universal priesthood of all Christians, looks to draw special interest. More than twenty years ago, Noel Titus underlined the same idea in his paper, *The Ordained Ministry and the Christian Koinonia,* when he writes that the ministry of the church has been the topic of considerable discussion in recent years.[1]

At the present time, in an era of consumerism, when people developed a consumerist mentality, religion and the priest can be seen as a spiritual institute or a person who offers spiritual service to satisfy the religious needs of people.

This understanding is accepted by Evangelicals since the role of the priest or pastor is not a sacerdotal one, but more of a duty to feed the flock spiritually and to help each believer to develop his or her spiritual calling. Since Christ as High Priest sacrificed his body for the benefit of humanity, every believer has to offer his energy and personal gifts for their neighbor's benefit. In an age of selfishness, in an individualistic and materialistic era, this teaching can be a revolutionary teaching if it is well developed and wisely sustained.

The importance of the study of this subject, from the Evangelical and the Orthodox perspective, can better us to understand both the Evangelical spiritual heritage and the Orthodox tradition. If we prove to have an interest in this topic, we can study the ecclesiology of both traditions and we can notice the "common ground" along with the differences between these two theological approaches. Furthermore, understanding this subject, from a theological and historical perspective, will offer us the opportunity to rethink the importance of Christian service, for in this postmodern time, the priest is a servant of God and people.

---

[1] Noel Titus, *The Ordained Ministry and the Christian Koinonia,* The Journal of Religious Thought, vol. 44, Summer-Fall 1987, Howard University School of Divinity, p. 64.

From a practical perspective, the concept of "universal priesthood" can hold a main impact in postmodern society since all Christians have to be "priests" as workers in their work place, in the schools as students or in other public areas of life. The concept of "universal priesthood" is an important theological force which was released since the Reformation, and thus during the history of the church when the true meaning of this concept was understood.

It is important to remember Dietrich Bonhoeffer's words, that the church is the church only when it exists for others.[2] At the same time, the function of the priesthood only gets its true meaning when it is directed for other people.

In this article I will develop the concept of priesthood from an Evangelical and Orthodox perspective. The Evangelical movement began during the sixteenth century when the Catholic priest Martin Luther, 'divorced' by the Roman Catholic Church, influenced with his new attitude a large mass of people in Germany and abroad. We will notice that Luther was more prolific in writings and debates on this subject than Calvin, though Calvin produced a *magnum opus* as *Institutio Christianae Religionis*.

2. The Evangelical Movement and Its Perspective upon the Concept of Priesthood

The concept of the priesthood of all believers was a powerful ideal for the Evangelical movement from the beginning.[3] From long ago they saw the importance of lay people as an active spiritual body in the social and ecclesial life. Actually, the term *lay* is not the best term to designate a group of Christians, for all Christians, lay, priests or pastors have the same value before God, and they are all children of God.[4] Karl Barth says that the term 'laity' is one of the worst in the vocabulary of religion and ought to be banished from Christian conversation.[5]

According to the Evangelical understanding, spiritual conversion is reflected in a high spiritual standard, a clear responsibility for personal behavior and a

---

[2] Dietrich Bonhoeffer, *Letters and papers from Prison*, New York, Touchstone, 1997, p. 382.
[3] Deryck W. Lovegrove *The Rise of the Laity in Evangelical Protestantism*, London, Routledge, 2002, p. 149.
[4] Paus Stevens defines 'lay' by *function* (does not administer the Word and sacraments), by *status* (does not have a 'Rev.'), by *location* (serves primarily in the world), by *education* (is not theologically trained), by *remuneration* (is not full-time and paid) and by *lifestyle* (is not religious but occupied with secular life) – usually in terms of negatives. (Paul R. Stevens, *The Other Six Days*, Grand Rapids, Mich.: W.B. Eerdmans, 1999, pp. 24-25).
[5] *Theologische Fragen und Antworten* (1957), quoted in R.J. Erler and R. Marquard (eds.), trans G.W. Bromiley, *A Karl Barth Reader*, (Grand Rapids: Eerdmans, 1986), p. 8-9.

great dignity for humanity. In this way, the Evangelicals developed the concept of universal priesthood, as the liberation of the individual by placing the responsibility for salvation on the believer's side. Actually, the Evangelicals sustain mainly four assumptions: (1) The authority of the Bible as God inspired Word for Christian living; (2) The act of redemption through Jesus Christ's sacrifice. Salvation is an act of unmerited divine grace received through faith in Christ, excluding for salvation any kind of penance or good works; (3) The personal experience of conversion and (4) The importance of spreading the good news of the gospel.[6] All these four issues are the central core of Evangelical beliefs. Besides this core, the Evangelicals share a number of doctrines with other Orthodox Christians: the doctrines of Trinity, the virgin birth of Christ, Christ's incarnation and bodily resurrection, miracles, the church as the body of Christ, the sacraments as sign of grace, immortality of the soul and final resurrection.[7]

The priesthood concept of all believers offered the base for an open worship and service, universal priesthood carries the concept that leaders (bishops, ministers, or elders) are *not to demand,* but they can encourage believers to confess their sins, since confession is a biblical teaching (James 5:16). This kind of priesthood brings equal privileges and equal responsibility to exercise in love their different spiritual gifts for the good of all.[8]

We have to notice that the opinions regarding the importance of the universal priesthood are not the same with different Evangelical theologians. For instance, for some, this concept is central in Evangelical theology, but for others like J.M. Ross, the doctrine did not get special attention until recently. He sustained that this doctrine is not fundamental in Christian thought and he warned those who try to put this doctrine in a central place or to think that the doctrine held a main role in the Reformers thought, will be disappointed because the doctrine did not get a prominence until the ladder half of the nineteenth century.[9] He sustained his point of view by stating that the doctrine was supposed to be characteristic of the English Free Church, and is difficult to find it in any representative writings about the priesthood of all believers in that tradition.

---

[6] For further information see *Evangelicalism* in *Christian Theology An Introduction*, by Alister E. McGrath, 2. ed., Cambridge, Blackwell Publishing Inc., 1997, pp. 121-124.

[7] *Evangelical Dictionary of Theology*, pp. 406-407.

[8] Gordon R. Lewis, Bruce A. Demarest, *Interrogative Theology*, Grand Rapids, Michigan, Zondervan, 1996, vol. 3, p. 274.

[9] J.M. Ross, "The priesthood of all Believers", in *The Expository Times*, Published by SAGE, 1951, p. 45.

This concept cannot be found in the Westminster Confession of Faith, neither the Savoy Declaration.[10]

For the Evangelicals, every Christian is a priest called to bring a "living sacrifice, holy, acceptable unto God" (Rom 12:1). The concept of the priesthood of all believers, along with the supremacy of the Bible and justification by grace, stay together at the heart of Protestantism.[11] Although, the medieval church developed the sacerdotal concept of the priesthood where the priest was seen as mediator between people and God, and in this way divided Christians into two classes, the clergy and the lay people, the Protestant theology of justification by faith pulled down these two Christian classes which distinguished and equalized the differences between all Christians. Church history shows that during at the height of the Middle Ages, the clerical theory was elevated to such a degree that any concept of a wider or universal priesthood was virtually obscured. Actually, R. Niebuhr explained the distinction between a priest-minister who ministers in an historical church and a preacher-minister of the Reformation in this way: firstly, from Chrysostom to Pius XI, there accentuated the importance of the work of administering the sacraments, he is a minister of sacraments, in this way he is always the mediator between God and humanity, while secondly, the preacher-minister of the Reformation churches found his main function in preaching. Regarding the authority, the priest authority is institutional, his ordination is mentioned first, then his personal discipline of life, and the study of the Scriptures, but for the Reformed preacher, ordination plays no such role in his accreditation, as do the study of the Bible, because he obtains the actual power from the Bible and from his discipline of the life.[12]

Evangelicals do not promote a hierarchy, nor a priestly succession, but sustain the concept of universal priesthood, or the priesthood of all believers. They share the same concept with Eduard Schweitzer who underlined the idea that the writers of the New Testament consistently refused to make any distinction between an official ministry of a select person and that of any believer.[13] From the Evangelical perspective, the doctrine contains twofold aspects: firstly, the vertical dimension where every believer has direct access to God without a

---

[10] The online version of this article can be found in http://www.ext.sagepub.com.

[11] J.M. Ross opinion sustain that this concept is less important as some theologians supposed. (J.M. Ross's article The Priesthood of all Believers, in The Expository Times, p. 45. The online version of this article can be found at: http://ext.sagepub.com).

[12] H.R. Niebuhr, *The Purpose of the Church and Its Ministry*, in http://www.religion-online.org.

[13] R.E. Schweitzer, 'Ministry in the Early Church' in D.N. Freedman (ed.), *Anchor Bible Dictionary*, vol. 4, New York, Doubleday, 1992, p. 836.

mediator, just like a priest in the ancient time,[14] and secondly, the horizontal dimension, the activist dimension where every believer based on his or her calling has a ministry to perform. William Robinson notice that the concept of "calling" in the New Testament always refers to all Christians and not to what we style ministries, for all Christians are ministers "called" to ministry.[15] Every born again Christian is called to develop these two dimensions; worship before God; and of serving before people. Evangelicals sustain the idea that all believers have direct access to God; this privilege does not cancel the teaching ministry, confession or the leadership concept in the church. This understanding of the priesthood concept creates a new kind of brotherhood where every Christian has responsibility for his or her fellow neighbor, and who also has a duty to represent their needs before God, to pray for others, to intercede with God, to proclaim the Word and also the confession of sins. By this teaching and practice the clerical class disappeared and the lay activities increased. By the personal spiritual gifts and vocation of every Christian, the hierarchy is smoothed into a Christian democracy, and the risk to appear as a professional clergy class disappears. In Paul Stevens' definition the "clericalism" is the domination of the ordinary people by those ordained, trained and invested with privilege and power, while the "anticlericalism" is the domination of the laity and the rejection of ordained church leadership.[16]

The priesthood of all believers is a comprehensive concept because it is a spiritual privilege, a moral obligation, and a personal vocation.[17] For every Christian it is a great privilege, and a spiritual benefit to be a priest of God and to access in His presence, but this privilege also brings responsibilities. Every Christian is responsible to embody the gospel, to minister for the church and for the society where he or she is living. Since every Christian has received a spiritual gift from God, every one has the responsibility to perform functions with that gift, to minister and to be a spiritual sustainer of fellow Christians. According to the Biblical teaching, every Christian has the grace for service toward God, toward fellow Christians and toward society. Paul speaks of believers generally as servants of God, and by their service the church is enabled to grow in maturity.[18] According to the Evangelical understanding, all Chris-

---

[14] The most quoted Bible texts for sustaining the doctrine of the priesthood of all believers are: Ex 19:6; Ps 50:23; Ps 51:17-19; Ps 141:2; 1Pet 2:5-9; Heb 13:10-16.

[15] William Robinson, *Completing the Reformation*, Lexington, The College of the Bible, 1955, pp.19-20.

[16] Paul R. Stevens, *The Other Six Days*, p. 52.

[17] Cyril Eastwood, *The Priesthood of all Believers*, Minneapolis, Augsburg Publishing House, 1962, p. 80.

[18] C.G. Kruse, 'Servants of God', in *Dictionary of Paul and His Letters*, Gerald F. Hawthrone, Ralph P. Martin, Daniel G. Reid (editors), Downers Grove, ILL, *IVP*, 1993, p. 870.

tians are "a royal priesthood" (1Pet 2:9) and "a holy priesthood" called "to offer spiritual sacrifices, acceptable to God by Jesus Christ" (1Pet 2:5). To fulfill the priestly ministry means that someone has to share in the continuing high-priestly work of Christ by offering themselves in love and obedience to God and in love and service of men.[19] The call of Christians to priesthood is a means to provide a service in society, therefore mixing the spiritual life with the social life in a daily personal experience. The intercessory prayer of the believers is seen as the censer on the altar, is also a priestly work (Rev 8:3). We can conclude with Paul Stevens who developed in his book, *The Other Six Days,* the concept that there are three dimensions of priestly ministry for the people of God: first, is the priestly ministry of access to God through worship and intercession, second, is the priestly ministry through service in the world, and third, is a priestly ministry in daily life. According with his view we bless God with worship and we bless the world with the presence of God.[20]

In the Evangelical world, the priesthood office embraces a large perspective, for every born again Christian is a priest, thus a part of the universal priesthood. According with Paul R. Stevens, we look in vain in the New Testament for a theology of the laity, because there are neither laypersons nor clergy.

> The word 'layperson' *(laikoi)* was first used by Clement of Rome at the end of the first century, but was never used by an inspired Apostle in Scripture to designate second-class, untrained and unequipped Christians...Ironically the church in its constitution is a people without laity in the usual sense of the word, but full of clergy in the true senses of the word – endowed, commissioned and appointed by God to continue God's own service and mission in the world.[21]

In conclusion, although the Eastern Orthodox teaching does not reject the concept of universal priesthood, they have not developed it either. From the Evangelical perspective the universal priesthood is not opposite and does not exclude the officer elected.[22] Both churches, the Evangelical and the Eastern Orthodox Church agree that the priesthood function is to bring spiritual sacrifice to God, and the root of the teaching is based on the Bible.

---

[19] T.W. Manson, *Ministry and Priesthood: Christ's and Ours*, London, Epworth Press, 1958, p. 70.

[20] Paul R. Stevens, *The Other Six Days*, Grand Rapids, W.B. Eerdmans, 1999, p. 180.

[21] Paul R. Stevens, *The Other Six Days*, p. 5.

[22] Sergius Bulgakov, *The Orthodox Church*, London, Centenary Press, 1935, p. 56.

3. The Roots of the Evangelical Concept of Priesthood

> *"Luther's greatest contribution to Protestant ecclesiology was his doctrine of the priesthood of all believers."*[23]
>
> Timothy George

We find the roots of the Evangelical concept of priesthood in the Reformers writings, especially in Luther's. When we study the priesthood concept during the church's history we realize that the 'priesthood' title does not seem to be applied to Christian ministries until the third century. Very clearly Loraine Boettner affirms that, first century Christianity did not have a priest, for not anywhere in the New Testament does it use the word 'priest' to describe a leader in his service.[24] During the third century, Cyprian (d. 258) Bishop of Carthage used in a paradigmatic way the Old Testament priesthood for a new perspective upon New Testament imagery. An interesting historical perspective was brought on this topic by H. Kranmer when he wrote:

> The first prominent theological thinkers on behalf of the Church were laymen of great ability. To mention only a few of the very prominent: Tertullian, Cyprian, Augustine. Cyprian and Augustine, having become bishops so to speak by surprise, where essentially, by their whole education and long 'secular career', laymen.[25]

After the medieval times, when the priesthood concept reached the highest importance, especially in the Roman Catholic Church, the Reformers rejected in general the term 'priest' because it came to be seen in connection with the Mass.[26]

The Reformers, especially Martin Luther brought a new perspective about the priestly ministry, even to the point of risking his life. Luther played a very important role in Christian history by his courage to expose the unbiblical practice of the medieval Church, and by his new theological approach, especially for his study and conclusions about the theology of the Apostle Paul. His effort was to represent Christian experience, not as hierarchical statutes, but as a personal and open experience of the grace of God for every believer. For that purpose, his foundation was theology linked with practical involvement. This new theological approaching opened a large gate for a liberating movement for all

---

[23] Timothy George, *Theology of the Reformers*, Nashville TN, Broadman Press, 1988, p. 95.

[24] Loraine Boettner, *Roman Catholicism*, Phillipsburg, The Presbyterian and reformed Publishing Company, 1962, p. 50.

[25] H. Kraemer, *A Theology of the Laity*, London, Lutterworth Press, 1958, pp. 20-21.

[26] Watson E. Milles, in *The New International Dictionary of the Christian Church*, p. 802.

Christians, for church laity, and at the same time it causes a denial of the control of the institutional church. Luther could not accept the idea that salvation is encapsulate in the Roman priesthood office and diffused through the sacraments, so he added the universal priesthood of believers in contrast to Roman claims for an exclusive priesthood of the ordained clergy.[27] As Theodore A. Gill writes, "Martin Luther made the priesthood of all believers a touchstone for the true church and a mark of the Reformation's faithfulness to an original Christianity too long subverted."[28]

In his theological incursion, besides theological concept as *sola scriputra, sola fide,* Luther also developed the concept of the priesthood of all believers.[29] Luther turned seriously to the Bible and developed his teaching based firstly on the Word of God. His teaching about individual conversion, the authority of Scripture and justification by faith, all these concepts empowered the laity because they put the individual outside of institutional frameworks. As Moses in the Old Testament called the nation of Israel to be a nation of priests, Luther understood the church in the same manner, as a gathering of priests and the priesthood of all believers and this was a central teaching of his.[30] We can say that the concept of universal priesthood in Luther's writings sprung out from his understanding of the concept of justification. In Luther's theological thinking, if justification is true only by personal faith, the sacerdotal and all clergy ministries remain without biblical support.

Martin Luther articulated his doctrine about the priesthood of all believers during the year 1520, when he waited the bull of excommunication, especially by his writings: *Treatise to the Christian Nobility of the German Nation, The Babylonian Captivity of the Church,* and *A Treatise on Christian Liberty.* He defined for the first time the notion of the priesthood of all believers[31] in his; *Treatise to the Christian Nobility of the German Nation* (1520) writing. He did not accept the medieval belief that Christians were to be divided in two classes: the clerics and the remainder of the Christians. We are not wrong to say that when Luther rejected the concept of hierarchy within Christianity, actually he

---

[27] *International Dictionary of Pentecostal and Charismatic Movements,* S. Burgess (Editor), p. 613.

[28] Priesthood of Believer, Theodore A. Gill, reprinted in *Theology Today,* vol. 15, no. 3, Oct. 1958, pp. 302-303.

[29] Carl Raschke, *The Next Reformation,* Grand Rapids, Michigan, Baker Academic, 2004, p. 26.

[30] Idem. p. 26.

[31] M. Luther, *To the Christian Nobility of the German Nation* in *Luther's Works,* ed. J. Pelikan and H.T. Lehmann, 55 vol., St Louis, Concordia; Philadelphia, Fortress Press, 1955-1986, vol. 44, pp. 127, 129.

democratized the church, he gave the authority to the congregation saying that "Christ takes both the right and the power to judge teaching from the bishop, scholars, and councils and gives it to everyone, and to all Christians equally when he says, *"My sheep know my voice"* (Jn 10:4)."[32] More than that, ordination has value and takes place only through the authority of the universal priesthood, not through the bishop's authority to ordain.[33] In other words, the authority for ministry did not come from a dominant position of the bishop, but from below, from the universal priesthood of the church.[34]

In his book, *The Babylonian Captivity of the Church,* Luther wrote very boldly against the Roman Catholic Church, he based his universal priesthood teaching on the practice of the baptism.[35] The baptism played an important role in the Christian life since all baptized Christians are in the spiritual priesthood (1Pet 2:9). He wrote: "We are all priests, as many of us are Christians. But the priests, as we call them, are ministers chosen from among us. All that they do is done in our name."[36] For Luther it was not an external appearance as a head shaved, or hair cut short that transformed someone into a priest, but union with Christ, like a marriage, through baptism. The position of the priest is obtained by baptism, because in that way, someone is incorporated in Christ, and becomes one with Him, who is the only true High Priest. Based on that spiritual unity the Christian becomes a priest, belonging to the priesthood of all believers.

In his, *Commentary on the Book of Isaiah,* Luther says that the title priest must not be applied to a particular person in the New Testament, but those who build up the ruins and convert people are the priests.[37] In his understanding, all Christians who worship God are consecrated and fit for the priestly office, and from this point on, there is not any difference between the consecrated and unconsecrated, because the Spirit of God consecrated all of them, they are priests taught by the Lord.[38] The genesis of the universal priesthood came not from the apostolic succession but from the true spiritual union between Christians and Christ. This spiritual union with Christ and the act of crucifying the old nature was the necessary condition for every Christian to fulfill his calling. Based on

---

[32] *Luther's Works*, Am. ed., vol. 39, pp. 306-307.
[33] *Treatise to the Christian Nobility of the German Nation* (1520), *LW* 44, pp. 127-128.
[34] *Luther's Concept of the Ministry: The Creative Tension*, Mark Ellingsen, Journal Word & World, vol. 1, no. 4, Fall 1981, p. 342.
[35] Luther rejected the authority of the Roman Catholic Church to rule over the Christian except if the Christians agree that ruling (See *LW*, vol. 36, p. 112).
[36] *The Babylonian Captivity of the Church*, (1520), *LW* 36, p. 113.
[37] *Lectures on Isaiah*, Ch. 40-66, *L.W.*, vol. 17, J.J. Pelikan, H.C. Oswald & H.T. Lehmann, Ed., *LW*, Saint Louis, Concordia Publishing House, p. 337.
[38] *Minor Prophets III: Zechariah*, *L.W.* vol. 20, J.J. Pelikan, H.C. Oswald & H.T. Lehmann, Ed.

this historical event of crucifixion, is at the same time mystical, resulted a brotherhood linking between Christ and Christians. The logic of Luther was clear: "Since Christ is the priest and we are His brothers, all Christians have the authority, the command, and the obligation to preach, to come before God, to pray for one another, and to offer themselves as a sacrifice to God."[39]

By his teaching regarding the universal priesthood, Luther eliminated the celibate priestly strata and involved the Christians in evangelization with a greater accent on the Christian responsibility.

The concept of priesthood seen as an intermediate spiritual group between the laity and God vanished. It seems that the concept of universal priesthood appears as a contradiction in terms, because the priest by definition is almost singular. Luther views the priesthood in its spiritual dimension because faith is a vibrant and a vertical connection between Christians and Christ. As a result of this vertical dimension the Christian, as an individual, is able to develop horizontal relationship with other Christians.

Developing the priesthood of all believers, Luther proved his ability to make every Christians important. For a long time, the Christians seemed to be unimportant, until Luther propagated the doctrine that every Christian is someone else's priest, thus, the ecclesiology received a new force. No one is left outside of Christian work, but everyone has his or her special calling.[40] He dismissed the medieval idea that there are two different classes of Christians: the priest's class seen as spiritual and the lay's class seen as a temporal Christian class.

In spite of his courage and bold attitude against the Roman Catholic Church, Luther did not go further in applying the concept to daily and practical life. Emil Brunner shows that neither Luther nor any other of the Reformers took this "universal priesthood" seriously in practice.[41] This is an interesting affirmation for when studying Luther's writings very often we find allusions to the priesthood of all Christians. At the same time, Brunner can be right in his affirmation because theoretically Luther developed the above concept, but prac-

---

[39] *Luther's Works*, American Edition, vol. 36, p. 145.

[40] We can notice here H.R. Niebuhr the four elements of someone's calling: (1) the call to be a Christian, who is the foundation for the following callings; (2) the secret call, when a person fill in his or her heart the invitation of God; (3) the providential call, who stress the equipping of the person with the talents necessary for the exercise of the office; (4) the ecclesial call, the summons and invitation extended to a man by some community or institution of the Church to engage in the work of the ministry. (H.R. Niebuhr, *"The Purpose of the Church and Its Ministry"*, in http://www.religion-online.org).

[41] Emil Brunner, *Dogmatics III*, Cambridge, James Clarke & Co., reprinted in 2002, p. 99.

tically we cannot see how Luther applied this concept, how he involved lay preachers in the ministry.[42]

Trying to simplify Luther's conception we can understand that he developed two lines of thought when he spoke about the priesthood, of two kinds of authority: authority *from below* and authority *from above*. As a minister with authority from below, the pastor is a facilitator of the congregation to minister the Word and Communion. As a minister with authority from above, the pastor has the right to exercise authority over the congregation, to have a prophetical function, because the ministry is directly instituted by Christ. This way of thinking distinguished pastor and laity and stresses the pastoral ministry. In spite of this, all Christians are "a royal priesthood", but not all of them share the same spiritual gifts, not all have the calling to preach the Word and to administer Communion. His reason for non-implication of the lay people in the ministry was to keep order in the church, and to raise a barrier against chaos. Therefore, for someone to preach and administer Communion it was necessary to be ordained, otherwise he would not have a reason to minister. Luther says that "There must be bishops, pastors, or preachers...otherwise, what would happen if everyone wanted to speak or administer, and no one wanted to give way to the other? It must be trusted to one person, and he alone should be allowed to preach, to baptize, to absolve, and to administer the sacraments."[43]

In Luther's understanding the priestly office consists in three parts: to teach or to preach God's Word, to sacrifice, and to pray. Anyone who pretends he is a priest but does not exercise these functions does not deserve to be called a priest, because this title is a high one, the priest is "an angel of God" (Mal 2:7). His responsibility or first duty is to imitate Christ in teaching people God's Word and doctrine, not his own.[44] Christ bestows the title of priests upon all Christians because they all are called priests after Him. Luther was so convinced about this that he was ready to say that in the virtue of baptism every Christian is called a priest, just as much as Apostle Peter or Paul. The name "priest" ought to be the common possession or property of believers just as much as the name "Christian" or "child of God".

---

[42] The same attitude is adopted by Steven Paul to explain "the incomplete Protestant Reformation". He notice following factors: the focus of the Reformation was more on the soteriology than on ecclesiology; the replacement of priest with the preacher, the adopted the Catholic seminary system, the kingly ministry eclipsed by church ministry, the ordination for full-time church worker and not an adequate recognition of lay ministry. (Stevens Paul *The Other Six Days*, pp. 45-48).

[43] *Luther's Works*, Am. ed., vol. 41, (St. Louis: Concordia Publishing House and Philadelphia: Fortress Press, 1955) p. 154. He says also that is obvious that "All are priests, but not all are the pastors" (*L.W.*, Am. ed., vol. 13, p. 65).

[44] Idem, pp. 307-328.

In spite of his democratic attitude regarding the involvement of every Christian in ministry, he was cautious that the church does not become an anarchical gathering. He was totally against those "who qualify themselves and preach whatever they please"[45]. For instance, even though anyone can understand and preach the Word, still this *minister verbi divini* has the right to preach in the church, but has not the right to draw the attention of the congregation upon his own person by assuming this office on his own. The congregation has to recognize someone's calling to preach. Luther did not recognize as preachers the "sectarians" who claimed that they had been called to preach their doctrines from place to place, even though they were saying that their calling was directly from the Holy Spirit. For Luther, they were just liars and impostors.[46] The preacher has to "be called and chosen to preach and to teach in the place of and by the command of others"[47].

All Christians are priests, even though they do not wear special garments and external accessories, they are priests because Christ, the High Priest ordained Christians as priests, and the Holy Spirit clothed them in His power and bestowed spiritual gifts on them. Many of those who claimed that they were priests, according with Luther, have never read a single word in Scripture, and some of them do not know the Children's Creed or the Ten Commandments. The real priests are united with Christ and suffer for the sake of Christ and for the sake of the Gospel.

This concept of universal priesthood put the pastor under a certain pressure: on one side he is one of the Christians appointed by the congregation and on the another side, he is called by Christ to exercise authority over the church. We find the aspect of the pastor as a member of the community in the first part of Luther's activity, and then we can notice the new accent that gives authority to pastors, based on their spiritual union with Christ, as in the second part of Luther's activity. Some suggested that after the Peasant Revolt (1524-1526), Luther was forced to change his previous attitude regarding the pastor's ministry.

An important implication of Luther's thinking about the universal priesthood was the concept of liberty. This means that Christians are not saved by any kind of good works, therefore they are free from any kind of obligation, resulting that salvation is purely a genuine faith in Jesus. The good works, the Mass and other Christian activity will follow genuine faith, but will not precede it. Good works are important, but these will follow as a response to God's prior grace in Christ.

---

[45] *Sermon*, 1531, *L.W.*, (J.J. Pelikan and H.T. Lehmann, et al., eds.), vol. 51, p. 224.

[46] Justo L. Gonzalez, *A History of Christian Thought*, vol. 3, Nashville, TN., Paternoster Press, 1988, p. 64.

[47] *L.W.*, (J.J. Pelikan and H.T. Lehmann, et al., eds.), vol. 39, p. 310.

Another implication of Luther's thoughts regarding the universal priesthood is the democratization of this office for all Christians. In this way, every Christian has a duty to watch and help prevent his or her neighbor from living in sin. For him every Christian has the right to teach, instruct, admonish, comfort and rebuke his neighbor with the Word of God. This responsibility becomes greater when we are speaking about the family environment when "The father and mother should do this for their children and household; a brother, neighbor, citizen, peasant or any other."[48]

The next great reformer, John Calvin, protested against the Roman Catholic Church as Luther did before him. He agreed with Luther in his basic theological doctrinal teaching about justification by faith, the prominence of the Bible, and the priesthood of all believers.

It is surprising that in spite of large theological writings, Calvin did not say as much as Luther about universal priesthood. Stevens Paul sustained the idea that the priesthood of all believers was not decisive for either Calvin's thinking or his practice in congregational life.[49]

Calvin declared universal priesthood openly in his famous, *Institutes,* when he wrote, "For we who are defiled in ourselves, yet are priests in him, offer ourselves and our all to God, and freely enter the heavenly sanctuary that the sacrifices of prayers and praise that we bring may be acceptable and sweet-smelling before God."[50] He maintained the same attitude of rejection regarding the ecclesial hierarchy as Luther had, and he was still virulent against Roman Catholic priesthood especially against the Pope, but his focus was on theology and not so much on the church politics or on the ecclesiological field. The original to note: when comparing Calvin with Luther regarding the priesthood is observing their different perspective and approach to the subject. Luther focused on the functional role of priesthood from a human perspective, but Calvin from Christological perspective. For Calvin, more important than the priesthood of all Christians was the priesthood of Christ. He is the High Priest who established a new covenant, with better promises (Heb 8:6), He is our substitute and ransom (Heb 7:27). The priesthood is spiritual since Christ opened, by His blood, a new way of entrance in the Most Holy Place for every Christian (Heb 10:19). The Christian's calling, as new priests in Christ, is to continually offer spiritual sacrifices (Heb 13:15-16).

Calvin underlined the priesthood of all believers in connection with Christ's priesthood based on 1Pet 2:9, that "Now ye are royal priests, and, indeed, in a

---

[48] Idem, p. 332.

[49] Stevens Paul, *The Other Six Days*, p. 178.

[50] J. Calvin: *Institutes of the Christian Religion*, vol. 1, ed. John T. McNeill, trans. and index. Ford Lewis Battles, Philadelphia, The Westminster Press, 1960, p. 502.

more excellent way, because ye are, each of you, consecrated in Christ, that ye may be the associates of his kingdom, and partakers of his priesthood."[51]

In Calvin's theology, the term elder or *presbuteros* is equivalent for priest, and the ministry of the elder is to bring as sacrifice the body and the blood of Christ, to make prayers and to bless God's gifts. Those who boast themselves that they are Christ's priests, are unjust before Christ because only He was consecrated of God, His priesthood is endless, He has not a successor. Calvin stressed clearly that "In Him we all are priests (Rev 1:6; 1Pet 2:9) to bring Him praises and thanksgivings, to give ourselves to Him."[52] He did not use the word 'priest' for the ordained minister but he insisted upon the divine origin and permanent necessity of the ministry of the Word and sacraments. Calvin, as Luther, the minister was also a servant of the Word who applied the biblical teaching to daily life. Reinhold Niebuhr concluded, "For the ministers of the Reformed churches 'preaching' was a symbolic word; it meant not only public discourse but every action through which the gospel was brought home and men were moved to repent before God and to trust in Him."[53]

It is important to know that the teaching about the universal priesthood did not reject the government of the church because the famous, *Augsburg Confession* (1530), in Article 14, underlined that "Concerning church government it is taught that no one should publicly teach, preach, or administer the sacraments without a proper call."

Another important theological document from the sixteenth century was, *The Second Helvetic Confession* (1566). This, *Confession,* was a major Reformed confession, accepted as a standard of faith for Switzerland, France, Scotland, Hungary and Poland and well received in the Netherlands and England, which had a clarification about the universal priesthood in the XVIII-th chapter. The chapter XVIII-th, contains, *The Ministers of The Church, Their Institution and Duties.* In this chapter, is made the clarification between the office of a priest and the calling of the priest. In a brief but very clear presentation. it is written that "Christ's Apostles called all who believe in Christ *priests*, but not on account of an office, but because, all the faithful having been made kings and priests, we are able to offer up a spiritual sacrifices to God through Christ (Ex 19:6; 1Pet 2:9; Rev 1:6)". The clear reason is that only Christ remained a priest forever, and He did not appoint any priests in the church of the New Testament.

---

[51] J. Calvin, *Commentaries on the Catholic Epistles*, trans. J. Owen, Grand Rapids: Eerdmans, 1948, p. 75.

[52] *Institutio Christianae Religionis*, Jean Calvin, vol. 2, Oradea, Ed. Cartea Crestina, 2003, pp. 658-659.

[53] H. Richard Niebuhr, *The Purpose of the Church and its Ministry*, in http://www.religion-online.org.

He strongly prohibited dominion of his disciples over other people, but commanded humility (Lk 22:24ff; Mt 18:3f; 20:25ff). All believers are priests, in, *The Second Helvetic Confession,* is made a clear distinction between the priesthood and the ministry: it is common that every Christian is a part of the universal priesthood, but not everyone is called into the ministry. For the ministry God calls dedicated people to teach and administrate the sacraments. The Old Testament priesthood with the external anointing, holy garments and ceremonies was abolished, but the ministers are stewards of the mystery of God. Only Jesus has all the power, and he does not share his power with people.[54]

4. The Roots of Orthodox Perspectives and the Evangelical Teaching about Priesthood

The Evangelical and Orthodox perspective about priesthood is encapsulated into its ecclesiology. As I have stated from the beginning, every Christian who is interested in the study of Evangelical ecclesiology will notice that this portion of theology is less developed than other theological themes, such as soteriology or anthropology. I do not have a clear basis for the lack, but I can presume that the reason for the weak development of the Evangelical ecclesiology can be found in the activism of the Evangelicals toward the fulfillment of the missionary task or in the individualistic attitude developed in the free Evangelical churches. Neither has Orthodox theology developed in large scale the priesthood teaching, for all of its doctrines are based on priestly ministry.

The biblical ground for the Orthodox tradition regarding the priest and priestly ministry is found in the priesthood office in the Old Testament (*kohen*). The main responsibility of the Old Testament priests was to mediate between the people of Israel and God bringing sacrifices and teaching the Law of God. Other priestly duties were to worship God, and most of all, to live a holy life.[55] The Orthodox priest, in virtue of his special grace, has the spiritual power to mediate between people and God, to be a pillar of stability and unity for the church congregation. Beside the Old Testament scriptures, the Orthodox teaching about priestly ministry is based on the t writings. Arguments of patristic literature are drawn from the works of John Chrysostom, "On the Priesthood", Ambrose, "On Debt of Priests" or Dionysius the Areopagite, "About Debt Priests".

The Evangelical understanding and teaching about the priesthood concept is based on the New Testament texts and was developed historically from the Reformers in the sixteenth century. In this understanding, every believer became a

---

[54] http://www.ccel.org/creeds/helvetic.htm.
[55] *New International Dictionary of New Testament Theology*, vol. 2, Colin Brown general editor, Grand Rapids, Michigan, Zondervan, 1986, p. 232.

priest in a mystical way due to his or her spiritual unity with Christ and holds personal communion with God. Out of that unity springs the universal priesthood which is seen by the ministry of intercession, by offering spiritual sacrifices in worship, praise, thanksgiving, and by service to those in need.

In the New Testament narrative, the word priest (*hiereus*) office is found only for Jews and Gentiles, not for a Christian minister. The exception to this rule is the book of Hebrews where Christ is Priest (Heb 5:6; 6:20) and High Priest (Heb 2:17; 3:1; 4:14; 5:5, 10; 8:1; 9:11). The high priest ministry of Jesus is an important doctrine in the book of Hebrews. We can find a clear motif for this, for the book was addressed especially to the Hebrew people who knew the religious ritual at the temple in Jerusalem.

The universal priesthood is an important concept in Evangelical teaching and practice, although we must notice that the New Testament does not provide many biblical texts about the priesthood of all Christians.[56]

Evangelicals see in Jesus' prayer, prior his crucifixion (Jn 17), an image of His 'High Priestly prayer' because Jesus says that He consecrates Himself for their sake (Jn 17:19). The verb *hagiazo* used here is also used for the sanctifying of priests and of sacrifices in Old Testament (Ex 28:38, 41; 29:1, 21; Num 18:9).[57]

This concept of High Priest referring to Christ is developed later in the epistle of Hebrews. In the New Testament the person of Christ is seen as the culmination of the High Priest function by His sacrifice and by His mediator ministry between God and men. Only Jesus Christ is the High Priest who sacrificed His own body for the salvation of humankind (Heb 5:10). To be part of the universal priesthood from an Evangelical perspective means to enjoy of special union with Jesus in God's redemptive purpose in the world.[58]

In Paul's letters the word *hiereus* appears metaphorically and is referring to devotional, compassionate, financial and evangelistic activities (Rom 15:16,27; Phil 2:17, 25, 30; 2Cor 9:12), and the term for office is used by Paul exclusively for the governing role played by Christ in the church (Col 1:18).[59]

---

[56] There are other terms from the Levitical cults which are appropriated for Christian activity as: "sprinkled" and "washed" come from ritual consecration of the priests (Heb 10:22; cf. Ex 29:21) or "firstborn" from the Levites as the first born of Israel (Heb 12:23).

[57] *New International dictionary of New Testament Theology*, vol. 3, p. 38.

[58] Findley B. Edge, 'Priest of Believers', *JRT*, no. 1, vol. XL, Jan. 1963.

[59] R. Banks, 'Church Order and Government', in *Dictionary of Paul and His Letters*, Gerald F. Hawthrone, Ralph P. Martin, Daniel G. Reid (editors), Downers Grove, ILL, *IVP*, 1993, p. 134.

A reason for such a lack of scriptural texts referring to the priesthood can be explained by the nonexistence of the priesthood office by Christians during the first century. I refer here to the nonexistence of any kind of Christian priesthood office because although there were a large number of Hebrew priests, yet out of them Luke says that "a great company of priests were obedient to the faith" (Acts 6:7).

There also cannot be found a rigid structure or hierarchical scheme between the Christians, since it is known that by his or her faith they have an opportunity to make intercession, to worship God directly and to become a spiritual member in the "body of Christ" (1Cor 12:12-13). Actually, we can not find the term 'priest' for a particular ministry among the Christians in the New Testament. Even the calling of disciples by Jesus can be seen as the example of the calling of laity ministers, to serve and not to dominate.[60]

A biblical text used as support for the universal priesthood concept is found in Peter's writings. The description of the general body of believers as *'a holy priesthood'* and *'a royal priesthood'* (1Pet 2:5, 9), constitutes the formal basis of the doctrine we study. As a 'holy priesthood', the Christians have a holy function: "to offer spiritual sacrifices acceptable to God through Jesus Christ" (1Pet 2:5). The worship opportunity for every Christian is based on the 'holy priesthood' prerogatives. By his words Peter enlarged the priesthood ministry concept from a small number of servants toward the whole community of Christians. According to his understanding, the priesthood ministry no longer was reserved for a select group, but belongs to all God's people, sanctified or made holy by the Spirit (1:3). By this image, the whole community has the right of approach to God.[61] Every Christian has open access to God in intimate knowledge and has the prophetic task in proclaiming the knowledge of God.[62] It is obvious that the general priesthood, as a concept, is intrinsically opposed to clerical pretensions but it is not anti-ministerial because soon after the church was born, two needs appeared: the spiritual service and the administrative service, in other words, there was a need for people to be fulfilled by worship and a need for the body to be fulfilled by service. Knowing those needs, the universal priesthood concept makes way for all Christians to minister according with their spiritual gifts, and this is an important gain for the whole spiritual work. The author of Hebrews sees Christians as priests who are able to enter into the Holy of Holies (Heb 10:19, 22), and to continually "offer up a sacrifice of praise to God, that is the fruit of lips that acknowledge his name" (Heb 13:15).

---

[60] Bob E. Lyons, *Kingdom of Priests*, Cleveland TN., Pathway Press, 1977.
[61] Donald Guthrie, *New Testament Theology*, Leicester, Inter-Varsity Press, 1981, p. 783.
[62] *The New International Dictionary of New Testament Theology*, Colin Brown (Ed. gen), Grand Rapids, Michigan, Zondervan, 1986, vol. 3, p. 37.

In an indirect way, Paul refers to the priesthood of all believers when he encouraged the Christians in Rome "to present your body as a living sacrifice, holy and acceptable to God, which is your spiritual worship" (Rom 12:1). The new kind of sacrifices consists not in slaughtered animals, but in personal sacrifices, holy and acceptable to God. Paul's special calling was "to be a minister" (*leitourgon*) of Christ for the Gentiles in the priestly service of preaching the gospel, so that the offering of the Gentiles may be acceptable, sanctified by the Holy Spirit (Rom 15:16).[63]

Paul also accentuated the solidarity in ministry since all the Christians are members in one spiritual body and they have a task to fulfill (1Cor 12:12-14).

In his prologue to the book of Revelation, John resumed Jesus Christ's work for His followers in two clear directions: first, He cleansed them from their iniquities and secondly, He made them "kings and priests" (Rev 1:5-6). In this way, Christ called them out from humanity and designated them for the service of God. The same formulation "kings and priests" appears in Revelation 5:10, where this high status for Christians is a clear result of Christ's atonement sacrifice.

This holy universal priesthood receives a special anointing, an anointing from the Holy Spirit who teaches and abides in the Christians' hearts (1Jn 2:20, 27).

In conclusion, the teaching about the universal priesthood is an important concept for the Christian tradition since it brings Christians together to minister, to worship and to serve those in need.

5. The Role of the Priest from the Orthodox and Evangelical Perspective

Those who are interested in studying the topic of priesthood from Orthodox dogmatic theology, may find that although the doctrine of the priesthood is not given much attention, there is found however, almost all of the Orthodox tenets are developed in connection with the priesthood teaching.

The tradition of the Orthodox Church, which is a rich one, is perceived as having come from God and includes the revelation of God for our salvation.[64] The content of the apostolic tradition is the content of Scripture applied essentially to human life, or started through the Church.[65]

---

[63] *The New International Dictionary of New Testament Theology*, Colin Brown (Ed. gen), Grand Rapids, Michigan, Zondervan, 1986, vol. 3, p. 38.

[64] *Învățătura de Credință Creștină Ortodoxă,* București, Editura Institutului Biblic și de Misiune al Bisericii Ortodoxe Române, 2000, p. 30.

[65] Dumitru Stanilloae, *Teologia Dogmatica Ortodoxa,* vol. 1, Bucuresti, 1996, p. 45

In studying Evangelical theology, there is not found such an old tradition as in the Orthodox theology since the Evangelicals are focusing exclusive on the teaching of Scripture as it was preached by the Reformers during the sixteenth century.

A point of convergence between the Evangelical and the Orthodox perspective is that both traditions focus in their teachings about priesthood on the person of Christ as High Priest (Heb 2:17; 3:1; 4:14-15; 5:5) and the Lamb of sacrifice (Jn 1:29, 35). The priestly ministry is one where it meets the supreme sacrifice, perfect forgiveness and saving grace.

The role of the Orthodox priest held a central position in this Christian tradition. The act of consecration of the priest for ministry in the Orthodox tradition is a mystery shared by the laying on of hands by the bishop invoking the Holy Spirit, through which by unseen grace the priest receives the grace of priesthood. Consecration is one of the seven sacraments practiced in the Orthodox Church, and through this mystery the priest receives the spiritual power to mediate for people before God in a special way. The ritual of consecration of a new priest in the Orthodox tradition is very complex including the Bishop's prayer from the altar, clergy songs accompanying the ceremony, the agreement of the people present by the words "He (the new priest) is worthy", and the presentation of the new robe for the new priest. The climax of the ceremony of ordination of a new priest is the prayer *"Divine Grace"* spoken by the bishop, invoking the grace of the Holy Spirit to come down over the kneeling candidate. The indelible character of the consecrated priest will continue to be upon him, even if that priest will be removed from service.

In the New Testament we find the practice of ordination in the sense of "putting aside" someone for a particular service (Acts 13:3). The purpose of the consecration is not to create a special class of servants or successors, but to recognize those who God has previously chosen for this ministry as answer to the prayer of the church.[66] According to the Evangelical understanding, by the act of laying on of hands, the ordained minister is not included in the apostolic succession, but he "is sent" to do a spiritual work necessary for the body of Christ. The Evangelicals ritual is much simpler including a sermon about pastoral responsibility of pastor or priest followed by the prayer of consecration by the laying on of the hands by the group of pastors.

In the Orthodox Church, the priest has the key position because he received "a surplus of grace", more than other believers; he represents Christ in the Church and in the sacraments through which Christ has committed to the church. The priest is a guarantor of the unity of the church because of his special grace that he

---

[66] John Tipei, „Ideea de succesiune in ordinea rabinica şi în hirotonirea creştină: un studiu comparativ", *Pleroma*, anul V, nr. 2, 2003, p 90.

possesses. Because of this special grace he is enabled to share Holy Communion, forgiveness of sins, and unity of believers as members of the spiritual body which head Christ is. All of these attributes of the priest make the believers to have an attitude of reverence and obedience to the Orthodox priest. The priest is also a "visible element" that unites the spiritual world through the Church liturgy.

There are three levels of ordained ministers in the Orthodox tradition: deacon, priest and bishop. For each level there is a very complex ordination ministry performed by the bishop. A difference between Evangelical and Orthodox perspective is that there are three levels of ordained people in Orthodoxy (bishop, priest and deacon) and only two levels of ordained people in Evangelical tradition (pastor and deacon).

Another difference between Orthodox and Evangelical tradition is that in the Evangelical tradition there is not a priest who posses a special spiritual power and grace to forgive the sins of the people, since every believer is a priest and in this way having the opportunity to come before God in repentance, and asking for personal forgiveness. In the Orthodox tradition the priesthood holds a special charisma, a spiritual power and a special authority to deliver people from corruption and giving help for their spiritual renewal. Another interesting issue is the concept of universal priesthood in Orthodox and Evangelical tradition. The concept of universal priesthood is emphasized in Evangelical theology, but only partially developed in the Orthodox tradition. For both traditions, the universal priesthood is not a church office, but a gift given by God to all Christians who have experienced spiritual regeneration.

In the Orthodox perspective the universal priesthood is represented by the laity who are incorporated into Christ through baptism, then received as evidence is the mystery of chrismation, as the personal relationship with the Holy Spirit. The universal priesthood has the opportunity to say "Amen", which is the right of the people of God par excellence. The universal priesthood in Orthodox tradition exists only in a spiritual sense not in a charismatic one because only the ordained priest holds a particular dose of grace.

The concept of universal priesthood in Evangelical theology was highlighted by reformers during the sixteenth century, in particular by Luther who was an opponent of clericalism. According to the universal priesthood concept, every believer is holy because of his or her faith in Christ and has the right to address God in prayer, in the name of Jesus Christ, without the need for an intermediary. The Christians are called "holy" because they were called out of the worldly life and their life was sanctified as "service for God".

From the Evangelical perspective, the concept of universal priesthood does not preclude the service of believers with their charisma. For instance, the pastoral function is not canceled, because the New Testament contains the references to the ministry of representation and the faithful are called to obey their leaders (Heb 1:17, 1Pet 5:8). But although the authority of the pastor is a delegated authority from God and recognized by the believers, he does not have an additional grace different from the rest of congregation.

One final aspect that I want to emphasize is of a philological nature. The Greek term presbuteros, appears 18 times in New Testament texts with reference to church leaders. In the Orthodox Romanian New Testament, the term was translated with "elder", "priest" (hereus) or it was transliterated with "presbyter" (presbuteros). The inconsistency in translation proves the uncertainty for the use of this term. The term "priest" (hereus) as equivalent for "presbuteros" was used until 1951, only in five texts out of 18 occurrences. Later on, the use of the term "priest" (hereus) translated for "presbuteros" was used very often, until it became the only acceptable term. Then, the number of occurrences decreases, but not significantly. The term "elder" that appears in earlier versions, did not appear in translations by the latter half of the twentieth century. In response to this situation Emanuel Contac, who studied the phenomenon, offers an explanation for the removing of the word "presbyter" in the Orthodox translation, appears "as an attempt to differ the Orthodox translation from the Protestant translation, perceived as a foreign body in the spiritual life of the Romanian people."

6. A Comparison between Orthodox and Evangelical Priesthood Concepts in Light of Biblical Teaching

I intend to develop briefly some of the characteristics and ministries of the Orthodox priest and from that point to find the Evangelical perspective for this issue. I will draw attention upon three main Orthodox teachings about priesthood: the apostolic succession, the church hierarchy and the sacramental position of the priest. These ecclesiastical concepts as apostolic succession, ecclesiastic hierarchy and sacramental priesthood are the core of the Orthodox teaching about priesthood.

The apostolic succession is an important doctrine for the Orthodox tradition. The Orthodox teaching of the apostolic hierarchy and the sacramental priesthood was established by Jesus' authority, not by any democratic process. The teaching developed in the Orthodox tradition is based on some New Testament events: by the event when Jesus had chosen the twelve Apostles (Lk 6:12-16) and by the empowerment of them by Jesus when He breathed the Holy Spirit upon them (Jn 20:22).

Later on, the Apostles of Jesus, endowed with *graceful spiritual power,* appointed bishops, priests and deacons.[67] The duties of the bishops, according

---

[67] George Remete, *Dogmatică Ortodoxă*, p. 326.

with the Orthodox perspective, who received the *graceful spiritual power* when they were consecrated, was to appoint new bishops, priests and deacons, to preach the Word of God and to lead the Christian community. In this way, an apostolic succession is born, an ecclesiastic hierarchy and a sacramental priesthood. Every Orthodox priest, in virtue of his ordination is in line with the former priests and bishops. The line of succession, according to this teaching, goes back to the first century. Without being in the hierarchical apostolic succession, no priest has the spiritual power to perform the sacraments and no Orthodox Christian has opportunity to be partakers of Christ. The inner factor of this succession is Christ Himself and the Holy Spirit, the outside factor of this succession is the church who is shepherded by the bishop. According with the Orthodox teaching, the source of the sacramental priesthood is Jesus Christ's unseen priesthood (Heb 4:14; 5:5; 9:1).

Evangelicals reject the doctrine of apostolic succession arguing that the Apostles' authority was unique, specific for their time. When we compare the concept of priesthood in the Eastern Orthodox Church and in the Evangelical movement we can easily see that the former developed a strong ecclesiastical hierarchy based mainly on the apostolic succession limited to a few elect priests, while the later developed a great laity force by empowering the lay people to express an active spiritual life, to bring personal testimonies, vivid missionary service and a great desire to bring a new and deeper kind of spirituality inside the community. If the Orthodox priest invites people to come to him and to the church to gain spiritual benefits as forgiveness of sins, spiritual teaching, spiritual grace and the mystery of Communion, the Evangelicals are going to have people, bringing the Word of God to where they reside, to where they are. Evangelicals encourage the Christians to work accordingly with their gifts, for the purpose of serving is "to prepare God's people for works of service, so that the body of Christ may be built up" (Eph 4:12).

The Evangelicals' argument against the apostolic succession teaching is that only God had chosen Apostles, not men. Jesus Christ chose the twelve Apostles after a night spent in prayer (Lk 6:12-16). After Judas' death, when Matthew replaced him and was enrolled with the eleven Apostles, for the enrollment they casts lots and the result was considered as God's answer for their request (Acts 1:24-26). Paul's calling to be an Apostle was not by any elder or bishop, but by a special and direct call from the resurrected Jesus, without an apostolic succession (Gal 1:1). Except for these few exceptions there are not biblical text suggesting the apostolic ministry and office can be inherited or pass on by apostolic succession.

It is true that Christians have the important duty to transmit the apostolic faith to the following generation (2Tim 2:2), but the apostolic office finished when the last Apostle died. We cannot find in the New Testament an instance when an Apostle ordained or consecrated another Apostle.

The Evangelicals also reject the church hierarchy seen as a pyramid with lay people on the bottom of the pyramid and the bishop on the top. Before God all Christians are equal, because of the image and likeness of God, regardless of their abilities or qualification. As a biblical proof, the Evangelicals remind us when Jesus was teaching the twelve Apostles that no one has the right to rule above another but to serve others (Lk 22:24). Not a pastor or a priest has a greater or a special grace than other Christians, contrariwise, every Christian can have a special calling or spiritual gift for certain ministries. By the empowerment of lay people in Evangelical churches, it has created a new kind of ecclesiology without a rigid hierarchy, but with a special trust and openness for a large mass of people to minister. The church operates with equal spiritual standings because there is no rank between Christians, all are united by faith in Christ and not by any political affiliation, economic status or educational attainment.[68] An important key concept in the Orthodox tradition is the sacerdotalism of the priest. Although the New Testament does not promote the teaching about a priestly sacerdotal position, in the Orthodox tradition, the priest hold this position in virtue of the grace received when he was ordained, in this way he is a "Christ-bearer". In the Orthodox Church only the priest has the right to give Holy Communion. The deacon does not have this right; the only exception is when there is not a priest present in the church. From an Evangelical perspective, since there is not a biblical explicit teaching about the sacerdotal priesthood, Communion is not presented as a repeated sacrifice of Christ, therefore there is not a reason to promote the sacerdotal teaching.

For Evangelicals the priest is not a person who possesses a special grace, but is a consecrated minister who has the duty to preach, to administer Communion and to be involved in worship with the whole congregation. The Evangelical pastor is not claiming that he is a dispenser of grace for the congregation.

It is true that between Evangelicals we are not meeting the sacramental position as in the historical church, that is the Orthodox and the Catholic Church. The pastors are praying and blessing the wine and the bread for the Holy Communion but since Evangelicals do not preach nor promote transubstantiation, they do not claim to hold a sacramental role. The pastor does not hold a special position, "no special accent falls on the administering, and not a word is said of a differentiation between the one who administers and the one who receives."[69] Emil Brunner's conclusion is that "The priest/bishop who adminis-

---

[68] Gordon R. Lewis, Bruce A. Demarest, *Interogative Theology*, vol. 3, Grand Rapids, Michigan, Zondervan, p. 273-274.

[69] Emil Brunner, *Dogmatics III*, p. 65.

tered the means of salvation has taken the place of the brotherhood that celebrated the Lord's Supper."[70] Norman Geisler noticed that "it took many centuries for monolithic Episcopal government to gradually emerge from the simple self-governing independent New Testament church."[71]

A special theological issue is the forgiveness of sins. For every Christian the weight of carrying their sins is above his or her spiritual power, therefore the need of a confessor is of a great need. In the Orthodox tradition, the priest has the power and the ability, based on the special grace bestowed upon him and based on his sacerdotal ministry to receive confessions of people, to promote the sacrament of penance and to make intercession between people and God to obtain the forgiveness of their sins. Using the Scripture of the New Testament, "If you forgive the sins of any, they are forgiven them; if you withhold forgiveness from any, it is withheld" (Jn 20:23), the Orthodox teaching states that the priest has the power of the forgiveness of sins because of his succession with the Apostles of the first century.

The Evangelical teaching is that every Christian who carries the burden of his or her sins has the right to come before God in faith in Jesus' Name, who is the only "one Mediator between God and men" (1Tim 2:5), to repent of sins and to receive the spiritual forgiveness.

According with Evangelical narration, only Jesus, who was God in flesh, has the power to cancel and forgive the sins of people (Mt 9:6; Mk 2:7, Lk 5:21-24). The believers are involved in this ministry of reconciliation by preaching the message of salvation through Jesus Christ's sacrifice. As I wrote previously, we cannot find any biblical Scripture to enable spiritual leaders to forgive other's sins.

7. The Power of Universal Priesthood Concept during History

Some ideas and concepts prove its power throughout the centuries. This affirmation is valuable for the priesthood concept also. A very important change in the Christian's rhetoric about universal priesthood concept occurred soon after Luther's era finished. The rhetorical language regarding the concept of universal priesthood lost its power and consistency. We can understand Luther's reason for stressing so vividly this concept in his theological fight with the Roman Catholic Church hierarchy, but later on, when the new movement shaped its identity theoretically it was no longer an important task to develop that theme.

---

[70] Emil Brunner, *Dogmatics III*, p. 69.
[71] Norman Geisler, *Systematic Theology*, vol. 4, p. 142.

Luther's sermons and writings about the priesthood of all believers can be seen as the seed for further development of the Evangelical movement. For the opponents of Evangelicals, Luther's teaching about the priesthood of all believers was a "Pandora's Box" that could not be closed again for the people understood their new status offered by the universal priesthood concept. From the Evangelical and historical perspective, the universal priesthood concept opened the way to the great revivals in England and America.

The Anabaptist leader Menno Simons, used the concept of the priesthood of all believers in his work, *Foundation of Christian Doctrine* (1539-1540). According to his understanding, Christians are priests because they were sanctified by Christ's sacrifice and they are called to live a sanctified life. As priests, they are to avoid evil lusts, to purify their own bodies daily, to suffer when it is necessary for the Lord and to live a life of prayer and thanksgiving. He stressed the importance of the new life was proved by adult baptism and withdrawing from the secular world.[72] The Anabaptists practiced this kind of universal priesthood for they do not make a distinction between an academically educated ministerial class and the laity, "Each member was a potential preacher and a missionary."[73]

During the seventeenth century the appearance of the Quakers marked the first formal rejection of the lay-clerical distinction within the modern church. George Fox, the Quaker's outstanding leader expressed three truths regarding the Christian's life, which he received while he was praying: (1) None are true believers but those who passed from death unto life by being born of God; (2) For someone to be a minister of Christ there is needed a spiritual anointing because the qualification for ministry is given not by ecclesiastical study, but by the Holy Spirit; (3) God does not dwell in temples made with hands, but in human hearts.[74] We take note that Fox promoted the same anti-hierarchical attitude as Luther and Calvin and stressed the pneumatological dimension in Christian life. His great influence upon the Quakers can be seen in their serious attitude regarding religious life, prayer, genuine worship, integrity and personal discipline. The Quakers ecclesiology was peculiar because they did not make a distinction or a division between clergy and laity; they promoted the concept that every one has a vocation to be a lay minister and to practice the free ministry.[75] They practiced the universal priesthood concept by personal or group

---

[72] J.D. Douglas (gen. ed.), Earle Cairns (cons. Ed.), *The New International Dictionary of the Christian Church*, Grand Rapids, Michigan, Zondervan Publishing House, 1996, p. 650.

[73] W. Schaufele, "The Missionary Vision and Activity of the Anabaptist Laity", *The Other Six Days*, p. 178.

[74] Richmond P. Miller, *Transmission of Faith Through Quaker Worship*, p. 182.

[75] Leo Rosten (ed.), *A Guide to the Religions of America*, New York, Simon & Schuster publisher, 1955, p. 123.

testimonies, corporate worship, a time of quietness, simplicity, better social relations, integrity and a strict and serious education.

The Quakers left their finger print on spiritual and social life since they shared, with all born again Christians, the responsibility in worship and organization. We can understand their open opposition to slavery that gave William Wilberforce his great success. Other contributions were; their eagerness to open the first asylum in England, to minister to the prisoners, an important role in the evangelization of North America in the mid-seventeenth century and an opposition to war. Out of these practical works of the Quakers we can see a force released when the theological concept as universal priesthood is practiced.

Robert Barklay, a Quaker theologian and apologist in his work, *Apology for the True Christian Divinity*, writes that in the spiritual and mystical body of Christ, all the Christians are members according to the different measures of grace and of the Spirit's diversity administered unto each member.[76] For Quakers, the outward authority of a priest cannot replace the supreme authority of the Spirit. Barklay's conclusion was that "We are for a holy spiritual, pure and living ministry where the ministers are both called, qualified and ordered, acted and influenced in all the steps of their ministry by the Spirit of God."[77]

Another early Evangelical movement which started during the seventeenth century, that practiced the universal priesthood and called people to attempt purification of the self and of society as well, was the Puritans. The importance of the Evangelical conversion experience was an important article of faith amongst the first Puritans who settled in New England.

The Puritans expressed the power of universal priesthood practiced on the daily basis but lost a large extent of the rhetorical language of the universal priesthood. They exercised a great impact upon society since they applied their religious views and disciplines at work, in the home, in carrying out social action and in education.[78] The concept of the priesthood, in the Puritanism thought, lead towards the full democratic potential of the doctrine only when Puritanism became free from the religious establishment. An important gain resulting from Puritanism was the emancipation of laity by their social involvement, and by their personal writings, since every one was encouraged to write his or her

---

[76] *Apology for the True Christian Divinity*, London, 8. ed., printed by J. Phillips, George-Yard, Lombard-Street, 1780, p. 272.

[77] Robert Braclay, Apology for the Chrisitan Divinity, Glenside, Quaker Heritage Press, first published in 1678, p. 288.

[78] Thomas D. Lea, "The Hermeneutics of the Puritans", *JETS* 39/2 (June 1996) p. 272. Thomas Lea is professor of New Testament at Southwestern Baptist Theological Seminary.

spiritual experience. For instance, J. Bunyan was one who wrote his spiritual biography, *Grace Abounding*, during the year 1666.

Another group, the Pietist Christians, remained in history to be remembered by their humble spirit, by their devotional exercises and sincere love for people. The Pietist leader Philipp Jakob Spener (1618-1648), was an important figure; he published during the year of 1675 the book, *Pia Desideria*. For his task to improve the pastoral care, he revived the concept of the 'priesthood of all believers' and used the term 'spiritual priesthood'. He introduced during the year of 1670, a small prayer booklet and established study groups, *collegia pietatis*, for fellowship and encouragement in faith and practice.[79] He says that the freedom to live Christian lives is based not in our own capacities but in God's empowering encounter.

A notable bible Evangelical writer, at the beginning of the eighteenth century, was Mathew Henry. He remained famous by his, *Commentary On The Whole Bible*, finished shortly before his death in 1714. In his commentary on the Epistle of 1Peter, he sustained that all true believers are a holy priesthood, sacred to God, serviceable to others, endowed with heavenly gifts and graces.[80]

When Evangelicals are speaking of their forefathers they undoubtedly refer to the Methodist leader during the eighteen century, John Wesley. The majority of historians are seeing the eighteenth century Wesleyan movement in England as the "Evangelical revival".

John Wesley like Richard Baxter, in the previous century, promoted the universal priesthood concept. Chares Wesley referred to the priesthood of believers in his Eucharistic Hymns:

> Ye royal priests of Jesus, rise,
> And join the daily sacrifice;
> Join all believers, in His name
> To offer up the spotless Lamb.[81]

During that time, people who recognized that something special happened in their lives were encouraged to share their spiritual experience, give testimonies, to pray and to sing. John Wesley asked the lay preachers to write their personal conversion, and these testimonies were published in the, *Arminian Magazine*.[82] This practice was another form of expressing the universal priest-

---

[79] Peter C. Erb (ed.), *Pietists: Selected Writings*, New York, Paulist Press, 1983, p. 8.
[80] Matthew Henry, *Commentary On The Whole Bible*, Waynesboro, Georgia: Operation Mobilization Literature, 1995, p. 978.
[81] J.M. Ross, "The Priesthood of all Believers", *The Expository Times*, 1951, p. 45.
[82] Deryck W. Lovegrove (ed.), *The Rise of Laity*, London: Routledge, 2000, p. 82.

hood concept. It is obvious that when the lay preachers started to preach, that criticism sprang up often out of the jealousy of the clergy. The clergy warned people against these lay ministers accusing them that they did not have a formal education to preach or to minister, they were not learned and skilled in their ministry, they undermined the church's order and they are responsible for spreading a false teaching among the people. In some cases, they called these itinerant preachers blasphemers. William Burton Pope (1822-1903), trained at the Wesleyan Theological Institution in Huston, in his, *Compendium of Christian Theology* (3 vols.), an authoritative textbook on dogmatic theology in the Wesleyan tradition, developed a very high doctrine of the ministry. Curiously, he did not write much about the subject of the universal priesthood.[83] He explained the development of the church hierarchy in his, *Compendium,* and concluded that the Reformation brought the only good argument of the Scripture against the hierarchical system of the Catholic Church. In his book he writes that the ancient Temple with the sacrifices and all various rituals had been replaced by Christ. Burton was critical when he wrote about the distinction between the clergy and laity in the churches because in his understanding there was not a separate order of priesthood since "all we are priests through fellowship with Him"[84] but he warned against excesses of the lay power, especially in the congregational system where the power of the pastor is reduced to a very slight element in comparison with the body of the laity.

The Baptist movement held an important role in the Evangelical movement. We can count the Baptists "champions of universal priesthood" because their sustained concept of liberty between all Christians. There was no priestly office since the beginning of the Baptists, because the whole community is a congregation of priests.[85] For them no other authority, creed or confession, can hinder the direct communion with God. The priesthood function does not belong to a privileged clerical class, but is a status of every Christian who turned to God from a sinful life.

John Smith, the founder of the English Baptist movement, in his writing, *Differences of the Churches of the Separation,* sustained the idea that the church is a kingly priesthood and the Christians are "kings and priests"[86]. In his under-

---

[83] J.D. Douglas (gen. ed.), Earle E. Cairns, (cons. ed.), *The New International Dictionary of the Christian Church,* Grand Rapids, Michigan: Zondervan Publishing House, 1996, p. 793.

[84] William Burton Pope, *Compendium,* vol. 3, p. 171.

[85] For additional information about the Baptist's perspective upon the concept of universal priesthood concept see *London Confession* (1644), *Second London confession* (1677), *New Hampshire Confession* (1833).

[86] John Smyth, "Differences of the Churches of the Separation", *A Sourcebook for Baptist Heritage,* H. Leon McBeth (ed.), Nashville: Broadman Press, 1990, p. 15.

standing, Christ exercised the threefold office: king, priest and prophet. The universal priesthood of all Christians was based actually on the priesthood of Jesus Christ. The threefold ministry of Christ has to be seen in the marks of the church: Word, sacraments and discipline.[87] As spiritual priests, the Christians offer spiritual worship and sacrifices acceptable to God by Jesus Christ. This spiritual priesthood possesses spiritual gifts as: prophecy, prayer, praise, worship and thanksgiving. In the church there exists and works together both groups of Christians, elders and brethren. For Baptists the priesthood of believers is a cardinal belief and a "most cherished distinctive".[88] They developed the concepts that every Christian has the right to interpret the Bible for his own benefits, to vote in the church's business and has obligation to develop his own religious beliefs. This liberty and democratization of the priesthood was reiterated in the, *Second London Confession* (1677),[89] where it is written that not only the bishops or pastors are fit to minister the Word, but also gifted people filled by the Holy Spirit, approved and called by the Church. All the members of the community were bound to develop for the good of the church the practice of their spiritual gifts, by communion, love and edification.[90]

An outstanding Baptist preacher during the nineteenth century, namely "the prince of preachers" was C.H. Spurgeon (1834-1892). He preached a sermon about "The Kingly Priesthood of the Saints" based on Revelation 5:10, where he says that we are the priests that are a divinely chosen people. He had an objection when he spoke about the class of clergymen because he sustained that all saints are priests. For someone to stand up and say he is a priest is a falsehood in Spurgeon's understanding because he detested the distinction between clergy and laity. He says that those who are called by divine grace are priests by divine constitution.[91] Every saint is a priest at God's altar, and is bound to worship God with the holy incense of prayer and praise. The priest's divine service is to bring spiritual sacrifices and to worship God. Although Spurgeon was a famous preacher during his time and preached thousands of sermons, when we research Spurgeon's sermons we realize that the great preacher did not have much to say about the concept of priesthood.

---

[87] Malcolm B. Yarnell, III, *'Changing Baptist concepts of royal priesthood John Smith and Edgar Young Mullins'* in *The Rise of Laity in Evangelical Protestantism*, p. 238.

[88] Findley B. Edge, "Priesthood of Believers", *JRT*, vol. LX, no. 1, p. 9, 1963.

[89] http://www.iclnet.org/pub/resources/text/history/lond1689.con.txt.

[90] William L. Lampkin, *Baptist Confession of Faith*, Valley Forge, Judson Press, 1969, pp. 285-289.

[91] *The Kingly Priesthood of the Saints*, by Charles Spurgeon, http://www.reformedsermonarchives.com/sp.

Another important Baptist leader who had something to say about priesthood was Edgar Young Mullins (1860-1928).[92] In Mullins definition, the church is "a voluntary association of believers united together for the purpose of worship and edification, and is the spiritual home of the saved."[93] From this perspective he sustained the existence of the universal priesthood, since every soul is capable of meeting with God without any human mediator. For him the New Testament church was rooted in freedom. Developing the concept that every Christian is a free person and has personal rights, Mullins canceled any distinction between laity and clergy. In the church there existed a "priesthood of all believers" where we all together regardless of the power or influence, are bound together and have the same equal privileges. Mullins did not annulated the pastoral ministry for the sake of universal priesthood but he writes that the pastors are not masters, but servants; they are not rulers but guides, they are not officials clothed with authority, but teachers. They are simply first among equals, selected to perform certain duties because of their special fitness, and not because they exercise any authority.[94] His clear warning underlined that whenever a church interposes between the child and the Father, through sacrament, through human priesthood or hierarchy, through centralized government, through authoritative oligarchies of any kind in spiritual affairs, it ceases to conform to the Kingdom of God, and becomes a juvenile court of an orphanage instead. He was very critical to the office of priest based on the hierarchical ladder. I will say that Mullins critical attitude regarding the clergy can be seen when he sustained that the priesthood is of pagan in origin, not Christian, he is an "exclusive manipulator of sacraments".[95] In the church there are not hierarchical classes because all Christians are priests together, no human priest may claim to be mediator between man and God, all believers are brothers and sisters in Christ, not masters and slaves, all share the same spiritual blessings.

The twentieth century with its political turmoil and atheistic philosophy did not quench the religious flame, by the contrary, during that century great Evangelical theologians as Louis Berkhof, Emil Brunner and Karl Barth wrote important theological writings.

An important Evangelical theologian, among the American Calvinist was Louis Berkhof (1873-1957). He had 38 years of teaching and writing, but he

---

[92] E.Y. Mullins served as president of Southern Baptist Theological Seminary (1899-1928), the Southern Baptist Convention (1921-1924), and Baptist World Alliance (1923-1928). His important work is *Axioms of Religion* (1908).

[93] E.Y. Mullins, *Why Is Christianity True?*, Philadelphia, American Baptist Publication Society, 1905, p 156.

[94] E.Y. Mullins, *Baptist Theology in the New World Order*, p. 404.

[95] Deryck W. Lovegrove (ed.), *The Rise of Laity*, p. 247.

did not stress the concept of the priestly office very clearly. In his, *Systematic Theology,* based on biblical text, it seems he followed Calvin's manner for he wrote about the priestly office of Christ but without extending his research toward the universal priesthood of all Christians. It is obvious in Berkhof's understanding based on the Bible teaching that Jesus Christ is the real Priest: "[Christ] can be called the *only real priest.*"[96] Christ's unique status of priest resulted from His atoning work: He is both, the priest and the sacrifice. No one else can replace Christ's work and sacrifice. Following Christ's pattern, Christians can do a priestly work by the ministry of intercession and by spiritual sacrifices as praise and worship. Berkhof shares that the intercessory work of Christ relates to our moral condition and sanctifies our service in the Kingdom of God.[97] As the universal priesthood, Christians are called to be active in their daily work, in testimonies and in the intercessory ministry, but without Christ's support everything is powerless and finishes in vain. The spiritual union between Christ and Christians, not human abilities, provide the reason for the priesthood of all Christians. This union is "intimate, vital and spiritual. He is the source of their life and strength, of their blessedness and salvation."[98]

One of the greatest theologians of the twentieth century among Evangelical theologians was Emil Brunner.[99] Emil Brunner did a large theological and historical study about the, *Development of Ekklesia into Church,* in his third volume of *Dogmatics.* In this lengthy chapter he wrote about the transforming process, during the centuries, of the *Ekklesia* that initially was an open Christian fellowship, but later it transformed into a rigid institutional *Church* with a totalitarian authoritarian structure.[100] Actually he writes that the Roman Catholic Church is not identical with what we know as the *Ekklesia* of the New Testament, but something fundamentally different. He marks two essential steps in that direction: first the deviation of the Lord's Supper concept from its original significance toward a sacramental understanding, and second, the transforming

---

[96] Louis Berkhof, *Systematic Theology,* Edinburgh, The Banner of Truth Trust, reprinted in 1988, p. 366.

[97] Idem, p. 403.

[98] Idem, p. 449.

[99] Emil Brunner (1889-1966) was an eminent and highly influential Swiss Protestant (Reformed) theologian. He was appointed as Professor of Systematic Theology at the University of Zurich from 1924 until his retirement in 1953. He was a substantial contributor to the World Conference on Church, Community and State in Oxford in 1937. He wrote his three volume magnum opus, *Dogmatics* (volume one: *The Christian Doctrine of God,* volume two: *The Christian Doctrine of Creation and Redemption* and volume three *The Christian Doctrine of the Church, Faith and Consummation*) where he developed his theological thought.

[100] Emil Brunner, *Dogmatics,* vol. 3, translated by D. Cairns and T.H.L. Paker, Cambridge, James Clarke & Co., 2002, p. 59.

of the first century church where the Holy Spirit bestowed spiritual gifts for serving in a rigid institutional organization. Brunner underlined that the primitive Lord's Supper is fundamentally different from what was called later the Sacrament, a concept unknown to the New Testament, or the mystery of the Eucharist.

Regardless of the concept of priesthood, Brunner did not see the priesthood as an office bestowed for a few leaders of the church, but as a special calling for all the Christians. When he developed the meaning of the Lord's Supper he says that:

"We find in the Ekklesia brotherhood nothing of a distinction between a bestower and a recipient, between priests and laity. Paul never says that in the Lord's Supper which the Ekklesia celebrates, someone, and in fact always the same person, took over the role of Jesus and thereby was lifted into prominence above the rest of the crowd."[101]

For his ecclesiological task, Brunner looks back to the Christian community of the first century where he does not distinguish any kind of hierarchy. The ecclesia is a community of brotherhood where Christians are celebrating in unity the Lord's Supper. This was not a *sacramentum* to gain a dominating significance over other ministries as spoken of in the Word, but an act of fellowship, a means to strengthen the hope for the Parousia.

The universal priesthood of the Christian is seen in the brotherhood network where there is not seen a differentiation between Christians, where all are equal in worship, fellowship and ministry. As a motif to sustain the equality of all Christians, Brunner writes that "The brothers in Christ are all holy in the sense of being *called to be saints* by God and because the whole life was sanctified as *lateria*"[102] according with personal sacrifice (Rom 12:1). Four centuries before, the concept of "calling" played an important role also in Calvin's theology.

Brunner's understanding was that the church of the first century was a charismatic fellowship where the Holy Spirit distributed for each person a special *charisma* and different *diakoniai*. All of these, spiritual gifts and ministries were given to the community because it is necessity for the Body of Christ. In spite of different *charisma* there was no rank among the Christians, and no power to command. Brunner did not agree with Clement's affirmation in, *First Epistle of Clement,* who states that once the leaders were appointed by the Apostles, the leaders have the right, the jurisdiction of leadership in the community, and all the Christians have to obey them because it has been decreed.

---

[101] Emil Brunner, *Op. Cit.* p. 64.

[102] Idem, p. 66.

These leaders stand over the congregation in virtue of their office. Also, Brunner suspected Ignatius' affirmation that says that "Where the bishop is, there the church is". He did not accept the Roman Catholic teaching that the real church is present in the form of a sacred priestly and sacred legal institution. That teaching, according with Brunner's understanding, was a decisive step of deviation from Ecclesia of the New Testament. The universal priesthood cannot develop into the monarchical bishop concept, *one* bishop *one* community, because the universal priesthood is a necessary liberation from the rigid principle that in one place, in one town there *must* be only one church. In Brunner's understanding, the liberty and dynamic presence of the Holy Spirit was replaced with the rational juristic spirit of Rome and the priest-bishop who administrated the sacraments actually replaced the brotherhood who celebrated the Lord's Supper. His argument was the same as Luther's a few centuries before, from the Epistle of Titus 1:5, when Paul instructed his younger disciple Titus, to "appoint elders in every town" (Titus 1:5), not only one elder in a town, but if need be a few elders.[103] The spiritual presence of Christ between the Christians makes that gathering become a fellowship. Actually in the Apostle Paul's teaching and practice we cannot find such monarchical understanding of the concept of the church. Furthermore, Jesus Christ says that "Where two or three are gathered together in my name, there I am in the midst of them." (Mt 18:20).

Finally, Emil Brunner wrote later that the bishop is in the place to guarantee the tradition, and in this way the bishop gets power and authority over the people. He identified this dominion of the Bishop of Rome over the whole Church was one main reason which lead to the division of the Church into an Eastern Church that is free from the Western Roman Church. We can conclude that the universal priesthood of all Christians was abolished as a result of lifting a bishop over other bishops and transforming the *ekklesia* from an organic spiritual body into an institution with a rocky structure.

In Brunner's understanding the church is not an institution, but it is the community of the faithful, those who through Christ are called to be saints. For him there is not any distinction between Christians, there is not any distinction between those who are clergy and those who are not, since all are called to be saints. He describes the Anabaptist fellowship as a priestly people because in the community the emphasis was that the true church is nothing more than the believing, priestly people. The believers made the true fellowship of faith, a universal priesthood of all believers and not that of a church institution. Later, when the Free Churches of America emerged, as in part descendents of the Anabaptist movement, in part European Churches, they accentuated the free-

---

[103] *Luther's Works*, Am. ed., vol. 36, p. 155.

dom from the State and voluntary membership. In this way the Christians who adhered to these new churches were very involved in missions, they made themselves heard in the church and joined in the church's work. The result was that the American churches are, according with Brunner, laymen's churches. In the Free Churches the element of fellowship or brotherhood developed and the universal priesthood is a great gain. Brunner states that this concept had a decisive influence in formation of the American democracy.

We cannot close this chapter without noticing the most important religious event during the twentieth century: the Pentecostal and Charismatic movement. These two Evangelical movements that stressed especially the pneumatological doctrine proved once more the force of the universal priesthood. The Pentecostal movement started as a frail and unnoticed revival within the poorer classes of people, but soon its zeal and passion for evangelization exercised an important influence in American society and abroad. Since its beginnings this spiritual refreshing movement demonstrated in a dynamic way how God use untrained people to accomplish spiritual renewal. Actually, Pentecostals found a scriptural support for their anti-hierarchical position in Christ disciple's equality and also in the first century church leaders who belonged to the masses of people, those who were simply lay people who had made a commitment to Jesus Christ.[104] It's not a secret that the Pentecostals were reluctant to creeds, for reasons of divisions between brothers,[105] and also to hierarchy, because Jesus says that "Whosoever will be chief among you, let him be your servant." (Mt 20:28). Even in the Pentecostal movement the theoretical teaching of the priesthood of all believers did not get special attention, but in practice this doctrine held a central position. The concept of universal priesthood motivated the lay people to become more involved in the ministry, to carry the leadership burden, or to do social service. From the very moment when someone was saved he or she must of necessity begin a life of service. Bob E. Lyons states, that there has to be compatibility between the pulpit and the pew, the lay people are not useless but the church has the task to equip the laity that they may fulfill their right place in the economy of God.[106]

He underlined that laity are not second-rate clergymen, and every lay person is called to witness to his or her faith in God. The lay advantage is that they, as the functioning people of God, contact more people in need of salvation than does the clergy. In that respect, lay people must know the Word of God, to have good direction and guidance from the local church, to know the dynamic

---

[104] Bob E. Lyons, *Kingdom of Priests,* Cleveland, TN., Pathway Press, 1977, p. 35.

[105] Steven J. Land, *Pentecostal Spirituality*, Sheffield Academic Press, Journal of Pentecostal Theology, 1994, p. 18.

[106] Bob E. Lyons, *Kingdom of Priests*, p. 49.

presence of Jesus Christ in his or hear heart and to posses the power of the Holy Spirit. A well known saying between Pentecostals is that the sheep by nature give birth to the lambs, not the shepherd. The pastor's duty is to feed the flock and to protect the sheep. The practical lesson is that the work of soul winning is not limited to the professional minister, but is shared between the clergy and laity. This conclusion drives people to understand that the lay people are people of God, called to be servants in His Kingdom and not second-rate citizens of the Kingdom.[107] They have to know their Lord, to have a strong experiential relationship with Christ and to have a love for people.

The Pentecostals were seen as people of prayer, but this concert prayer finds its biblical roots in the priesthood of all believers.[108] All of them regardless of social class or intellectual ability are a holy priesthood called to praise the Name of the Lord and to be intercessors for their fellow brothers and sisters. The Pentecostals are aware of the unfortunate possibility to notice a conflict between the clergy and the laity that will result in slowing the expansion and development of the Kingdom of God.[109]

The baptism of the Spirit made every Christian a servant of Christ and leveled any difference between the Christians. The spiritual baptism and the call of the Spirit to ministry, has no "respect of persons". [110]

Since the beginning of the movement, the Pentecostals stressed eschatological expectation; they were eschatological people who accentuated the urgency of the mission. It is relevant for the Pentecostal movement to underline that the exponential growing of the Pentecostal movement during the twentieth century, which can be explained not by a special class of trained teachers, but by the involvement of lay people in spreading the Gospel by the universal priesthood fulfilling the spiritual mandate. The Pentecostals understand their missionary mandate in a practical way, as agents of reconciliation, not just to renew the church, but to worship God, to be prayer warriors and to reconcile the world with God.[111]

The lay people have an important role to play since the laity as priests are equal to but distinct from that of the professional clergy. Bob Lyons writes that it is

---

[107] Idem, p. 33.

[108] Idem, p. 94.

[109] Idem, p. 53.

[110] Roger Heuser and Byron D. Klaus, 'Charismatic Leadership Theory: A Shadow Side Confessed', *Pneuma: Journal of the Society for Pentecostal Studies,* vol. 20, no. 2, Fall 1995, p. 174.

[111] Idem, p. 174.

equal in the sense that clergy and laity both have a calling from God, but there are different levels of administration and authority in the Kingdom of God.[112]

It has to be said that the Pentecostals assumed, at the beginning of the movement, some risks by involving lay people in the preaching ministry. There was also involved in preaching and ministry, people who did not have a calling for that ministry, unfortunately some of them developed a kind of popular theology without a clear hermeneutics study. But, in spite of that assumed risk, the Pentecostals developed by the work of the Holy Spirit and today bring spiritual refreshing and comfort for many people. Today there are many Pentecostal seminaries and faculties of theology in most countries of the world. Some are opening new Pentecostal churches in former communist countries releasing spiritual power for renewal of the society.

The Charismatic renewal movement can be described as a lay movement without any traditional roots and without a hierarchical structure. This spiritual renewal movement put a great accent on the direct guidance of the Holy Spirit in the lives of Christians. The Charismatic gatherings provide the framework and encourage the Christians to manifest their gifts as prophecy, worship or witness. They focused on the Pentecostal experience and the Holy Spirit's ministry that endows men and women with spiritual power. Inside of the Charismatic movement, any laymen can place hands on those who want to receive the fullness of the Holy Spirit. According with their understanding, God is doing a mighty work today bound neither by office nor by the rank of people. Unfortunately Charismatics did not pay, until now, enough attention for forming a corpus of doctrine and as a result the radical laicizing of church life began. That is true because in the, *Dictionary of Pentecostal and Charismatic Movements*, they do not have an article about Charismatic theology or about the universal priesthood of the believers.[113]

8. Apology for the Priesthood of All Believers In finishing this presentation about the priesthood concept from the Evangelical and Orthodox perspective, we can draw some important conclusions. In the Eastern European Orthodoxy, and also in the Roman Catholic Church, the priesthood concept roots can be traced back to the Church Fathers, and is based mainly on the apostolic succession teaching forming an ecclesial hierarchical structure. In the Evangelical movement, which is rooted in the Reformers' teaching, the concept was simplified and linked with scriptural expressions as "holy priesthood" and "royal priesthood" (1Pet 2:5, 9), but we notice also a lack of New Testament material

---

[112] Bob E. Lyons, *Kingdom of Priests*, p. 57.

[113] David F. Wright, 'The Charismatic Movement The laicizing of Christianity?' *The Rise of the Laity in Evangelical Protestantism*, Deryck W. Lovegrove (ed.), London, Routledge Publisher, 2002, p. 257.

about the concept of priesthood. A reason in developing the concept of universal priesthood is due to Paul's attitude, as seen that most of his letters are addressed to the believers, not exclusively to the Apostles. The role of the ministries, according to Paul, is to "equip the saints for the work of the ministry". (Eph 4:12). The congregation recognized the minister's calling and also the congregation has the duty to correct or discipline him if his behavior is not in accordance with the Word of God.

I have endeavored within this study to expound that the Evangelicals do not sustain the common ancient teaching of a mediated class of priests between the people and God employed by other men to represent them before Him. Contrary to that, Evangelicals followed Luther's theology that Christians by virtue of their relation to Christ have direct approach to God, there is no need of another person to intervene or to mediate between him and God; every man and woman has the privilege at anytime be by himself or herself to be in a personal relationship with God.

Emphatically, Steven Paul says that the difference between the two Christian groups, lay and ordained, even though it is a foreign concept of the New Testament teaching, exists in practice.

When you enter the church today there are two 'people' – laity, who receive the ministry, and 'clergy' who give it. But when we enter the world of the New Testament we find only one people, the true *laos* of God, with leaders among the people.[114]

The concept of universal priesthood, which is not rejected by any Christian church, is very important from a theological and practical implication in this postmodern time. When it is practiced seriously it can bring important gains for individuals or for society, or unfortunately, if it is not clearly understood, it could bring adverse results.

We can notice some good outcomes when the concept of the universal priesthood is preached and practiced.

Firstly, the concept of priesthood of all believers, potentially can lead toward a spiritual revival. Since the Reformers time, the Evangelicals released an incredible spiritual power with incredible results by developing the concept of the universal priesthood. The great spiritual awakening in Europe and in America during the eighteenth and nineteenth century, or the explosion of the Pentecostal movement with its dynamic force during the twentieth century could not have been possible without a clear understanding of the universal concept of priesthood.

---

[114] Paul R. Stevens, *The Other Six Days*, p. 26.

As a pastor I can see the results of combining the willingness of born again lay people who want to be active for the Kingdom of God, with biblical truth and with the power of the Holy Spirit. These three elements are necessary for spiritual results. Without a biblical teaching any kind of awakening can be a flame of short duration, with a small impact and without a force to touch a whole generation of people. A pastor who is busy with everything in the church; visiting and counseling people, helping the poor, ministering the Word, doing administrative work and so on, will in a short time collapse. In contrast, if he is working to equip the believers as universal priests, to do their ministry, the benefit is greater and the believers realize their responsibility. The lay people need to do more than just sustaining the church financially or being part of the service, for the work is too great to be done by a small number of people. Working together brings a sense of unity, of acceptance and empathy toward those around us.

Secondly, practicing the universal priesthood concept will bring an advantage for society and a direction for Christians. As I have demonstrated in this paper those who understood the practical aspect of the universal priesthood cannot remain uninvolved, but to the contrary, they become active in society. The priesthood concept is strongly attached to the concept of sacrifice and serving. Having Christ's example of High Priest for humanity who came on the earth, "Not to be ministered unto, but to minister and to give his life a ransom for many" (Mk 10:45), Christians who understand the real meaning of priesthood will live sacrificially and not selfishly

As a vivid example I presented the Quakers who as universal priests were very active in their opposition against slavery; they were instrumental in opening the first asylum in England; and sacrificially worked among prisoners.

It is not difficult to notice that the world we live in is a world of suffering and needs. The street children, poor families, drug addicts, alcoholics, sick and elderly are waiting to see a Good Samaritan or an army of universal priests who will care for them. Christians who are living a godly life, who are attending weekly to the church service, need clear direction and a purpose to focus upon. Many pastors, often do not realize the potential of a large number of Christians who are able and ready to imitate Christ in practical service for others.

Thirdly, the priestly concept will impact families and the new generation, for it helps the lay people to bring theology down from the pulpit to their own families, since every parent is a priest in his own family and from the family to express that calling to the society. The Puritans, as I demonstrated earlier, remained an example of serious family life, where the father was a real priest for his children, teaching and instructing them for their future. The spiritual life inside Christian families was lifted up because the father as a priest for his family has the responsibility to lead the family in home Bible study and prayer. Likewise, the mother has a great influence by her perseverant prayers and by cultivating in her life in the fruit of the Spirit as love, joy and peace. In this way a theological concept, as the universal priesthood, was not only hypothetical but also practical as a concept which could influence families, society, and lifestyle, as well as in the morality arena. We are aware of the turmoil over family life in this time but when the parents are priests for their children, teaching and serving their needs, and when the marriage faithfulness by a spirit of serving defeats the selfishness of the human nature, the families get a greater victory.

There can appear certain risks when we truly want to practice the concept of universal priesthood. I underline here two issues: the risk of the development of a kind of popular theology and the risk of churches splitting. History shows that when lay people get authority sometimes tension arises between the lay people and the leaders or pastors. Anytime and anywhere when the laity was in charge to do priestly activity, especially when they were in charge of preaching the gospel, there appears the risk to develop a popular theology, a shallow theology. To eliminate that risk, it is the pastor's duty to equip the lay people with good biblical knowledge. Church history proved that forbidding people to have access to the Bible was a loss, not a gain, because while trying to eliminate the risk of popular teaching it hindered the development of the community

To proclaim and sustain the universal priesthood furthermore, means to assume the risks and to take the risk because this teaching is a biblical teaching with wonderful results for pastors who can see the grace of God by using lay Christians for missions. Another benefit is for lay people who can be involved in all kind of missions, seeing their utility for church and society. The German scholar, Eduard Schweitzer, who studied carefully ecclesiology at the beginning of twentieth century, shares that the church based on the universal priesthood concept, without two classes of Christians, laity and clerics, can be practiced and feasible biblically as long as "such churches would not exclude any kind of order to prevent it from dissolving into disorganized chaos; the "Charismatics" would not elevate themselves and their gifts above other members, and the authority of the basic gospel would not be disputed either by new religiously experienced revelation or by any adaptations to modern popular trends."[115] I conclude that his concept can be a model to be studied but not without difficulties in practice as long as human nature dominates the people hearts. When the universal priesthood concept is practiced the gain for the church and for society can be overwhelming.

---

[115] R.E. Schweitzer, 'Ministry in the Early Church' in D.N. Freedman (ed.), *Anchor Bible Dictionary*, (6 vols.; New York: Doubleday, 1992), IV, pp. 835-842.

The universal priesthood can be an answer for society and churches in this postmodern time when individualism touches millions of people. The priesthood of all believers has to be practiced in relationship within the church, for the benefit of its members, and through that church for the benefit of the world outside.[116] Knowing and practicing the concept of universal priesthood is a privilege for all Christians which gives dignity, hope, joy and overwhelming blessings to every believer.

In conclusion of this study, I can report that the differences between the Orthodox and Evangelical churches, on the ground of the theology of the priesthood, is still a matter of continued study and theological research. We can notice the risk of losing the direct communion between the believers and God if we develop a theology of intercessor clergy.

In Romania before the year 1989, the difficulty of dialogue between these two traditions was deep because of the communist political system who aimed to divide Christians and to weaken the churches. If there is a will for openness and reciprocal understanding, the theologians of both traditions will need to promote mutual respect and love, to study the priesthood conception and to make the effort to understand the other's tradition. Furthermore, mutual loves is needed for reciprocal acceptance and humbleness to embrace Paul's advice: "And if on some point you think differently, that too God will make clear to you. Only let us live up to what we have already attained." (Phil 3:15-16).

Bibliography

Braclay, Robert, *Apology for the Christian Divinity*, (first published in 1678), Glenside, Quaker Heritage Press.

Berkhof, Louis (1988), *Systematic Theology*, 13th edition, Edinburgh: The Banner of Truth Trust.

Boettner, Loraine (1962), *Roman Catholicism*, Phillipsburg, NJ: The Presbyterian and Reformed Publishing Company.

Bonhoeffer, Dietrich (1997), *Letters and papers from Prison*, New York: Touchstone.

Bulgakov, Sergius (1935), *The Orthodox Church*, London: Centenary Press.

Bruce, F.F. (1964), *The Epistle to the Hebrews*, The New International Commentary on the New Testament, Grand Rapids: Eerdmans.

---

[116] *The Priesthood of all Believers,* P.G. Mathew, 1996. http://www.gracevalley.org/articles/Priesthood.html.

Brunner, Emil (2002), *Dogmatics III*, D. Cairns and T.H.L. Paker (transl.), Cambridge: James Clarke & Co.

Calvin, Jean (1960), *Institutes of the Christian Religion*, vol. 1, ed. John T. McNeill, trans. and index. Ford Lewis Battles, Philadelphia: The Westminster Press.

_____ (1948), *Commentaries on the Catholic Epistles*, trans. J. Owen, Grand Rapids, Michigan: Eerdmans.

Douglas, J.D. and Earle, E. Cairns (eds.) 1996, *The New International Dictionary of the Christian Church*, Grand Rapids, Michigan: Zondervan Publishing House.

Eastwood, Cyril (1962), *The Priesthood of all Believers*, Minneapolis, Augsburg Publishing House.

Elwell, A. Walter (2003), *Evangelical Dictionary of Theology*, Grand Rapids, Michigan: Baker Academic a Division of Baker Book House Co.

Erb, C. Peter (1983), *Pietists: Selected Writings*, New York: Paulist Press.

Erler, R.J. (1986), *A Karl Barth Reader*, Grand Rapids: Eerdmans.

Ferguson, B. Sinclair and Wright, F. David (ed.), *New Dictionary of Theology*, (1991), Leicester: Intervarsity Press.

Freedman, D.N. editor (1992), *Anchor Bible Dictionary*, vol. 4, New York: Doubleday.

George, Timothy (1988), *Theology of the Reformers*, Nashville TN.: Broadman Press.

Justo, L. Gonzalez (1988), *A History of Christian Thought*, vol. 3, Nashville, TN.: Paternoster Press.

Guthrie, Donald (1981), *New Testament Theology*, Leicester: Inter-Varsity Press.

Hawthorne, F. Gerald, Martin P. Ralph, Reid G. Daniel, editors (1993), *Dictionary of Paul and His Letters*, Downers Grove, ILL: *InterVarsity Press*.

Heuser, Roger and Byron, D. Klaus (1995), *Charismatic Leadership Theory: A Shadow Side Confessed, in Pneuma: Journal of the Society for Pentecostal Studies*, vol. 20, no. 2.

Land, J. Steven, *Pentecostal Spirituality* (1994), Sheffield: Sheffield Academic Press, *Journal of Pentecostal Theology Supplemental Series*.

Lawson, John (1980), *Introduction to Christian Doctrine*, Wilmore, Kentucky: Francis Asbury Publishing Company, Inc.

Lea, D. Thomas, (1996), *The Hermeneutics of the Puritans*, JETS.

Lewis, R. Gordon, Bruce A. Demarest, *Interrogative Theology*, Grand Rapids, Michigan, Zondervan, 1996.

Lovegrove, W. Deryck (2002), *The Rise of the Laity in Evangelical Protestantism*, London: Routledge.

Lyons, E. Bob (1977), *Kingdom of Priests*, Cleveland TN.: Pathway Press.

Maddox, L. Randy (2003), *Formation for Christian Leadership: Wesleyan Reflections*, Portland, Oregon: ATLA.

Manson, Thomas W. (1958), *Ministry and Priesthood: Christ's and Ours*, London: Epworth Press.

Matsoukas, A. Nikos (2006) *Teologie Dogmatică și simbolică*, București: Bizantină.

McGrath, Alister (1997), *Evangelicalism in Christian Theology An Introduction*, Cambridge: Blackwell Publishing.

Mullins, E. Young (1905), *Why Is Christianity True?* Philadelphia: American Baptist Publication Society.

Niculcea, Adrian, *Teologia Dogmatică Ortodoxă Comparată*, Constanța, 2001.

Pelikan, Jaroslav, *Credo*, Iași, Polirom, 2010.

Stevens, R. Paul (1999), *The Other Six Days*, Grand Rapids, Mich.: W.B. Eerdmans.

Smyth, John (1990), 'Differences of the Churches of the Separation', in H. Leon McBeth, *A Sourcebook for Baptist Heritage*, Nashville: Broadman Press.

Titus, Noel (1987), 'The Ordained Ministry and the Christian Koinonia', *JRT* 44.

Raschke, Carl (2004), *The Next Reformation*, Michigan: Baker Academic, Grand Rapids.

Remete, George, *Dogmatica Ortodoxă*, Alba Iulia, Reîntregirea 2000.

Ross, M.J. (1951), 'The priesthood of all Believers', in *The Expository Times*, SAGE Journals, 63.

Rooke, W. Deborah (2000), *Zadok's Heirs: The Role and Development of the High Priesthood in Ancient Israel*, Oxford: Oxford University Press.

Ward, W.R. (1992), *The Protestant Evangelical Awakening*, Cambridge: Cambridge University Press.

* * * *The Columbia Encyclopedia* (2007), Sixth Edition, New York: Columbia University Press.

* * * *Învățătura de Credință Creștină Ortodoxă* (2000) București, Editura Institutului Biblic și de Misiune al Bisericii Ortodoxe Române.

http://www.mb-soft.com/believe/txn/augsburg.htm.
http://www.ccel.org/creeds/helvetic.htm.
http://www.gracevalley.org/articles/Priesthood.html.
http://www.luthersem.edu/word&world.
http://www.reformedsermonarchives.com/sp.
http://www.religion-online.org
http://ext.sagepub.com
http://swartzentrover.com/cotor/E-Books/holiness/Compendium/compendium Christian Theology/vol.3/pdf

Abbreviations

ATLA	*American Theological Library Association*
NIDNTT	*New International Dictionary of New Testament Theology*
JETS	*Journal of the Evangelical Theological Society*
JRT	*Journal of Religious Thought*
JPT	*Journal of Pentecostal Theology*

Abstract

This comparative study of the concept of priesthood will be viewed from the different approaches of the Evangelical and Eastern Orthodox Church. In an era of theological dialogue and ecumenism, this study is seen as a theological and practical challenge. The historical Eastern Orthodox tradition, with its strong roots in the patristic literature, and the dynamism of universal priesthood which erupted in the German Reform movement enlarged during the great awakening, are strong realities, beyond any question mark.

A large portion of this article is provided from the Reformers perspectives on the priesthood teaching as taught by Luther and Calvin. Included is the Orthodox perspective on the priesthood concept as it shows close relationship between hermeneutics of biblical texts, especially those in the Old Testament, the writings of the Church Fathers and the vigorous Church tradition. The writings of John Chrysostom, Ambrose or Dionysius the Areopagite, emphasizing the mediator role of the priest, are fundamental for understanding the priesthood concept from an Orthodox perspective. The Evangelical perspective on this topic is more subjective, where the priest does not hold a hierarchical position but develops a subjective linking with the divinity as a spiritual unity with Christ, by offering spiritual sacrifices in worship, praise, thanksgiving, and various services towards others.

It is worthy to note that while both traditions emphasize Jesus Christ's role of High Priest in biblical texts like the Gospel of John (17:19) or the Epistle to the Hebrews, the Evangelicals emphasize Peter's reference to the royal priesthood concept (I Pet. 2:9). A clear difference between the two perspectives lies in the fact that ordination in the Orthodox tradition is very laborious, while in the Evangelical tradition the same ministry is quite simple. In the Orthodox tradition, the Bishop invokes the presence of Holy Spirit upon the new priest, the clergy sings adequate songs, the Christians repeat the formula "He is worthy" and, finally, the new priest having received the priesthood grace, receives his new robe. In the Romanian Evangelical tradition the ritual is characterized by simplicity; it includes a sermon about pastoral responsibility and ends with a prayer of consecration with the laying on of hands by a college of pastors. The Evangelicals do not embrace the concept of apostolic succession nor the concept of sacerdotalism, while these concepts are highly emphasized in the Orthodox tradition.

However, despite the ecclesiological and ministerial differences between the two Christian traditions, postmodernity provides the framework for an open and honest dialogue between the Orthodox and the Evangelical theologians. Furthermore, social needs require the active involvement of both clergy and laity. There is a need for those who have the priesthood grace and those who belong to the universal priesthood to be active and helpful in bringing hope to those in need, according to Jesus Christ's eternal patterns of service.

Contributors

IACOB COMAN is Associate Professor of Church Dogmatics at the Pentecostal Theological Institute of Bucharest, Romania, where he also serves as the Academic Dean of the Faculty of Theology. He holds a BTh (1996) degree from the Emanuel University of Oradea and two doctorates: a PhD in Fundamental Theology and Church Dogmatics (1999) from the Babeș-Bolyai University of Cluj-Napoca and another PhD in Philosophy (2009) from the Romanian Academy, The "Constantin Radulescu Motru" Institute of Philosophy and Psychology. Dr. Coman is a prolific author in theology and poetry. He has written seven books and about 40 articles and studies in theology and five books in the area of Christian poetry and hymnology. His publications include Theo-Doxa-Logia and Teologie fundamental și metafizică. Dr. Coman is ordained with the Seventh Day Adventist Church of Romania and serves as Pastor of the Târgu-Mureș community, being also known as an international evangelist. He is married to Lia Ildiko and have together two children – Roberth and Ruth.

CHRISTIAN KRUMBACHER serves currently as the Pastor of the Gemeinde Gottes in Trossingen, Germany. He holds a BTh (1986), a MA in Theology (2003) from the Pentecostal Theological Seminary in Cleveland, Tennessee, USA, and a M.Div. (2010) from the Columbia International University, Columbia, USA. (German branch: Akademie für Weltmission, Korntal, Germany). Being of German descent, originally from Romania, Christian immigrated to Germany in his childhood. With a pastoral experience of over 25 years with the Gemeinde Gottes organization, he also serves as Regional Overseer in the South of Germany. Christian is married and has five children.

EUGEN JUGARU serves as a Lecturer at the Pentecostal Theological Institute of Bucharest, Romania, teaching Systematic Theology. He holds a Bachelor of Theology (1996) degree from the "Babeș-Bolyai" University of Cluj-Napoca and a PhD (2011) in Dogmatic Theology from the "Lucian Blaga" University of Sibiu, Romania. Dr. Jugaru published a number of articles in theological journals and presented several papers to seminars and conferences in Romanian universities and abroad. He is ordained in the Pentecostal Church of Romania and serves both as pastor and as leader in the regional structures of his denomination. Eugen is married to Dana and have together three children – Theodora, Laura and Cristian.

JOHN FLETER TIPEI is currently Associate Professor of New Testament at the Pentecostal Theological Institute of Bucharest, Romania. He had served as the President/Rector (1997-2010) of the same institution and the founding Senior

Editor (1999-2010) of the Pleroma, a journal for theological research published by the Pentecostal Theological Institute. Dr. Tipei holds a M.Div. degree (1987) from the Pentecostal Theological Seminary in Cleveland, Tennessee, and a PhD in Biblical Studies (2000) from the Sheffield University, UK. He has written five books, over 30 articles in theological journals and magazines and has translated and edited over 20 books. His publications include The Laying on of Hands in the New Testament: Its Significance, Techniques and Effects (2009). Dr. Tipei is an Ordained Bishop with the International Church of God, Cleveland, Tennessee and worked for the past 20 years in Romania as missionary-teacher, pastor and leader in the regional and central structures of the Pentecostal Church of Romania. He is married to Rodica and have together five children.

The Greek New Testament for Beginning Readers

The Byzantine Greek Text & Verb Parsing

Maurice A. Robinson
William G. Pierpont
John Jeffrey Dodson
(Eds.)

The Greek New Testament for Beginning Readers contains a number of valuable features:

- A readable, non-italic font for the main body of Greek text
- Footnotes containing brief definitions of words occurring less than fifty times
- Word frequency counts to help the reader decide if a word should be memo-rized
- Footnotes showing how to parse all verbs occurring less than fifty times
- An alphabetized list of all other verb forms with parsing information
- A lexicon showing proper names and all words occurring fifty times or more

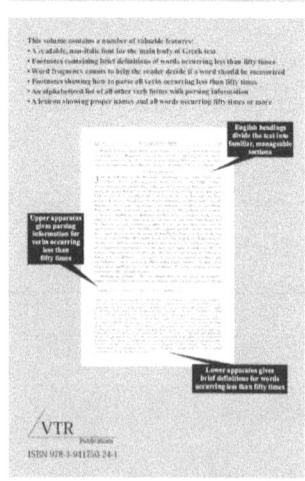

Hardcover · XII/781 pp. · 23,4 x 15,6 cm
ISBN 978-3-941750-24-1
€ 39,95

VTR Publications
Gogolstr. 33 · 90475 Nürnberg · Germany
info@vtr-online.com
http://www.vtr-online.com

www.ingramcontent.com/pod-product-compliance
Lightning Source LLC
Chambersburg PA
CBHW060341170426
43202CB00014B/2843